The Logic of Estrangement

# The Logic of Estrangement

## Reason in an Unreasonable Form

Julius Sensat
*University of Wisconsin—Milwaukee, USA*

First published 2016 by
PALGRAVE MACMILLAN

Palgrave Macmillan in the UK is an imprint of Macmillan Publishers Limited, registered in England, company number 785998, of Houndmills, Basingstoke, Hampshire RG21 6XS.

Palgrave Macmillan in the US is a division of St Martin's Press LLC, 175 Fifth Avenue, New York, NY 10010.

Palgrave Macmillan is the global academic imprint of the above companies and has companies and representatives throughout the world.

Palgrave® and Macmillan® are registered trademarks in the United States, the United Kingdom, Europe and other countries.

ISBN: 978–1–137–56557–0

This book is printed on paper suitable for recycling and made from fully managed and sustained forest sources. Logging, pulping and manufacturing processes are expected to conform to the environmental regulations of the country of origin.

A catalogue record for this book is available from the British Library.

A catalog record for this book is available from the Library of Congress.

*For Trudy, without whom not*

# Contents

# List of Tables

# Acknowledgments

I am grateful to the publishers of the following articles for permission to re-use material from them as a partial basis for the chapters indicated:

Marx's inverted world. *Topoi*, 15(2):177–188, 1996 (Chapter 6).

Reification as dependence on extrinsic information. *Synthese*, 109(3):361–399, 1996 (Chapters 4 and 6).

Classical German philosophy and Cohen's critique of Rawls. *European Journal of Philosophy*, 11(3):314–353, 2003 (Chapter 7).

Work on the first two of these articles was supported by the National Science Foundation and the Graduate School at the University of Wisconsin—Milwaukee. Work on the third was supported by a sabbatical award in 2003 from the University of Wisconsin—Milwaukee. Work on Chapters 2 and 3 of the book was supported by a sabbatical award in 2011 from the University of Wisconsin—Milwaukee. Work on Chapter 7 was supported by a fellowship during 2005–2006 from the Center for 21st Century Studies at the University of Wisconsin—Milwaukee.

I wish to express my heartfelt gratitude to several people who have helped me greatly by way of insightful comments and suggestions at various stages of composition: Bill Bristow, Bernie Gendron, John Koethe, Marc Linder, Blain Neufeld, Frederick Neuhouser, Nataliya Palatnik, Bill Wainwright, and an anonymous reviewer for Palgrave Macmillan. I am also grateful to my students and to various colloquium audiences to whom I have presented material that found its way into the book. Special thanks to Terese Agnew for permission to use her brilliant 'Portrait of a Textile Worker' as the source for the book's cover image. Finally, I am grateful to Brendan George and Esme Chapman of Palgrave Macmillan and Vidhya Jayaprakash of Newgen Knowledge Works for their accomplished and supportive editorial and project-management activities throughout the publication process.

# A Note on Translations and Citations

I have consulted and often followed available English translations of the writings of Kant, Hegel, and Marx [47–55; 58; 67; 70–72; 84–87; 89–93; 147], but I have modified them where noted. In citing Kant's writings, I have referred to the Prussian Academy edition of his collected works [66] by volume and page number, except for the *Critique of Pure Reason*, where I have used the customary A/B references. I have also cited an English edition together with the German, but without the English edition's page numbers when it also contains the German pagination.

# 1
# Introduction

In a letter to Arnold Ruge of September 1843, Marx says:

> Reason has always existed, just not always in reasonable form. The critic can therefore start out from any form of theoretical and practical consciousness and develop from existing reality's *own* forms the true reality as its ought and its ultimate purpose [*Endzweck*] [93, p. 143 (translation modified); 95, part 1, 2:487].

It may be tendentious, for reasons I will explain in a moment, to read this passage as concerned with estrangement and its overcoming. Tendentious perhaps, but, I would argue, fruitful. For it enables us to understand the passage as expressing two ideas traceable back through German idealism to Kant's critical philosophy and forward through the thought of Lukács [81], the critical theorists of the Frankfurt School (Horkheimer and Adorno [63; 64], Marcuse [82]) and their successors (Habermas [42–45], Honneth [60–62]), and, I maintain here, John Rawls [110–119]. The first is that of estrangement or alienation, understood as reason in an unreasonable form, and the second is that of the potential of philosophy or critical social theory to play an integral role in overcoming it. On this reading, these thinkers do not always use the language of estrangement, but they are nonetheless concerned with it. For example, Kant does not use the term when he speaks, in a manner reminiscent of Rousseau, of 'passions' that wreak devastation in a self-incurred 'dominion of evil', in which persons act as though they were 'instruments of evil' [66, 6:97]. Nor does Rawls use it when he evaluates alternative conceptions of the social minimum by reference to their comparative 'strains of commitment' [117, §38]. In fact, he hardly uses the term at all. Even Hegel, who treats estrangement as a pivotal phenomenon, does not explicitly refer to it when he discusses the emergence of a 'rabble' within his system of ethical life [52, §244; 57, 7:§244.] Yet we can plausibly take it to be topically central in all of these cases. And these thinkers all attribute an important social role to philosophy or critical theory, whether it be defense or vindication of reason in public life (Kant, Hegel, Rawls), reconciliation to the social world (Hegel, Rawls), the self-consciousness of transformative social practice (Hegel, Marx, Lukács, the Frankfurt School, Habermas, Honneth), or the elaboration of ideas to form a basis of democratic social unity (Rawls).

The possibly tendentious character of these assertions lies in their treatment of estrangement as reason in an unreasonable form, since a more typical characterization—understandably, especially with respect to Marx—would refer instead to a self-induced separation of human beings from their essential nature, which then assumes a hostile or alien form, one that suppresses or distorts the realization of their freedom.[1] On this view, social criticism on grounds of estrangement consists in showing how social practices create or sustain such a separation and how social change could enable a reunification. Yet whether one (1) understands modernity to have entered a 'post-metaphysical' period (Habermas), (2) maintains that in a democratic society, appeals to fundamental metaphysical or philosophical-anthropological doctrines are not available within the space of public reasons (Rawls), or (3) simply insists on a strict distinction between the factual and the normative,[2] one can reasonably question whether there is a defensible concept of human nature or the human essence—even a historically variable one— that could fund a concept of estrangement that could serve as a basis for social understanding and critique. I do not deny that Hegel and Marx make use of essentialist language and express essentialist ideas.[3] However, I believe that ideas in their writings can be extracted from this context to fashion a concept of estrangement that can support social understanding and exercise a critical function through the idea of an irrational or unreasonable embodiment of reason in the social world. As I have claimed, the same could be said, I think, of other figures

---

[1] See, for example, the discussions by Wendling [149, chap. 1] and Schacht [129, chaps. 2–3].

[2] For example, Schacht [130].

[3] For example, Hegel, when he says that in the ethical realm, individuals '*actually possess their own* essence' [52, §153; 57, 7:§153], or Marx, in his early treatment of estranged labor [89, pp. 322–334; 95, part 1, 2:363–375], where he says that such labor estranges man 'from his spiritual essence, his *human* essence' [89, p. 329; 95, part 1, 2:370].

standardly read as contributors to the tradition of critical social theory, though I do not argue for this claim in what follows. Moreover, once we recast the concept of estrangement in this way, there is no reason to exclude Kant and Rawls from the fold, and I do defend this claim here (Chapters 2 and 7).

When is reason in an unreasonable form? Here we can take our cue from Kant. He takes reason to be a system of principles for theoretical and practical reasoning, judgment, and action. This system itself specifies standards that assign to each of its possible uses certain interests, bounds, prerogatives, and relations of priority or subordination with respect to other possible uses. It is possible to use principles of reason in ways that violate these standards. For example, Kant views it as unreasonable to subordinate duty to inclination, pure to empirical practical reason. If such violations take place as part of a social practice, then we can speak of the practice as embodying reason in an unreasonable form.

Many theorists of estrangement have taken it to play at times a historically productive role. Certainly Hegel and Marx understand it in this way.[4] It is not immediately clear how the concept of a separation of human beings from their essential nature can by itself account for this feature of estrangement. On the other hand, the view of estrangement as reason in an unreasonable form can easily accommodate it. In the *Phenomenology of Spirit*, in the social world that he calls self-alienated spirit, Hegel sees forces of development that eventually make possible an overcoming of society's alienated condition and a realization of freedom. It is plausible to claim that for Hegel this process of sociocultural development (or *Bildung* as he calls it) is driven by reason in an unreasonable form.[5] Similarly, Marx, for whom capitalism is a system of estrangement, nonetheless holds that it is responsible for the development of society's productive powers. As we'll see, Marx views this process as driven by reason in an unreasonable form, because it is a process in which technical or instrumental reason is put into the service of capital. Even Kant's theory of history—as a process in which humanity's 'unsocial sociability' drives human sociocultural development that eventually makes it possible to approximate the realization of an ethical community—fits into this mold, for unsocial sociability is for Kant a

---

[4] This point is stressed by Sayers [128].

[5] Consider, for example, his discussion of 'absolute freedom and terror' in the aftermath of the French Revolution. More generally, the idea of reason's 'self-othering' as progressive suffuses the Preface to the *Phenomenology*.

realization of reason in an unreasonable form. It is a matter of a socially reinforced tendency to give empirical practical reason priority over pure practical reason. Moreover, Rawls follows Hegel's lead in understanding the idea of toleration to be made possible by the Reformation, the ensuing rise of religious pluralism, and the latter's consequent devolution into religious war. What is religious pluralism without toleration if not a realization of reason in an unreasonable form?

Thinking about estrangement in this way also allows us to retain two important ideas from the more standard characterization. The first is that estrangement is a self-incurred condition in which agents turn their own agency into a force that blocks or distorts the realization of their freedom. The new conception construes freedom as the freedom of reason, the freedom that is realized when persons assume control over and responsibility for their judgments and actions. When agents realize their reason in an unreasonable form, they compromise their own freedom. The second idea is that the elimination of estrangement and the full realization of freedom require a social transformation. In this case we think of the transformation as establishing conditions of social unity enabling agents to hold one another to mutually acceptable standards. Since we can retain these two ideas in the new conception, I will accordingly understand estrangement to be marked by three interrelated features:

1. It is a social condition in which reason is realized in an unreasonable form.
2. It is a condition in which agents unwittingly turn their own agency into a force against itself, a force that blocks or distorts the realization of their freedom.
3. It can only be eliminated through a kind of social unity.

Besides conceiving of estrangement in these terms, my investigation restricts its purview in two ways. First, while a comprehensive study would trace the idea of estrangement back to ancient times, the focus here takes in the late eighteenth century to the present. Second, within this period, one can distinguish a concept of what might be called social estrangement—whereby agents unwittingly construct an alien social world—from one of 'existential estrangement'—whereby agents live individual lives that are their own but are nonetheless inauthentic or alien. While the former is anticipated in Rousseau's thought and finds expression in Hegel's philosophy and the ideas of Marx and the subsequent tradition in critical social theory, the latter develops largely through a reaction to Hegel's thought on the part of Kierkegaard, Nietzsche, and Heidegger, among others. Though there may indeed be important connections between the two sets of ideas,[6] my focus is on the former.[7] In addition, as I've indicated, I maintain that the tradition including them should be expanded to include Kant and Rawls.

Aside from the fact that there are anticipations of the idea of estrangement in Rousseau that influence Kant's thinking, Kant's critical program explicitly takes itself to be the self-critique of a reason at odds with itself and needing to put itself into reasonable form. The project concerns not only theoretical aspirations but practical endeavors as well. For example, as we'll see in Chapter 2, Kant concerns himself with social circumstances in which moral evil bears the marks of estrangement. He also has the resources for a challenging defense against Hegel's striking charge that *morality* as he characterizes it is a form of estrangement. Kant concedes that morality can appear to be an alien imposition, but he takes this appearance to be a mere semblance that provides false— we might say 'ideological'— support for the condition of estrangement provided by systematic moral evil. We can fruitfully read much of his practical philosophy as aimed at dispelling such support. Kant's most ambitious and significant contribution to this effort, in my judgment, is his attempt in the *Critique of Practical Reason* to disclose an a priori entryway into a circle of equivalences containing our status as morally responsible, our rationality (in a strong sense), our transcendental freedom, and our autonomy. For Kant this circle provides us with an indispensable self-conception linking us to morality (Section 2.2.1). He supplies a moral psychology supporting this self-conception (Section 2.2.2), an assurance that morality makes adequate room for human happiness (and thus for empirical practical reason) (Section 2.2.3), and an argument that the presuppositions of morality are compatible with the unity of reason (Section 2.2.4).

For Hegel, however, the appearance of Kantian morality as alien is not a mere semblance but rather reflects three genuine forms of estrangement (Section 2.3). I call two of these 'motivational estrangement' and 'content estrangement', respectively. The charge of motivational estrangement is that the Kantian structure of motivation unduly separates moral from empirical interests and puts them into unnecessary conflict with each other. The charge of content estrangement is that

---

[6] Schmitt [131].

[7] For an account of the latter that also does not presuppose a normative concept of the human essence, see Jaeggi [65].

Kant's so-called pure practical reason is incapable of providing moral content on its own and can do so only by presupposing the reasonableness of the background social world. Hegel roots these two forms of estrangement in a third form, which I call 'moral individualism' and which treats moral deliberation as fundamentally and self-sufficiently a form of individual deliberation about personal maxims for dealing with given circumstances. The mature Hegel hopes to overcome or avoid all three of these conditions by taking a new approach to the realization of freedom—one in which basic social structure is crucial—and by laying out a system of ethical life in which self-interest bears an organic relation to the general interest.

I discuss the main elements of Hegel's theory of freedom in Chapter 3. For Hegel, the free will must will itself as its own object. This is only possible in a social world that is well-ordered by the concept of freedom. Such a world must realize three forms of practical freedom: personal freedom, moral freedom, and social freedom. Personal freedom is realized through the social recognition and exercise of rights of individuals to pursue their own interests, without interference from others. Moral freedom is realized through the power of individuals to determine through their own reflection what is right and to act on that determination. Social freedom is realized through self-conscious participation in forms of social cooperation that provide conditions for the realization of personal and moral freedom and conditions for their own existence and reproduction as well. Personal freedom must be rooted in moral freedom, which in turn must be rooted in social freedom. An attempt to provide the first without the second would realize reason in an unreasonable form, as would an attempt to provide the second without the third. Finally, a free social world must make available, through philosophy, speculative insight into the reason embodied in these forms. Such insight provides the self-consciousness essential to the full realization of the free will.

After presenting Hegel's theory, I raise some questions concerning whether it is successful (Section 3.6). Drawing in part from the young Marx's critique,[8] I try to confirm what seems to be an unresolved tension between separatist and integrationist characterizations on Hegel's part of the relation of civil society to the political state.

Next, in Chapter 4, I lay out Marx's mature conceptions of value and capital, as they are found in *Capital*. I stress their nature as conceptions

---

[8] *Critique of Hegel's Philosophy of Right* and 'On the Jewish Question' [93, vol. 3; 95, part 1, vol. 2].

of economic estrangement, and I try to show how Marx understands them to provide the basis of a critique of political economy for its ideological aspects. Marx contrasts commodity production, in which the 'value form' (*Wertform*) of the products of labor is the dominant interpersonal production relation, with a possible social world in which individuals in their everyday working lives bear thoroughly 'reasonable' (*vernünftige*) relations to one another and to nature [90, p. 173; 95, part 2, 6:110]. Since he conceives of commodity producers as acting rationally in making their economic decisions, he in effect regards the value form as a realization of reason in an unreasonable form, a form in which producers are dominated by their own production process, and hence a form of estrangement. Marx regards capitalism as a form of commodity production that develops and intensifies this estrangement. In confronting capital, workers confront their own labor in an alien, hostile form, one that requires them to work at the direction of another and to perform labor and even surplus labor as a mere means of maintaining their existence, and one that generates unemployment and poverty. Moreover, this estrangement has material-technical as well as socioeconomic aspects. Workers' social productive powers—science, technology, division of labor, and so on—are developed and applied at the expense of and in opposition to their individual productive powers. For Marx, all of these developments intensify the character of the production process as an unreasonable realization of human reason and a form of unfreedom.

After presenting Marx's account, I consider some features of Hegel's theory in light of it (Section 4.6). Implicit in Marx's analysis are potential criticisms of Hegel's views (1) on the compatibility of commodity production and freedom, (2) on the division of labor and machinery, (3) on the wage transaction as a form of freedom, and (4) on poverty and the existence of a 'rabble'. The most surprising of these criticisms is perhaps the first: If Marx is right, then given what Hegel himself requires for the social realization of freedom, there is no room in his system of ethical life for an economy based on the production of commodities, let alone capitalist production. The basic reason is that commodity production, as social production by private individuals, precludes knowledge at the stage of production whether and to what extent producing activities will count as part of the social division of labor, whereas Hegel's rights of moral subjectivity require that such contributions be the objects of self-conscious collective intention.

Marx's elaboration of value and capital as forms of estrangement in volume 1 of *Capital* rests on some simplifying assumptions about the quantitative determination of equilibrium prices and the equilibrium rate of profit in capitalist economies. Volume 3 relaxes these assumptions and attempts to provide a more generally applicable theory of price and profit determination, one that sustains the thrust of the earlier claims about estrangement. But Marx leaves these explorations in an incomplete and inadequate state—one, in fact, that contains a significant error. In Chapter 5 I try to indicate the lines of a more adequate theory, and I discuss its implications for the viability of Marx's account of estrangement. For example, I explore the extent to which Marx's claims that commodity production is a system of estrangement, that profits rest on the exploitation of labor, and that capital is workers' own labor in an alien form can be sustained in the more general setting. The discussion is perforce technical, but I make an effort to use clear, simple examples and always to say in plain English what is being argued. For readers who are interested, I provide in an appendix some of the more technical considerations supporting claims made in the chapter.

Chapter 6, on 'strategic estrangement', is an effort to develop a general conception of estrangement of which Marx's notion of economic estrangement is a special case. According to this conception, when agents act independently of one another in a social setting, their powers of reason can be active and realized, but in an unreasonable social form. Because of this social form, their action orientations together determine or constitute, in a way not under the control of reasoned reflection, macro-social tendencies with respect to certain features of their social world. The events governed by these tendencies work against the realization of their freedom. Since they unwittingly drive these tendencies, they are in effect restricting the scope of their own agency, the use of their rational powers, through the very exercise of these powers. In this respect, estrangement is an agency-induced social constriction of the powers of rational agency. For this kind of estrangement, the task of critical theory is to bring to light its existence, its roots in the social form of individuals' own agency, and the kind of social change required to eliminate it. Such knowledge, combined with the commitment to reason already present in the social world, could provide agents with a reason to make the transformation. Here again there are technical forays in the overall account, but I try to use clear examples and state in nontechnical terms what is being argued.

I provide the account for several reasons. First, it clarifies and straightforwardly explains several puzzling features that Marx attributes to value and capital—for example, that they rest on an 'occult power' and have a 'ghostly objectivity'. Second, as just noted, it provides a generalization of his conception of estrangement, one that can be applied to contexts that are not economic in any narrow sense; I sketch how it might be applied in the explanation of certain gender inequalities, for example. Third, it brings to light the importance of what I call independent agency—in contrast to joint or collective agency—as fertile ground for the development of estrangement. It thereby supports the analysis of Chapter 7, where the topic of independent agency comes up in a consideration of whether certain of Rawls's ideas are threatened by the possibility of estrangement. Fourth, it shows how estrangement can generate for itself a supporting ideology. Finally, it helps to clarify the possible grounds on which estrangement can be criticized.

Chapters 4, 5, and 6 provide an assessment of Marx's ideas that differs significantly from those of Habermas [42; 44; 45] and other influential critical theorists. At the same time, these chapters present Marx's treatment of estrangement in a way that makes its social-scientific viability and its status as critical theory apparent. Honneth [62, chap. 4] laments the fact that

> the organization of labour is now to be left to the globalizing forces of the capitalist labour market. The path thus demarcated…has paved the way for the sobering situation with which we are now confronted: the hardships of all those who not only fear losing their jobs, but are also concerned about the quality of their jobs, no longer resonate in the vocabulary of a critical theory of society [62, p. 58].

He proposes as a remedy a critique appealing to the normative necessity for workers to secure mutual recognition as participants in the social division of labour. He recognizes the Hegelian roots of such an idea, but he does not discuss Marx. A central aim of my treatment of Marx's ideas is to make clear their continuing relevance for just such a critique.

In Chapter 7, I turn to Rawls's political philosophy. Several similarities between Rawls's project and those of the philosophers studied in earlier chapters clearly indicate that he is concerned with estrangement. His effort to bring political reason into coherence and reconciling it with reasonable pluralism is similar to Kant's effort to provide a self-critique of reason. His conception of a well-ordered society that realizes democratic social unity echoes similar conceptions on the part of the earlier thinkers. Like Hegel, for example, he envisions a society that engages citizens' reason, draws willing allegiance to itself and thereby generates its own support, so that all citizens can with good reason find their social world and their place in it acceptable. What he takes to be the two moral powers of democratic citizenship, the capacity for a conception of the good and the capacity for a sense of justice, are akin to Hegel's conceptions of the personal and moral freedoms necessary to overcome estrangement. Moreover, he envisages important social roles for political philosophy. Two of these are (1) to reconcile us to the existence of reasonable pluralism, and (2) to extend the limits of real political possibility through the elaboration of realistic utopias. Finally, Rawls follows Marx in being concerned to avoid acceptance of ideological support for unreasonable social conditions. This concern makes an account of estrangement important to his project, because estrangement can sometimes generate for itself a supporting ideology.

Given this context, there are several ways an adequate treatment of estrangement and its relation to ideology could bear on Rawls's ideas: First, it could have significant implications for the assessment and critical development of his account of liberalism and justice. It could point to needed changes in that account's elaboration of its social ideals or in its proposals for implementation. For example, I make an effort to show that Rawls's conception of the difference principle implies a dualism between motives of self-interest and those of justice that is akin to the motivational estrangement that Hegel finds in Kantian morality, and that it closes off potential sources of egalitarian motivation (Section 7.3.2). I claim (Section 7.5) that this estrangement stems from a form of individualism that itself grows out of the role of Rawls's two fundamental interests of democratic citizenship in generating principles of justice through the original-position exercise, and thus getting rid of the estrangement would require a revision in the ideal of democratic citizenship so as to accommodate a more 'co-deliberative' interest. Moreover, the individualism is one that allows the emergence of economic and strategic estrangement. I also develop an argument that commodity production is incompatible with Rawls's ideal of a well-ordered society and hence cannot figure in an implementation of his conception of justice (Section 7.4.3).

Second, an adequate account of estrangement might underwrite rebuttals of some extant *criticisms* of Rawls's theory. In Section 7.3.1 I argue that G. A. Cohen's well-known critique of Rawls's treatment of the difference principle [24] fails and that its inadequacy is due in part to its use of an abstract moralism implicated in estrangement.

Third, it might turn out that estrangement-generated ideology is *already* a real social force supporting certain entrenched beliefs and attitudes standing in the way of acceptance of Rawls's ideas. Even here, where the problem does not lie in the putatively well-ordered society supported by his theory but in the way things are now, incorporating an account of estrangement and ideology into the theory might be needed, if political philosophy is to succeed at extending the limits of practical political possibility. For example, Murphy and Nagel refer to the persistence in 'our everyday thinking' of the libertarian idea that we have a strict, unqualified right to what we earn on a natural—i.e., government-free—market, and they take this persistence to explain the appeal of certain insufficiently egalitarian and indeed logically indefensible criteria of tax equity [100, pp. 31, 34–35]. They point out a fallacy that they think illegitimately shores up the idea, but they implicitly concede that their critique will not by itself lead people to relinquish it, because '[t]he moral ideas that do the work of legitimation have to be graspable and intuitively appealing, not just correct' [100, p. 188]. They do not investigate, however, whether the supposed comparative intuitive appeal of this idea has roots in economic estrangement, nor whether that explanation could undermine the appeal.

Fourth, it might also turn out that existing, estrangement-generated ideology finds its way into Rawls's theory itself. In Section 7.4.1, I argue that Rawls's conception of justice unnecessarily incorporates an instrumentalism about economic life that is an all too real phenomenon induced by existing commodity production and capital as forms of estrangement. And in Section 7.4.2 I make a similar claim about Rawls's characterization of the index of primary goods.

Chapter 7's analysis does not warrant on balance a pessimism about the long-term possibility of eliminating the estrangement standing in the way of democratic social unity. If the analysis is correct, however, it speaks in favor of significant revisions in Rawls conception, especially its ideal of democratic citizenship and its envisaged social implementation. My hope is that treating Rawls's work as a contribution to the conversation on estrangement and to the critical theory tradition will help to identify a way forward.

# 2
# Kantian Morality and Estrangement

Kant is an incipient philosopher of estrangement. Though he does not use the vocabulary of estrangement that became prominent in the nineteenth century, he offers an account of moral evil that accords it the marks of the concept, and he understands his moral philosophy as aimed at dispelling the semblance of morality as an alien imposition, a semblance that in his view helps to sustain socially systemic moral evil. I want to discuss his moral philosophy as an attempt to foster such a self-clarification.

## 2.1  Moral evil as estrangement

Recall the three interrelated features in our working definition of estrangement (Chapter 1):

1. It is a social condition in which reason is realized in an unreasonable form.
2. It is a condition in which agents unwittingly turn their own agency into a force against itself, a force that blocks or distorts the realization of their freedom.
3. It can only be eliminated through a kind of social unity.

Even though Kant does not use the term 'estrangement', moral evil on his conception is the substance of a phenomenon that can be understood in precisely these terms.[1]

---

[1] Velkley [148, pp. 41–42] discerns an incipient account of evil as self-alienation in Kant's writings, in a line of thought that goes back to Rousseau. See also Wood [155, p. 334].

(1) We noted in the last chapter that reason, for Kant, is a self-subsistent set of principles for theoretical and practical reasoning, judgment and action. While these principles set standards for their own use, it is possible to use them in violation of these standards. If such uses become an established social practice, we can speak of that practice as a realization of reason in an unreasonable form.

For Kant, moral evil or immoral action must be viewed as originating in a propensity of our free power of choice. This propensity is characterized by a 'supreme maxim'—a second-order maxim for adopting maxims that allows departures from the strict priority of moral incentives over those of self-love [70; 66, 6:21–22, 31–32]. The propensity thus reflects acceptance of ways of reasoning that do not respect the required priority of pure practical reason (that is, reason as a self-sufficient issuer of unconditional requirements on action), in which morality is rooted, over empirical practical reason (reason in support of the inclinations). In immoral action, then, persons guide their power of choice by reasoning that clashes with the requirements of their own practical reason. If such reasoning becomes socially systemic, then moral evil becomes the substance of a social practice that realizes reason in an unreasonable form.

For Kant, though we are individually responsible for our own immoral actions, the propensity to evil is basically a social phenomenon. It has social causes:

[O]nly in comparison with others does one judge oneself happy or unhappy. Out of this self-love originates the inclination *to gain worth in the opinion of others*, originally, of course, merely *equal worth*: not allowing anyone superiority over oneself, bound up with the constant anxiety that others might be striving for ascendancy; but from this arises gradually an unjust desire to acquire superiority for oneself over others [70; 66, 6:27].

It is not the instigation of nature that arouses what should properly be called the *passions*, which wreak such great devastation in [the human being's] originally good predisposition. His needs are but limited, and his state of mind in providing for them moderate and tranquil. He is poor (or considers himself so) only to the extent that he is anxious that other human beings will consider him poor and will despise him for it. Envy, addiction to power, avarice, and the malignant inclinations associated with these, assail his nature, which on its own is undemanding, *as soon as he is among human beings*. Nor is it necessary to assume that these are sunk into evil and are examples that lead him astray: it suffices that they are there, that they surround him, and that they are human beings, and they will mutually corrupt each other's moral disposition and make one another evil [70; 66, 6:94].

(2) This condition is a 'dominion of evil' [70; 66, 6:93], in which individuals act as though they were *'instruments of evil'* [70; 66, 6:97]. It is a condition that they unwittingly bring upon themselves:

> Human beings... mutually corrupt one another's moral predisposition, and even with the good will of each individual... they deviate through their dissensions from the common goal of goodness, as though they were *instruments of evil*, and expose one another to the danger of falling... under its dominion [70; 66, 6:97].

(3) Finally, this condition can be eliminated only through the social unity that characterizes a community collectively organized to realize and sustain morality:

> If no means could be found to establish a union which has for its end the prevention of this evil and the promotion of the good in the human being – an enduring and ever expanding society, solely designed for the preservation of morality by counteracting evil with united forces – however much the individual human being might do to escape from the dominion of this evil, he would still be in incessant danger of relapsing into it [70; 66, 6:94].

While I think that the above remarks by Kant establish that on his view, the propensity to evil is in important respects a social phenomenon, they do not explicitly point to any positive condition other than just the basic social fact of living among others. Kant gives no analysis of any very specific social arrangements (for example, capitalism) that might give rise to the propensity for evil based on competitive self-estimation. This lack may make it hard to conceive of the social unity that would eliminate the propensity to evil rooted in humanity's social nature, other than through an abstractly characterized ethical community.[2] It may seem that Kant does not provide anything more than a *transsocial* propensity to evil rooted in humanity's social nature, in which case it might be ineradicable (even asymptotically). Yet I think that Kant

---

[2] I owe this point to an anonymous reviewer for Palgrave Macmillan.

does draw an admittedly abstract but nonetheless definite social contrast between what he calls the 'ethical state of nature', in which the moral law is not a publicly unifying principle but is a law prescribed by each individual to himself, and an ethico-civil state in which its members prescribe the moral law publicly to themselves as a body acting collectively [70; 66, 6:95–96].[3] That said, however, Kant's treatment may be short on specifics that would assure us of the effectiveness and stability of such a public affirmation of what remains at bottom an individual morality.

Kant's treatment of the propensity to evil is quite sophisticated by game-theoretic standards. One way of putting his point is to say that morality realized as an individualistic system, where each person acts independently of the others, lacks stability, since the expectations supporting it are precariously balanced as on the point of a needle; uncertainty of any order, no matter how high—for example uncertainty on A's part concerning B's certainty of A's certainty of B's action—can take the system out of equilibrium and launch it into an alien dynamic, one driving immorality as a system of estrangement. Morality individualistically realized would thus be vulnerable to the strategic estrangement discussed in Chapter 6.

One might object to this account on the grounds that if morality is genuinely realized, then everyone has a perfectly moral disposition and ipso facto is insensitive to how he or she expects others to act. The problem with this objection is that it is working with an unrealistic conception—for Kant—of the realization of morality. For Kant, no one has or will ever have a holy will; the most that can be asked of an individual is a striving that results in a constant improvement in one's moral character. This fact raises the specter of a threshold level of temptation above which one would act immorally. In this situation, the worry that others will act immorally, or that they will expect one to act immorally, or that they will expect one to expect them to act immorally, and so on, can in principle raise the (expected) costs of acting morally to an unacceptably high level.

## 2.2 Moral philosophy as critical theory

While Kant thinks that the requirements of morality are accessible, as uncompromising demands—as requirements of pure practical reason— in ordinary moral thinking, he also believes that our attachment to

---

[3] This distinction between independent and collective agency will be important to our analysis of estrangement, particularly in Chapter 6.

them can waver in favor of our own needs and desires. To that extent, he thinks, they can seem to have an alien character. In part this semblance arises because the idea of reason as by itself providing a warranted and sufficient incentive for action is so different from the idea of reason as serving inclination, a function that is pervasive and plain, that we can easily come to question the legitimacy of moral demands, or at least their purity as unconditionally valid [70; 66, 4:404–405]. Several factors can work to reinforce such doubts. Among them are (1) the apparent reasonableness of needs and desires that come into conflict with moral requirements, (2) philosophical doctrines that would root morality in happiness as the moral good, (3) various strains of enlightenment thinking—such as naturalism, empiricism, and skepticism about the claims of traditional metaphysics—that question the possibility of pure reason as a source of practical cognition, (4) the explanatory programs of the empirical sciences, and (5) ordinary experience and reflection on the character of empirical knowledge. All these factors can seem to support the idea that reason is available for practical use only as empirically conditioned reason—reason in support of inclination.[4] In virtue of these challenges, a central aim of Kant's moral philosophy is to elicit a self-clarification that will display and strengthen our identification—already implicitly present—with the moral law in all its purity, so that we can firmly regard it as a full expression of our freedom and dignity.

Thus it is plausible to read Kant not only as concerned with moral evil as a social condition of alienation, a condition in which freedom is not realized, but also as thinking that the semblance of morality as an alien imposition can provide a kind of 'ideological' support for this condition. On this view, by exposing the semblance for what it is, philosophy can function as socially effective critique, eliciting a self-clarification that will enable individuals to see the unreasonableness of current practices—their character as estrangement—and to identify conditions and means for their transformation in an emancipatory direction. By functioning as critical theory in this way, Kant's moral philosophy would also provide resources for a response to Hegel's charge, discussed below (Section 2.3), that Kantian morality itself is a form of estrangement. We might put the issue this way: According to Kant, those who take morality to be an alien imposition are thereby in a condition of merely *subjective* alienation; morality merely *seems* to them to be an unreasonable form of their reason, a self-imposed limitation of their freedom, because of the way it constrains satisfaction of their seemingly

---

[4] For further discussion, see Stephen Engstrom's Introduction to the Pluhar translation of the second *Critique* [72, pp. xxvii–xxxii].

legitimate empirical needs, their empirical practical reason. For Hegel, however, this appearance is no mere semblance: such individuals are responding correctly to a condition of *objective* alienation.

Against this general background, Kant sets four tasks for himself that would help to dispel the semblance of morality as an alien imposition. They are first, to show that morality is fully expressive of our freedom rather than restrictive of it; second, to provide a moral psychology that allows for our susceptibility to taking a practical interest in the moral law; third, to show that morality nonetheless provides adequate accommodation for the realization of happiness as an objective good; and fourth, to integrate morality, with its unconditional validity and its implication of our freedom, into a coherent conception of reason as a whole. I will take up each of these tasks in turn.

### 2.2.1  Morality as the expression of freedom

Two of the central claims that Kant tries to secure in the crucial first chapter of the 'Analytic' section of the *Critique of Practical Reason* are first, that the fundamental law of pure practical reason has the following formulation:

> So act that the maxim of your will could always hold at the same time as a principle in a giving of universal law [68; 66, 5:30]

and second, that this law is given in us as the moral law by a 'fact of reason' [68; 66, 5:31]. Though Kant does not explicitly display an argument for the first claim, his reasoning seems to go roughly as follows. Distinguish between particular practical laws and the fundamental law. The fundamental law specifies the condition that a particular principle or maxim must satisfy to be necessarily valid for all rational beings. That condition cannot be one satisfied through the principle's 'matter', i.e., the object to be realized by acting on the principle. For such a condition could bind the subject to the principle only if the representation of the object as existing produced a feeling of pleasure in the mind of the subject. Such a condition would be an empirical one that is only contingently satisfied. Thus the principle would not necessarily be valid for all rational beings. So the condition must be satisfied through the form of the principle. But the form of a practical principle that is universally valid is nothing other than legislative or lawgiving form, the principle's capacity to give itself as universal legislation. So the requirement to act only on maxims with that form is the fundamental law of pure practical reason.

The two claims we've specified would root morality in pure practical reason. Yet they would not be enough to allay the sense that in opposing our inclinations morality requires the suppression of an essential part of ourselves and is to that extent a restriction of our freedom. For what can be said to someone who worries that freedom lies in unconstrained empirical practical reason, which the moral law constricts? It is not enough to point out that morality, as pure practical reason, necessarily has rational priority over empirical practical reason.

Kant does go on, however, to assert Theorem IV, which has two parts. For our purposes, we need consider only the first part:

> *Autonomy* of the will is the sole principle of all moral laws and of duties in keeping with them [68; 66, 5:33].

Here is the proof Kant offers:

> [T]he sole principle of morality consists in the independence from all matter of the law (namely, from a desired object) and at the same time in the determination of choice through the mere form of giving universal law that a maxim must be capable of. That *independence*, however, is freedom in the *negative* sense, whereas this *lawgiving of its own* on the part of pure and, as such, practical reason is freedom in the *positive* sense. Thus the moral law expresses nothing other than the *autonomy* of pure practical reason, that is, freedom, and this is itself the formal condition of all maxims, under which alone they can accord with the supreme practical law [68; 66, 5:33].

Kant's treatment is so brief and lacking in explicit reference to earlier claims taken to be established that it is not clear exactly what the theorem is supposed to assert, nor precisely how its proof is supposed to go. For example, does the theorem actually assert our autonomy, or just autonomy's status as morality's basic principle? And on which previous results does the proof of the theorem rest? It makes sense to interpret the theorem as asserting our autonomy, since Kant has just put forward the claim that morality is given in us by a fact of reason [68; 66, 5:31], and the proof claims that the moral law expresses 'nothing other than the *autonomy* of pure practical reason, that is, freedom'. But on these grounds, we should take the theorem to assert our freedom as well as our autonomy. Moreover, to claim that morality expresses 'nothing other' than our autonomy or freedom seems to take the proof even further.

I want to suggest that Kant is concerned to capture a circle of implications linking rationality (in the strong sense that includes pure practical reason), morality, freedom, and autonomy.[5] To be sure, given morality, we could use this circle to derive autonomy and freedom, but as we'll see, I want to claim that its significance goes beyond that fact. However, even if Kant does not have the circle in mind in his proof, he makes earlier claims that yield it, making it available for a proof of the theorem on the stronger interpretation suggested by what he explicitly says.

We can use the following abbreviations to make the circle perspicuous:

L  Our wills are determinable only by the mere legislative form of our maxims[6]

R  We are subject to the fundamental law of pure practical reason, i.e., we have rational wills (we have a faculty of pure practical reason)

M  We are subject to the moral law

A  We have autonomous wills

F  We have free wills.

The following six numbered propositions will lay a basis for the circle.

1. If R then L (by Theorem III)

Kant's Theorem III states: 'If a rational being is to think of his maxims as practical universal laws, he can think of them only as principles that contain the determining ground of the will not by their matter but only by their form' [68; 66, 5:27]. By way of proof, Kant argues that if the matter (the object to be produced) were the determining ground of the will, then the maxim would determine the will only subject to an empirical condition and thus could not be binding on all rational beings. But then the only thing left to determine the will is the maxim's legislative form.

2. If L then R (analytic)

---

[5] For discussion of a similar idea, see Sussman [145].

[6] This proposition is a paraphrase of the supposition of Kant's 'Problem I' (except that Kant apples it to 'a will' rather than to 'our wills') [68; 66, 5:28]. I mean it, as I think Kant does, as normative; it does not claim that we cannot determine our wills by something other than mere legislative form, but only that we ought not to do so.

3. If L then F (demonstrated solution to Kant's 'Problem I')

We may summarize Kant's proof of this proposition as follows: Anything that is determined by the causality of nature must lie in the empirical world (the world of appearances: things representable by the senses in time). But lawgiving form can be represented only by reason and therefore does not belong among appearances. Hence if lawgiving form is the only determining ground of a will, that will must be independent of the causality of nature i.e. it must be (transcendentally) free [68; 66, 5:28].

4. If F then L (demonstrated solution to Kant's 'Problem II')

In his proof of this proposition Kant argues that the matter of a practical law can be given only empirically, whereas a free will is independent of empirical conditions. Therefore its determining ground cannot lie in the matter of the law but must lie in its lawgiving form [68; 66, 5:29].

5. R if and only if M (*Groundwork* II)

In *Groundwork* II, Kant identifies the formulation in the second *Critique* of the fundamental law of pure practical reason with the categorical imperative as it is found in ordinary moral consciousness. In the Preface to the second *Critique*, Kant says that the work presupposes the *Groundwork* 'insofar as this constitutes preliminary acquaintance with the principle of duty and provides and justifies a determinate formula of it' [68; 66, 5:8].

6. R if and only if A (analytic)

We are now in a position to construct the circle. First, 'if morality then rationality':

7. If M then R (from 5)

Then 'if rationality then autonomy':

8. If R then A (from 6)

Then 'if autonomy then freedom':

9. If A then F (from 1, 3, 6)

Finally, close the circle with 'if freedom then morality':

10. If F then M (from 2, 4, 5)

Now use the fact of reason as an entry into the circle and use the circle to derive our autonomy and our freedom:

11. M (fact of reason)
12. A (from 7, 8, 11)
13. F (from 9, 12)

One might question at this point why it is important to close the circle. To derive our autonomy and our freedom we did not need to appeal to the closing link (10) or to any of the consequences of closure. So what's the point of closure? One answer is that this closing link is necessary to establish one of the claims Kant takes himself to have proved: that 'the moral law expresses nothing but the *autonomy* of pure practical reason, i.e., freedom' [68; 66, 5:33]. In principle, the circle might not have closed; we might have been able to derive freedom (or autonomy) from morality but not the converse. After all, doesn't the very reality of our freedom mean that we can exercise it in other ways than morally? Without deriving morality from freedom we would not have shown that the true expression or full realization of our freedom lies in morality. We would not have foreclosed the possibility that in certain respects the moral law suppresses freedom. We would not have shown that the moral law is the only principle that respects our status as free, the only law that is *competent* to determine a free will.[7] We would not then have provided an answer to the question that sparked our interest in Theorem IV in the first place: What can be said to someone who worries that freedom lies in unconstrained empirical practical reason, which the moral law constricts? Without adequately answering this question we cannot provide such a person with sufficient resources to overcome the semblance of morality as an alien imposition.

Moreover, closing the circle establishes the equivalence[8] or interdependence of four ways of thinking of ourselves: as rational, as autonomous, as free, and as morally responsible. Closure connects these ideas in a way that makes them of a piece, so that they stand or fall together. The fact of reason, in providing entry to the circle, opens up

---

[7] Compare Kant's formulation of Problem II, whose solution (4) figures in closing the circle (that is, in proving claim 10): 'Supposing that a will *is free*: to find the law that alone is competent [*tauglich*] to determine it necessarily' [68; 66, 5:29].

[8] Abusing notation slightly: $A \rightarrow B \rightarrow C \rightarrow A$ implies $A \leftrightarrow B \leftrightarrow C \leftrightarrow A$.

for us the possibility of a conception of ourselves in terms of these ideas. In addition, Kant would want to expand the circle in terms of several of the ideas in *Groundwork* II: ideas of persons as bearers of dignity, as ends in themselves and worthy of respect, as equally sovereign authorities with respect to the terms of social cooperation, and so on. The fact that all these ideas stand or fall together makes identification with the moral law, as opposed to a rejection of it as an alien imposition, a more attractive—Kant would say indispensable—option.

That the fact of reason provides entry to the circle needs closer examination. For it is not only *what* Kant expects us to accept in these pages that suggests a concern with estrangement, but also his *method* for securing acceptance. Consider the fundamental law of pure practical reason. Kant offers no proof of this law; in fact he thinks no empirical evidence or antecedently known rational principle is available from which it could be inferred [68; 66, 5:31]. The only thing that Kant says in its behalf is that in our moral thinking we have an incontrovertible consciousness of it as valid ('it thrusts itself upon us on its own as a synthetic a priori proposition' [68; 66, 5:31]). This 'thrusting' is what Kant means by a fact or deed of reason (*Faktum der Vernunft*) [68; 66, 5:31], reason's proving its reality 'through the deed' [68; 66, 5:3].[9] Many have read Kant's invocation of the fact of reason as a reversion to dogmatic rationalism. However, Kant's remark is not a direct affirmation of the law, much less a proffered proof, but an articulation of and stimulus to a meta-level reflection in which *we* recognize the law as given *in us* by reason.[10] Kant aims at enabling his readers to liberate *themselves* from the appearance of the moral law as an alien imposition by understanding themselves in terms of the order of interdependent concepts in which the concept of morality is imbedded. Once we enter the circle of concepts through the fact of reason, we can see that each concept—morality included—is presupposed by all the others and gains some support thereby.

For Kant, philosophy has a social role. It provides a defense of reason, i.e., a defense of the competence of socially organized persons to

---

[9] On the question of whether 'fact of reason' or 'deed of reason' is a better rendering of '*Faktum der Vernunft*', see Engstrom's discussion [72, pp. xli–xlii].

[10] Cf. Engstrom's remark: 'If the basic law of pure practical reason is a fact in the sense just indicated, then showing that pure reason is practical must be a matter of drawing attention to this law, of directing thought to it in a way that clearly reveals its basis in reason and thereby puts us in a position to achieve a reflective (philosophical) recognition of it as given in us by reason' [72, p. xlii].

assume responsibility for their judgments and actions, by holding themselves accountable to mutually acceptable standards. Kant says in the Doctrine of Method at the end of the first *Critique* that the claim of reason is 'never anything more than the agreement of free citizens' [71; 66, A739/B766]. If we take this idea seriously, then we should read Kant as seeking consensus rather than engaging in an exercise of showing true. By entering the circle of ideas in our reflection and coming back around to the fact of reason, we can come to understand its a priori nature as rooted in our mutual acceptance of those ideas. That is, its a priori nature is due to the fact that we inhabit a culture of 'persons' who as such 'always already' think of themselves and one another as worthy of respect, as ends in themselves, as free and equal, and so on. This reading brings Kant more into line with the critical theory tradition and shows what that tradition has seen in him.

In connection with the fact of reason and the question of alienation, we can draw a parallel between Kant and Hegel, whose *Phenomenology of Spirit* is explicitly concerned with facilitating the development of consciousness 'to a point at which it gets rid of its semblance of being burdened with something alien' [48, ¶89; 57, 3:80–81]. In this work Hegel aims at laying out a pathway of thought through which individuals can gain access to an order of ideas in terms of which they can achieve a warranted form of self-consciousness that is free of estrangement, namely that of 'spirit's consciousness of itself as spirit', or 'absolute knowing'. Similarly, Kant's fact of reason is purportedly a laid-out pathway of thinking that provides access to a non-alienating order of concepts. And just as in Hegel's case it is important that the order of concepts turn back on itself in his philosophical system to allow comprehension, from the newly achieved point of view, of the very course of thinking that provided individuals with access to that point of view in the first place, in Kant's case too it is important that the circle close by coming to include its point of entry, namely the fact of reason, our consciousness of the moral law as supremely authoritative. In these respects Kant is a philosopher of estrangement *avant la lettre*.[11]

### 2.2.2 Moral psychology

For Kant, by virtue of the fact of reason, in our moral thinking we are conscious of the moral law as supremely authoritative. This

---

[11] Franks further discusses the idea of a parallel to Kant's fact of reason in Hegel's thought [35, pp. 375–378].

consciousness even discloses our transcendental freedom to us, so that we are aware that in some sense we can act from that law. Moreover, we can even know, as we've seen, that the moral law is the only law competent to determine the will in a way that respects its independence of natural causality.

Yet there are some motivational questions that remain. Precisely because we have transcendental freedom, we can inquire about our susceptibility to act *from* the moral law rather than in some other way. What is it about us that makes us susceptible to taking a practical interest in the moral law rather than, say, viewing it merely as an intellectual curiosity, even granting its validity? Moreover, we are confronted by nonmoral incentives as well as moral ones:

> [W]e find our nature as sensible beings so constituted that the matter of the faculty of desire (objects of inclination, whether of hope or fear) first forces itself upon us, and we find our pathologically determinable self, even though it is quite unfit to give universal law through its maxims, nevertheless striving antecedently to make its claims primary and originally valid, just as if it constituted our entire self [68; 66, 5:74].

What motivational resources do we have for according our varied incentives the order and weight that morality would require? Given that Kant's account aims at a self-clarification, and in particular one that removes the apparently alien character of morality, these are important questions. Kant answers them by providing a moral psychology, a way of thinking of ourselves from the practical point of view, that he takes to supply a basis for identifying with an appropriate conception of the person.

This psychology attributes to the human being a 'free power of choice' and three 'predispositions to good' [70; 66, 6:26–28]. The latter are:

1. A predisposition to 'animality': a physical and purely mechanical self-love that does not require the exercise of reason. It is generally driven by instincts, such as those of self-preservation, propagation, care of children, and community.
2. A predisposition to 'humanity', which requires the use of rationality. It falls under the heading of self-love, and it disposes us to compare

our happiness with that of others. Under certain conditions it can give rise to social vices of envy, spite, and the like.[12]

3. A predisposition to 'personality', which is the susceptibility to respect for the moral law as of itself a sufficient incentive to the power of choice.

These predispositions cannot determine our will unless they are incorporated into our maxims by our free power of choice [70; 66, 6:23–24]. We must take all three as given, but we can and must assign them a priority or weight through the maxims we follow.

Each way of ordering the three predispositions defines a moral character. There is thus a conception of the person, a way of thinking about oneself, that corresponds to each ordering. A morally good person will accord unconditional priority to the predisposition to personality. Our free power of choice is not determined by this ordering. We must freely incorporate it into our maxims, and it is up to us whether we do so. Yet Kant thinks that there is a basis for identifying with the conception of the person founded on the moral ordering, for four reasons:[13]

1. The predisposition to personality is unconditionally good and incorruptible [70; 66, 6:28].
2. Unlike the other two predispositions, it is 'rooted in reason practical of itself, i.e. in reason legislating unconditionally' [70; 66, 6:28]. This makes it the only predisposition suitable to be ranked in an unconditionally prior position.
3. An ordering of the predispositions in which the predisposition to humanity is prior would not distinguish us from beings that are simply determined to act in rational pursuit of their happiness, as defined by given, naturally caused desires; it would not reflect our status as transcendentally free. Similarly, if the predisposition to animality were treated as prior, the ordering would not even reflect our rationality; it would not distinguish us from animals acting from instinct. But the predisposition to personality reflects our transcendental freedom; its unconditional priority is the only ranking that is appropriate to us as persons with a free power of choice.

---

[12] The sense of 'humanity' here is not the same as that found in the humanity formulation of the categorical imperative.
[13] Here I largely follow Rawls [116, pp. 296–298].

4. The predisposition to personality cannot be repressed; we are always susceptible to respect for the moral law as itself a sufficient incentive [70; 66, 6:35].

These considerations provide, Kant thinks, a basis for our identification with a conception of the person incorporating the moral ordering of the predispositions.

### 2.2.3   The accommodation of happiness

To dispel completely the apparently alien character of morality, Kant would have to show that morality provides sufficient room for the realization of happiness. For on Kant's conception, we are not only reasonable beings for whom moral worth or a good will is an unconditional good; we are also natural beings with desires and at the same time beings with powers of empirical practical reason. Our status as such gives rise to the natural albeit conditional good of happiness, understood as the satisfaction of our rationally organized desires. But precisely because of the priority of morality over happiness, of pure over empirical practical reason, it might be the case, for all that has been said so far, that the realization of morality leaves no room for the realization of happiness, in which case morality would estrange us from a fundamentally important aspect of ourselves. For we human beings, as beings in the order of nature, are inevitably interested in the actual, empirical consequences of our actions. That is, we have an interest in effecting changes in the natural world in accordance with reason's requirements, including those of empirical practical reason. Even though transcendental freedom belongs to us as intelligible beings, and even though good willing has value regardless of its effects, our will is not capable of being satisfied solely by the self-determination of our free power of choice through the form of a possible universal legislation. For the very settling on an action is always, for us, the adoption of an end as a contemplated effect in the empirical world.

> [I]n the absence of all reference to an end no determination of the will can take place in human beings at all, since no such determination can occur without an effect, and its representation, though not as the determining ground of the power of choice nor as an end that comes first in intention, must nonetheless be admissible as the consequence of that power's determination to an end through the law...; without this end, a power of choice which does not [thus] add to a contemplated action the thought of either an objectively or

subjectively determined object... can itself obtain no satisfaction [70; 66, 6:4].

Moreover, practical reason, like theoretical reason, has its own interest in systematic unity, and it seeks integration of actions, both those of a single agent over time and those of different agents. So practical reason must provide us with an ultimate or final end, one that is capable of unifying the various intentions of all moral agents and all chains of consequences into a coherent whole that gives individual conduct on a given occasion its ultimate meaning or point (Yovel [156, pp. 39–40]). This end must include the complete good, a world that realizes all that is objectively valuable, not only morality but also the happiness that is conditional upon it.

> [I]t cannot possibly be a matter of indifference to reason how to answer the question, *What is then the result of this right conduct of ours?* nor to what we are to direct our doings or nondoings, even granted this is not fully in our control, at least as something with which they are to harmonize. And this is indeed only the idea of an object that unites within itself the formal condition of all such ends as we ought to have (duty) with everything which is conditional upon ends we have and which conforms to duty (happiness proportioned to its observance), that is, the idea of a highest good in the world.... This idea... meets our natural need, which would otherwise be a hindrance to moral resolve, to think for all our doings and nondoings taken as a whole some sort of ultimate end which reason can justify [70; 66, 6:4-5].

Since without such a complete good justified as an end by reason, there would be a 'hindrance' to moral resolve, *morality itself must require it as an end.* To be sure, on any given occasion, we may need to be prepared to sacrifice our own individual happiness for the sake of the moral law. But our commitment to the moral law cannot be sustained unless we can think of moral conduct as having causality in the world and thereby contributing to the realization of an ultimate end that includes whatever happiness—our own or others'—is objectively valuable (for Kant this will be morally permissible happiness in proportion to virtue). For this reason, according to Kant, the moral law 'extends itself' to include human happiness as a necessary end [70; 66, 6:7n].

Thus for Kant, morality itself provides us with an ultimate end—the highest good—that is both a moral world and a happy world. Since we are commanded by morality to bring about this world, we are justified in believing that its realization is possible through our will.[14] Hence, Kant would argue, morality makes adequate room for happiness and thus does not estrange us from the empirical side of ourselves.[15]

### 2.2.4   The unity of reason

Yet this line of thought discloses a problem that has been lurking in the background since our discussion of Kant's view that the fact of reason discloses our freedom to us. The validity of the moral law presupposes our freedom. In addition, as we now learn, the validity of the moral law implies the possibility of the highest good. As we'll see presently, that possibility in turn has its own presuppositions, which together with that of freedom raise the possibility that morality will always have an alien character, in virtue of constraints they place on the ability of reason to attain a self-subsistent unity among its principles. If morality and its presuppositions preclude such unity, then morality will to that extent take on an alien character, since it will thereby require reason to be in an unreasonable form.

The problem of the unity of reason is the problem of determining how the theoretical and practical uses of reason are to be structured and related to each other if they are to cohere into a single faculty of reason capable of realizing the fundamental interests of each. The problem is to come up with a 'constitution' of reason whose principles assign to different forms of reason appropriate domains of authority and responsibility so as to insure the ability of reason as a whole to satisfy all of its interests, both theoretical and practical, pure and empirical. It is reason itself that tackles this problem, by giving a critique of itself.

The unity of reason is necessary for the autonomy of reason. A reason without a unifying constitution is a reason at odds with itself; it

---

[14] This belief is made possible by reasonable faith in the existence of God, not as a providential God but rather as guarantor of the effectiveness of the causality of our will in bringing this world into being. God guarantees the possibility of success, but success must be achieved through our action. Here I follow Yovel [156, chap. 2].

[15] Kant's argumentation could be challenged at a number of points. One problem relevant to our topic is that on Kant's view, the achievement of the highest good is not possible in a finite length of time, since it requires the perfection of our wills. Therefore, he thinks, what the moral law really requires of us is a struggle to achieve an endless historical approximation of the highest good. But such a continuous approximation is not the avoidance of alienation but at best a gradual reduction of its severity. On this matter, see Yovel [156, pp. 96–98].

is a self-alienated reason. Moreover, if pure practical reason is incompatible with the unity of reason, then there will always be a point of view within reason from which morality appears alien, insofar as it can only exist within a reason divided against itself. As we'll see presently, the existence of pure practical reason constrains the possibilities for the unification of reason, in virtue of the fact that it requires the acceptance of certain theoretical claims that speculative reason must regard as theoretically undecidable. Kant needs to show that these constraints can be satisfied.

The constraints arise because pure practical reason requires certain theoretical presuppositions. Kant calls them postulates of pure practical reason.[16] He characterizes them as having the following three properties:

1. They are theoretical propositions in that they are meant to capture what exists; they aim at being true.
2. They are theoretically undecidable in that no possible empirical or a priori considerations count for or against their truth.
3. They are practically necessary in that they are rationally necessary presuppositions for the acceptance as binding of an unconditionally valid practical principle, the moral law.

Kant claims there are three such postulates, asserting the existence of God, transcendental freedom, and immortality. That they are theoretically undecidable he takes himself to have shown in the first *Critique*, since they assert the existence of objects beyond the realm of possible experience. He takes them to be practically necessary as presuppositions of acceptance of the moral law (freedom) and the highest good as its a priori object (God and immortality).

The postulates are theoretical propositions that are theoretically undecidable but practically necessary. Without any priority relation that would assign either to speculative or to practical reason primacy, i.e., the prerogative of determining whether reason should accept these propositions, there would be a conflict within reason, with speculative reason calling for their rejection (where rejection is not 'taking to be false' but rather 'not taking to be true') and practical reason calling for their acceptance (taking them to be true). There would be a conflict because 'it is still only one and the same reason which, whether from a theoretical or

---

[16] My account of Kant's doctrine of the postulates in part follows Willaschek's treatment [150].

a practical perspective, judges according to a priori principles' [68; 66, 5:121], and one and the same reason cannot coherently both take the propositions to be true and refrain from taking them to be true. Without a primacy relation, the unity of reason would not be realized, and reason would be in a state of self-alienation.

However, the unity of reason requires a constitution that provides for the full realization of the legitimate interests of each form of reason. The interest of the speculative use of reason consists in regulating the understanding so as to provide maximum systematic unity to empirical knowledge in a way that respects the limits of our theoretical knowledge and thereby avoids speculative mischief [68; 66, 5:120–121]. The interest of the practical use of reason lies in 'the determination of the will with respect to the final and complete end' [68; 66, 5:120], i.e., the highest good. So an assignment of primacy cannot infringe on either of these interests.

It is clear that assigning primacy to speculative reason would not meet this requirement. Doing so would require rejection of the propositions, thereby denying the presuppositions of the categorical requirements of pure practical reason and precluding the latter from determining 'the will with respect to the final and complete end' [68; 66, 5:120]. The only remaining possibility is the assignment of primacy to pure practical reason. Would such an assignment infringe on the legitimate interests of speculative reason? Kant thinks not, because reason would be accepting the propositions only on practical grounds and for a practical purpose. It would not be denying that they are undecidable on evidentiary grounds and therefore not available for the sort of expansion of knowledge that would amount to speculative mischief.

Kant would thus argue that pure practical reason is compatible with the unity of reason, through the assignment to it of primacy over speculative reason in the constitution of reason.

## 2.3   Hegel: Kantian morality as estrangement

Kant expounds his conception of moral evil as estrangement in his *Religion within the Boundaries of Mere Reason*. It is there also that he understands a community in which morality is the basis of social unity to be the only remedy for this estrangement. In a remark alluding to a passage in this very work, Hegel surprisingly claims that Kantian *morality*—not *im*morality—is itself a form of estrangement. In the passage in question, Kant contrasts the 'despotism' of religious service through faith in statutory articles or the observance of arbitrary practices (whether these be of the 'shaman of the Tunguses', the 'European prelate', the 'sensuous Wogulite', or the 'sublimated Puritan and Independent in Connecticut') with the freedom [70; 66, 6:179] of those 'whose intention is to find this service solely in the disposition to good life-conduct' [70; 66, 6:175–179]. Hegel comments:

> [B]etween the Shaman of the Tungus, the European prelate who rules church and state, the Voguls, and the Puritans, on the one hand, and the man who listens to his own command of duty, on the other, the difference is not that the former make themselves slaves, while the latter is free, but that the former have their lord outside themselves, while the latter carries his lord in himself, yet at the same time is his own slave. For the particular—impulses, inclinations, pathological love, sensuous experience, or whatever else it is called—the universal is necessarily and always something alien and objective [55, p. 211; 57, 1:323].

While Kant's moral philosophy as sketched in Section 2.2, insofar as it aims at dispelling the appearance of morality as an alien imposition, provides resources for a challenging reply to Hegel's charge, Hegel would not be satisfied. He goes on to develop a critique of Kant's moral philosophy as built on a fundamentally deficient framework, one that separates universal and particular interests, puts them at odds with each other, and prioritizes them, all in a way that impoverishes both. As a consequence, Kantian morality is implicated in both a motivational form of estrangement and a form of estrangement connected with the content of morality. Moreover, a deeper analysis shows that these forms of estrangement are rooted in a kind of individualism that is itself a form of estrangement.

### 2.3.1  Motivational estrangement

In 'The Spirit of Christianity and its Fate' [55; 57, vol. 1], which contains the passage quoted above, Hegel objects to what he sees as the absolute heterogeneity[17] of moral and empirical interests in Kant's conception of morality, along with the strict priority of the former over the latter. Empirical interests have their own distinctive character and retain meaning for the subject regardless of whether their pursuit respects this

---

[17] For further discussion of Hegel's critique of dichotomy in Kant's thought, see Sedgwick [136].

priority or not.[18] Thus, from the point of view of empirical interest, morality is an alien constraint. Since pure practical reason and empirical practical reason are both reason, morality is the realization of reason in an unreasonable form.

It is worth noting in passing that in making this charge, namely that Kantian morality is a form of estrangement, Hegel need not reject Kant's idea that *immorality* can take on the form of estrangement. The important thing for Hegel is the absolute heterogeneity and opposition of moral and empirical interests. Any social structure that rests on and preserves these conditions is a form of motivational estrangement. Against empirical interest, morality can appear as an alien constraint, but equally, against the demands of morality, empirical interest can take on an alien form.

Thus for Hegel, in Kantian morality the universal (moral) and particular (empirical) interests of the individual come apart, with the former dominating the latter. There is no possibility for the realization of the former through the latter, the universal through the particular, as would be the case were there an organic relation between the two. But, Hegel believes, such realization is precisely what is required to overcome the alienation in Kantian morality. There must be a thorough unification or synthesis of these different aspects of the person into an integrated whole (as opposed to their mere 'juxtaposition' within a priority structure).

For the young Hegel of 'The spirit of Christianity and its Fate', such a synthesis can take place in a community united through love, in which 'the correspondence of inclination with the law is such that law and inclination are no longer different'. Hegel is quick to point out that this way of putting the matter is misleading: '[T]he expression "correspondence of inclination with the law" is...wholly unsatisfactory because it implies that law and inclination are still particulars, still opposites.' For he is referring to a 'righteousness of a new kind', a 'synthesis in which the law...loses its universality and the subject its particularity; both lose their opposition, while in the Kantian conception of virtue this opposition remains, and the universal becomes the master and the particular the mastered' [55, pp. 214–215; 57, 1:326].

---

[18] It is true that for Kant, only morally permissible ends have objective value, but this feature of Kant's view is itself a function of the dualism of moral and empirical interests and the priority of right in his doctrine. Besides, even for Kant, all ends determined by the rational organization of a subject's empirical interests have subjective value and to that extent meaning for the subject.

Hegel later drops the idea of a community united through love, but he retains the idea of a need to imbue the individual's particular actions with universal significance. He holds that this integration is achievable only through a kind of social unity in which the individual's particular activity is recognized, by the individual and by others, not as a merely independent pursuit but rather as participation in a system of cooperation that realizes and maintains a reasonable social world. In the *Philosophy of Right* he says:

> The state is the actuality of concrete freedom. But concrete freedom requires that personal individuality [*Einzelheit*] and its particular interests should reach their full *development* and gain *recognition of their right* for itself (within the family and civil society), and also that they should, on the one hand, *pass over* of their own accord into the interest of the universal, and on the other, knowingly and willingly acknowledge this universal interest even as their own *substantial spirit*, and *actively pursue it* as their *ultimate end*. The effect of this is that the universal does not attain validity or fulfillment without the interest, the knowledge and the volition of the particular, and that individuals do not live as private persons merely for these particular interests without at the same time directing their will to a universal end [*in und für das Allgemeine willen*] and acting in conscious awareness of this end. The principle of modern states has enormous strength and depth because it allows the principle of subjectivity to attain fulfillment in the *self-sufficient extreme* of personal particularity, while at the same time *bringing it back to substantial unity* and so preserving this unity in the principle of subjectivity itself [52; 57, 7:§260].

Shortly after this passage Hegel says: 'Everything depends on the unity of the universal and the particular within the state' [52; 57, 7:§§260, 261Z]. These remarks indicate that though Hegel no longer speaks of love as the basis of a society-wide free social unity that could overcome the alienation he finds in Kantian morality, he still wants to oppose the latter with a 'righteousness of a new kind', one that does not merely insert two distinct kinds of interest ('inclination' and 'the law') into a priority structure but rather rests on a conception of the reasonableness of the social order and the organic contribution that one makes to its realization and maintenance through the pursuit of one's particular interests.

### 2.3.2　Content estrangement

Hegel objects not only to what happens to the particular when it is separated from the universal, but also to what happens to the universal when it is separated from the particular. It becomes too abstract and formal, he thinks, to provide the necessary ethical content. The content then must come from an illicit source.

Kant's conception of morality as rooted in the fundamental law of pure practical reason requires that practical reasoning governed solely by that law be capable of determining the requirements of morality as its output or content. In particular, it must be capable of yielding that content without taking any moral claims as given. Only formal principles of valid practical reasoning, and not any substantive moral claims, can be appealed to at the highest level. More specifically, if we grant that the fundamental law of pure practical reason is given by the categorical imperative, this condition requires that all moral requirements be derivable through testing of maxims for permissibility by applying the categorical imperative to them. It is clear from Kant's treatment in *Groundwork* II that he envisages two ways that a maxim can fail this test:

1. The maxim 'cannot even be *thought* without contradiction as a universal law of nature' [69; 66, 4:424]
2. While the maxim can be thought without contradiction as a universal law of nature, it is 'still impossible to *will* that [the] maxim be raised to the universality of a law of nature because such a will would contradict itself' [69; 66, 4:424].

The first sort of contradiction (a 'contradiction in conception') is one between what the plan of action described by the maxim presupposes and the conditions necessary for the maxim to hold as a universal law.[19] The second sort of contradiction (a 'contradiction in the will') is one between willing the maxim to be a universal law and willing what one necessarily wills as a rational agent. Kant intends his 'deposit case' to exemplify a contradiction in conception:

> I have, for example, made it my maxim to increase my wealth by every safe means. Now I have a *deposit* in my hands, the owner of which has died and left no record of it. This is, naturally, a case for

---

[19] Here I follow Scanlon, in 'How I Am Not a Kantian', his contribution to Parfit [105, 2:116–139], at 2:118.

my maxim. Now I want only to know whether that maxim could also hold as a universal practical law. I therefore apply the maxim to the present case and ask whether it could indeed take the form of a law, and consequently whether I could through my maxim at the same time give such a law as this: that everyone may deny a deposit which no one can prove has been made. I at once become aware that such a principle, as a law, would annihilate itself since it would bring it about that there would be no deposits at all [68; 66, 5:27].

Acting on the maxim as anticipated presupposes that there is a practice of leaving deposits. But such a practice would not survive in a society in which people generally denied deposits that no one could prove had been made. People would not leave deposits whose disposition they could not safely entrust to others.[20]

Hegel raises a number of objections to this example and to similar ones. One of the most challenging is that the contradiction does not show that the action on the maxim is wrong unless the practice of leaving deposits (a practice Hegel refers to as 'property') itself can be justified. If the practice is unjustifiable, then the action may not be wrong, regardless of the verdict of the categorical imperative test. And if the practice is justifiable, then the action is wrong anyway, again regardless of the verdict of the test. The real issue is whether the practice is justifiable or not:

If property is not to be, then whatever claims to be property must be cancelled. But the aim is precisely to prove that property must be; the sole thing at issue is what lies outside the capacity of this practical legislation of pure reason, namely to decide which of the opposed specific things [that is, property or non-property] must be lawful. But pure reason [i.e., the test of the maxim] demands that this should be done beforehand, and that one of the opposed specific things shall be presupposed, and only then can pure reason perform its now superfluous legislating [47, p. 78; 57, 2:463].

---

[20] Kant's example is marred by the fact that the universal law he considers is not a generalization of the maxim he specifies. Yet it is arguable that a generalization of the correct maxim would also have as an effect that there would be no deposits, thereby providing Kant with what he needs to illustrate a contradiction in conception.

Hegel is saying that Kant's test can generate reasonable content only by presupposing a reasonable social world in the background, and thus it cannot solve the problem of content, since it must rely on substantive practical requirements as input in order to generate its output. Kant has not shown that pure practical reason is capable of providing the requirements of morality.

We've seen that Hegel finds estrangement in Kantian morality because of the problem of the alien domination of moral over empirical motives. Now we can see that in his view, the content problem creates another vulnerability of Kantian morality to estrangement, and it also opens up a possibility for morality to play an ideological role. Both of these consequences stem from the fact that content is unwittingly imported from outside the practical reasoning governed by the categorical imperative, in the presupposed reasonableness of the social world. The content has an unacknowledged and unevaluated source in the social world. Since the outcome of the reasoning is an action that (partly) realizes and reproduces the social world, that world is governed by a dynamic that could depart significantly from what reasoned reflection could certify. The dynamic would then be one that is alien to reason, even though it supervenes on the reasoning activities of individuals. In such a case reasoning governed by the categorical imperative would be a realization of reason in an unreasonable form, a form of estrangement. Moreover, since the derived content is not acknowledged as imported from the social world, that world is in effect treated as part of the natural environment of decision, and its irrationality or unreasonableness could end up being occluded. In such a case, Kantian morality would be playing an ideological role supporting the very estrangement it creates.

### 2.3.3   Moral individualism

For Hegel, the motivational and content estrangement we've been discussing are themselves forms of a more fundamental estrangement, one that rests on an individualism that prevents Kant's moral law from realizing the autonomy he claims for it.

Kant's pure practical reason (*Wille*) has a purely formal character. It abstracts from all content of the will and constrains only the form of volition, requiring only that it have the form of a possible self-legislation. How then does the moral law acquire its specific content? Since the law is purely formal, this content must be *introduced*, through a process in which the free power of choice (*Willkür*) incorporates *given, material* incentives and circumstances into maxims to be tested by the categorical imperative. In Hegel's view, the need for this process implies that pure practical reason as Kant presents it is not fully autonomous. It cannot engage in a '*lawgiving* of its own' [68; 66, 5:33, emphasis added]. Rather, it must determine itself by *testing* candidate laws whose origin lies in incentives and circumstances that are not themselves self-conscious products of its self-determining activity.

> [Practical reason] is the absolute abstraction from all matter of the will [*Wille*]; a heteronomy of choice [*Willkür*] is established by a content.... [T]he essence of pure will [*Wille*] and pure practical reason is to be abstracted from all content, and thus it is a self-contradiction to seek in this absolute practical reason a moral legislation which would have to have a content, since the essence of this reason is to have none [47, p. 76 (translation modified); 57, 2:461].

One might object that when we act from respect for the moral law, we act on an incentive that does not come from the outside but is generated by reason itself. So while actions aimed at an end pointed to by our inclinations do not fully realize our autonomy, our actions from duty do fully realize it.[21] But for Hegel this objection would miss its mark, on the grounds that before we can act from respect for law we must have a law to respect, and it is the origin of that law that is at issue here. In other words, for us to be able to act from respect for lawgiving form, there must be something—a substantive practical constraint or requirement, a content—that has that form, and Hegel is concerned with the origin of this content, this substantive moral law. And the generation of such a law requires the process described above, through which certain maxims

---

[21] This objection seems to be in line with a view held by Christine Korsgaard: '[A]ction from duty is more completely autonomous, or anyway more completely self-generated or reason-generated, than action undertaken for the sake of satisfying an inclination. Action from duty is, in a way, more completely "top down" since the incentive is generated by the activity of reason rather than adopted from nature. The thought of the moral principle in this case generates its own incentive, wheres when we perform a permissible action the moral principle operates on a natural incentive.... In [the case of acting from respect for law] we generate both form and matter, law and incentive, from our own activity' [73, pp. 55–57].

stemming from material incentives fail the categorical imperative test.[22] For example, Kant says:

> I ought to try to further the happiness of others... simply because a maxim that excludes this cannot be included as a universal law in one and the same volition [69; 66, 4:441].

We learn that we ought to further the happiness of others from the failure of a maxim oriented entirely toward self-interest to satisfy the categorical imperative. More generally, the point is that the requirements of morality are generated (or 'constructed') by practical reasoning that subjects the individual agent's rational interests to the supposed constraints of reasonableness imposed by the categorical imperative.[23] That imperative does not itself generate those interests but takes them as arising out of given input. Interpreters of Kant often realize this fact but do not see Kant's conception of autonomy as compromised by it. For example, Rawls says that

> earlier we said that pure practical reason constructs out of itself its a priori object.... We can now see that the phrase 'out of itself' is an exaggeration; the metaphor is bit out of control. To correct this, we say that pure practical reason, as represented by the three formulations of the categorical imperative, constructs its object from the

---

[22] Korsgaard supports this reading (perhaps inadvertently) when she says: 'Could a rational being resist the basic tendency to self-love and therefore deny that her inclinations do have standing?... [L]et us suppose that you could. What would follow? You won't be pursuing any personal ends of your own, so what maxims will you consider acting on? We encounter the perfect duties, duties to tell the truth and keep our promises and so forth, in the ordinary course of action, going about our business, but you now have no business. How about the imperfect duties? Presumably if you don't regard your own inclinations as having standing, you won't regard the inclinations of others as doing so either, and your duty to promote their happiness will disappear. So what are you going to do—the other imperfect duty, develop your talents and powers? Kant says that these are given to us for all sorts of possible ends, but now you have no other ends. The denial of self-love is a route to normative skepticism' [73, pp. 56–57].

[23] As Rawls says, 'Kant thinks of the agent who is working through the CI-procedure as primarily concerned with that agent's own interests' [116, p. 233].

materials (the matter) presented to it by rational maxims at step (1) [of the procedure for applying the imperative]' [116, p. 251].

Yet he nonetheless discerns a Kantian conception of autonomy that legitimately draws on the individual's capacity (1) to legislate the moral law through a form of practical reasoning that respects the categorical imperative and (2) to act in conformity with that legislation.

But Hegel does view Kant's conception as compromised, because rather than comprehending individuals' inclinations themselves as part of reason's own self-realization as such, i.e., as a self-conscious part of it, the conception represents them simply as given input to deliberation. Hegel thinks that if it is possible for reason to affect their formation, then reacting to them simply as given amounts to heteronomy. His key idea is that for autonomy to exist, we must be able to comprehend their formation as under the guidance of reason, through the self-conscious production and maintenance of appropriate generating conditions, thereby making it a self-conscious part of the will's activity of self-determination.

Of course, individuals acting by themselves cannot self-consciously produce all the inclinations that figure in their respective individual deliberations. But through social cooperation in the realization and maintenance of their social world, they can participate in this production. Hegel's idea is that individuals must engage in such cooperation if they are to enjoy autonomy. He regards autonomy as perforce a social achievement rather than a capacity possessed by individuals under all conditions.

Furthermore, what we've said about inclinations applies as well to other circumstances that get reflected in an individual agent's deliberations: the institutional environment and the set of feasible actions, for example. To the extent that the production of these circumstances can be brought under rational control through social cooperation, treating them simply as given amounts to heteronomy. It also amounts to estrangement, because when they are within the scope of agency, they must be viewed as outcomes of agency and thus as an expression of reason. They must be viewed as part of an overall process of will formation in which reason confronts itself in the form of something alien. This overall process is a realization of reason in an unreasonable form.

Thus for Hegel, Kant's conception of moral deliberation, as fundamentally and purportedly self-sufficiently a form of individual deliberation about personal maxims that arise out of given circumstances, is a form of individualism about practical reason, an individualism that is itself a form of estrangement.[24]

The motivational estrangement and content estrangement that we have discussed have their roots in this individualism. The fact that in Kant's fundamental deliberative exercise, individuals are concerned to advance rational interests having their source in circumstances external to the moral will requires that there be a heterogeneity and an opposition between moral and self-interested motivation that preclude the necessary organic relationship between them. And the fact that the fundamental deliberative procedure starts with social conditions taken as given makes necessary an importation of moral judgment on those conditions, an importation that belies the claim that the deliberative procedure alone generates all substantive moral requirements.

---

[24] It is no accident that Hegel discusses 'Reason as lawgiver' and 'Reason as testing laws' under the rubric 'Individuality which takes itself as real in and for itself' in his *Phenomenology* [48, ¶¶419–437; 57, 3:311–323]. Moreover, this label makes clear that the problem for Hegel is not individuality per se, but *individualism*—individuality that takes itself to be real *in and for itself.*

# 3
# Hegel: Actualization of the Free Will

## 3.1 Philosophy, freedom, and estrangement

For Hegel, the world is thoroughly intelligible, and as such it must realize a rational system of categories. Hegel's logic lays out what he takes to be this system. His philosophies of nature and spirit aim at explaining how the system is realized in natural and cultural phenomena. His term for the realized system is 'Idea' (*Idee*). The term is appropriate, because Hegel takes something from Plato. The Idea is the inner reason that makes the external reality, the reality of spatiotemporal objects, events, and actions, what it is. Hegel differs from Plato in not understanding the Idea as an intelligible world of forms separate from the sensible world and more real than the latter. He believes that forms are in things, as their immanent soul and essence. In this respect he draws a page from Aristotle. But in another respect he differs from both of these ancient philosophers and is distinctly modern: the realization of the Idea is for Hegel the self-realization of free reason—thought freely structuring itself, giving itself content, and actualizing itself. This process is one in which human beings can be participants; in fact it is only understandable in terms of responsible thinking in inquiry and action. For Hegel, a philosophically adequate account of this process both (1) carries out and completes Kant's attempted self-vindication of human reason and (2) articulates the actualization of human freedom.

The logic examines the Idea as 'concept' (*Begriff*), i.e., in abstraction from its embodiment in the natural and socio-cultural worlds. The Idea is the actualized concept, and thus it has two moments or aspects: its form of being purely as concept, and the shape that the concept assumes in its actualization. The philosophies of nature and spirit examine these shapes, with the aim of exhibiting how they realize the concept. To do this is to make manifest their character as Idea, which is, for Hegel, their character as free reason.

Hegel is the quintessential philosopher of estrangement. The idea of estrangement and its overcoming permeates his philosophy, because freedom is its central concern and for him freedom and estrangement are inversely related. Since reality is thoroughly intelligible, reason is at work in it, and hence it can be brought into reasonable form; but until it is, it is reason in an unreasonable form. In these circumstances, humanity has not fully actualized its freedom but rather is in a condition of estrangement. Moreover, philosophy itself plays can play an important role in bringing reality into reasonable form, thereby overcoming estrangement and realizing freedom.

As a knowing or acting subject, one is free for Hegel only when one is self-determining in the sense that all limitations are self-imposed rather than imposed by anything extrinsic or alien to oneself. This is not to say that one is free only when not related to an 'other'. On the contrary, freedom involves confrontation with an other, but it requires that one be 'with oneself' or 'at home' (*bei sich*) with or in that other, rather than estranged from it. So, for example, in attaining the standpoint of absolute knowledge, that of philosophical cognition, we rid ourselves of 'the semblance of being burdened with something alien' [48, ¶89; 57, 3:81]. We do so by grasping the object of consciousness as our own rational self-externalization and thereby becoming 'at home in [our] own other-being [*Anderssein*] as such' [48, ¶788 (translation modified, emphasis omitted); 57, 3:575]. In opening up the world to us as fully intelligible, the perspective of absolute knowledge dispels the sense that the world is indifferent or hostile to reason. Moreover, the social attainment of this perspective and its insight—through philosophy—is itself part of the self-realization of free reason in the world. It provides the form of self-consciousness essential to the full realization of freedom. Thus with the help of philosophy, we can achieve a kind of 'speculative freedom', thereby overcoming a form of estrangement.

While Hegel's political philosophy, which is part of the philosophy of spirit, aims at facilitating speculative insight and hence speculative freedom, its topical focus is on three kinds of practical freedom, whose realization Hegel calls the actualization of the concept of the (free) will.[1] We'll refer to them as personal, moral, and social freedom.[2] They correspond, respectively, to the three main divisions of the *Philosophy of Right*: 'Abstract Right', 'Morality', and 'Ethical Life'. Personal freedom is

---

[1] Helpful studies of Hegel's political philosophy are provided by Dudley [29], Honneth [61; 62], Neuhouser [102], Patten [107], Rawls [116], and Wood [153; 154].

[2] Following Neuhouser [102].

the freedom realized through the social recognition and the exercise of the rights of individuals to pursue their own individual interests, without interference from others. Moral freedom is the freedom realized by agents when they determine through their own reflection what is right and act on that determination. Social freedom is the freedom realized through self-conscious participation in forms of social cooperation that provide conditions for the realization of personal and moral freedom and for their own existence and reproduction as well. Social freedom is thus realized by a social structure allowing willing participation in the realization and maintenance of a free social world. These three kinds of freedom are related in the following way: personal freedom can be realized only as part of (the realization of) moral freedom, and moral freedom can be realized only as part of (the realization of) social freedom. Hegel tries to show that to consider personal freedom in abstraction from moral freedom is to render it indeterminate or unreasonable, and similarly for moral freedom in abstraction from social freedom.

Moreover, for Hegel, the full realization of social freedom, and thus of all three forms of practical freedom, is possible only with the realization of speculative freedom, at least in part. For the philosophy of right, as speculative philosophy, provides the self-consciousness integral to social freedom. A truly free social world requires a reflectively acceptable public conception of the social order as the substantial basis of individuals' freedom and thus as an order with which they can willingly identify. The philosophy of right, for Hegel, demonstrates this reflective acceptability; it thus provides the necessary public conception, which completes the social realization of freedom, the actualization of the concept of the free will, by making the social world more self-consciously rational. Philosophy thereby takes on an important social role. It is true that Hegel sometimes speaks of art and religion as providing the necessary self-consciousness, but he is clear that these are less adequate forms.[3] The full realization of social freedom requires the self-consciousness provided by philosophy, and if it is not explicitly

---

[3] 'The truth concerning *right, ethics, and the state* is at any rate *as old* as its *exposition and promulgation* in *public laws and in public morality and religion*. What more does this truth require, in as much as the thinking mind [*Geist*] is not content to possess it in this proximate manner? What it needs is to be *comprehended* as well, so that the content which is already rational in itself may also gain a rational form and thereby appear justified to free thinking. For such thinking does not stop at what is *given*... but starts out from itself and thereby demands to know itself as united in its innermost being with the truth' [52, p. 11; 57, 7:13–14].

shared by everyone, it must at a minimum be available in the public culture.[4]

With respect to the four forms of freedom we've discussed—personal, moral, social, and speculative—the implications for estrangement include the following: An attempted realization of any of these forms (except the last) in abstraction from the next would be a realization of reason in an unreasonable form, and hence a form of estrangement.

## 3.2   The free will as its own object

In the Introduction to the *Philosophy of Right*, Hegel claims that the object of the free will is the free will itself.[5] This claim has important implications for the understanding and assessment of his account of the three kinds of practical freedom and for marking the difference of his position from Kant's. How are we to understand this claim? How does Hegel support it? And what are these implications?

In §§5–7 Hegel presents the concept of the (free) will as the unity of two elements or moments. The first is

> the element of *pure indeterminacy* or of the 'I''s pure reflection into itself, in which every limitation, every content...is dissolved; this is the limitless infinity of *absolute abstraction* or *universality*, the pure thinking of oneself [52, §5; 57, 7:§5].

This characterization is obscure, but if we take Hegel's advice [52, §4R; 57, 7:§4A] and consult individual self-consciousness, we can isolate this element. Suppose you have assumed the practical attitude, i.e., you are engaged in making a decision. Present to your awareness will be certain 'contents' or 'limits'; perhaps they have been presented to you by nature or by your desires and impulses, or perhaps they stem from prior intentions you have adopted. Hegel would claim that in occupying the practical standpoint you think of yourself as detachable from these contents, as able to renounce the desires and impulses or to change your mind about the intentions. This conception of yourself is the element

---

[4] '[P]hilosophy with us is not in any case practised as a private art, as it was with the Greeks, for example, but has a public existence [*Existenz*], impinging upon the public, especially—or solely—in the service of the state' [52, p. 17; 57, 7:21].

[5] Hegel takes freedom to be a basic determination of the will, so that '[w]ill without freedom is an empty word' [52, §4A; 57, 7:§4Z]. So strictly speaking, 'free will' is a redundancy. Nonetheless, I will sometimes use this expression in an effort to make clear Hegel's meaning.

in question, namely the 'absolute possibility of abstracting from every determination in which I find myself or which I have posited in myself, the flight from every content as a limitation'. The second element is the 'transition [that occurs in willing] from undifferentiated indeterminacy to differentiation, determination, and the positing of a determinacy as a content and object'. The free will does not 'merely will'; it wills something, and in so doing it attains determinate existence [52, §5R; 57, 7:§5A].

The free will is a unity of these two elements for two reasons: First, the will must adopt some ends—the second element is necessary—because otherwise it remains empty and never steps into existence and realizes itself. But second, the second element without the first is insufficient. Were the will not conscious of itself as separable from its object, it could not think of itself as freely identifying with the object, freely accepting it as its end. Consequently, its production of the object would not count as a case of its own self-determination, but only one of external determination and hence unfreedom. To realize its nature as free, the will must give some determination to itself, it must 'negate' itself by assuming a fixed shape, but at the same time, it must remain 'with itself' in this limitation, thereby 'negating the negation.' Thus freedom is 'self-referring negativity' [52, §§7R, 23; 57, 7:§§7A, 23], or in other words, self-determination in and through an other.[6] The will's universality must realize itself in and through its determinate content, its particularity.

Thus the will is essentially, or 'in itself', this self-determining activity. After working out this account, Hegel considers what the will must be like if it is to be 'for itself what it is in itself'. For only as such is it fully actualized. In other words, he asks what the will must be like if it is to be conscious of itself as self-determining. He considers three possibilities:

1. It must be an immediate or natural will.
2. It must be a reflective or arbitrary will (a will with 'freedom of choice').
3. It must be a will that takes itself as its object.

The immediate or natural will takes its content to be immediately present: 'the *drives, desires, and inclinations* by which the will finds itself naturally determined' [52, §11; 57, 7:§11]. This content does not present

---

[6] This is a recurring theme in Hegel: negativity as the self-realizing power of the self, or as the activity of self-determining thought.

itself as rational but only as given by nature. Hence the will must think of itself as finite or externally determined rather than infinite, free, or self-determining, so it cannot be for itself what it is in itself.

The reflective will represents its content as determined through rational processing of the drives, processing that weighs or prioritizes them to fashion a conception of happiness, for example, or some other value [52, §17; 57, 7:§17]. However, the drives themselves are still represented as given. So on this conception the will, while a choosing will and hence infinite in form, remains tied to content appearing as 'determinations of its nature and of its external actuality' [52, §14; 57, 7:§14]. Once again the will must think of itself as determined or limited by content 'not derived from its own self-determining activity as such' [52, §15; 57, 7:§15].

Hegel calls the reflective will the 'arbitrary will', because even though reflection is involved, it is not rationally constrained to a determinate result, and it is based on drives taken as given: these drives

> conflict with each other in such a way that the satisfaction of one demands that the satisfaction of the other be subordinated or sacrificed, and so on; and since a drive is merely the simple direction of its own determinacy and therefore has no yardstick within itself, this determination that it should be subordinated or sacrificed is the contingent decision of arbitrariness – whether the latter is guided by calculations of the understanding as to which drive will afford the greater satisfaction, or by any other consideration one cares to name [52, §17; 57, 7:§17].

Hegel goes so far as to claim that the arbitrary will is self-contradictory:

> [F]reedom of choice proves to be a contradiction, because the form and content are here still opposed to one another. The content of freedom of choice is something given, and known to be grounded, not within the will itself, but in external circumstances. For this reason, freedom in relation to such content consists only in the form of choosing, and this formal freedom must be regarded as a freedom that is only supposed to be such because it will be found, in the final analysis, that the same external sort of circumstances in which the content given to the will is grounded must also be invoked to explain the fact that the will decides in favour of just this and not that [51, §145A; 57, 8:§145Z].[7]

---

[7]  See also Hegel [52, §§15R, 15A; 57, 7:§§15A, 15Z].

Only the third alternative, the will that wills itself as its object, is for itself what it is in itself [52, §§10, 21–23; 57, 7:§§10, 21–23]. For only on this conception does the will not adopt its object as something 'encountered,' something coming to it from outside 'its own self-determining activity as such' [52, §15R; 57, 7:§15R]. Thus according to Hegel, 'the will which *has being in and for itself* has as its object the will itself as such, and hence itself in its pure universality' [52, §21R; 57, 7:§21R].

At this point a puzzle arises whose solution is key to understanding Hegel's position. In saying that the will has itself in its pure universality as its object, Hegel sounds a lot like Kant, who claims that the moral law, as the law of a free will, requires acting solely from respect for the universality of pure reason, i.e., reason that pays no attention to empirical incentives unless they can be incorporated into a maxim that can be universalized. Though there are differences in the two positions, which we'll discuss in a moment, both rest on the claim that the concept of a free will is the concept of a will that wills according to the universality appropriate to it as a free will. But we've seen (Sections 2.3.1–2.3.2) that Hegel finds Kant's position problematic on two grounds: first, that the structure of motives it posits is alienating, a structure of estrangement, and second, that Kant's pure practical reason cannot give itself enough content to guide decision. How then can Hegel expect to avoid the same criticisms? The answer is that he will seek to overcome the individualism in which these two problems are rooted (Section 2.3.3) by conceiving of freedom as a social achievement, realizable only in a certain kind of social world.

It is worth noting that he shows awareness of the problem. He says the following in his lectures on the philosophy of history:

> The will is free only when it does not will anything different, external, alien to itself (for as long as it does so, it is dependent), but wills itself alone—wills the will. This is absolute will—the volition to be free. The self-willing will is the basis of all right and obligation—consequently of all statutory determinations of Right, commands of duty, and enjoined obligations.... But the next question is: How does the will assume a definite form? For in willing itself, it is nothing but an identical reference to itself; but, in point of fact, it wills something specific: there *are*, we know, distinct and special duties and rights. A particular application, a definite form of will, is desiderated; for pure will is its own object, its own application, which, as far as this showing goes, is no object, no application. In fact, in this form it is nothing more than *formal* will. But the metaphysical process by which this abstract will develops itself, so as to attain a definite form of freedom, and how rights and duties are evolved therefrom, this is

not the place to discuss. It may be remarked...that the same principle obtained speculative recognition in Germany, in the *Kantian* philosophy [54, 442–443; 57, 12:524–525].

Hegel does no more than allude here to his resolution of the difficulty. The easiest entry into what he has in mind is to consider how a choosing or reflective will might be transformed into a free will, a will that, in Hegel's terms, realizes its essence. The reflective will is dependent on alien drives, drives that affect it from outside its (merely) formal activity of self-determination. To realize its freedom it has to rid itself of any motivational dependence on this external affectation. In the abstract, we might consider two ways of doing so. One is for the will to purge itself of any reliance on sensuous motives in order to act solely out of respect for the universal validity of practical law. The other is for the will somehow to 'internalize' the drives, to make them a part of its own activity of self-determination. Hegel understands the first solution to be Kant's proposal; he regards it as vulnerable to the motivational and content problems we've discussed, and thus as unworkable. His own proposal is the second. What does it amount to?

We can elaborate on the proposal both in terms of the general 'metaphysical process' Hegel refers to above and in terms of the more specific issues of his moral and political philosophy. As far as the former is concerned, that Hegel opts for this solution is implicit in his general characterization of freedom:

The substance of spirit is freedom, i.e. the absence of dependence on an other, the self-relating of self to self. Spirit is the actualized concept that is for itself and has itself for object.... But the freedom of spirit is not merely an absence of dependence on an other won outside of the other, but won in it; it attains actuality not by fleeing from the other but by overcoming it.

This 'overcoming' is the transformation of a difference into a self-differentiation through which spirit

comes to be what it ought to be according to its concept, namely, the ideality of the external, the Idea that returns to itself out of its otherness; or, expressed more abstractly, the self-differentiating universal that in its difference is at home with itself and for itself [58, §382A; 57, 10:§382Z].

That Hegel refers here to self-differentiating universality is significant for understanding his differences from Kant. The philosophy of right concerns the realization of the concept of the will, where 'concept' has the specific meaning accorded to it in Hegel's logic:

> Philosophy has to do with Ideas and therefore not with what are commonly described as mere concepts. On the contrary, it shows that the latter are one-sided and lacking in truth, and that it is the concept alone (not what is so often called by that name, but which is merely an abstract determination of the understanding) which has actuality, and in such a way that it gives actuality to itself. [52, §1R; 57, 7: §1A].

So for Hegel the concept of the will is that of a self-actualizing, concrete universal—a self-reproducing, organic totality—and it is this character that Hegel thinks makes it possible to avoid the problems of motivation and content faced by Kant's position, which is stated in terms of a more abstract and formal kind of universality.

To see how this difference plays out in the specifics of Hegel's moral and political philosophy, consider the specific reference to the 'drives' in the following passage, which expresses the idea that purity of motive should be understood in terms of overcoming the otherness of the drives through their modification and incorporation into a system that realizes practical freedom:

> Underlying the demand for the *purification of the drives* is the general idea [*Vorstellung*] that they should be freed from the *form* of their immediate natural determinacy and from the subjectivity and contingency of their *content*, and restored to their substantial essence. The truth behind this indeterminate demand is that the drives should become the rational system of the will's determination; to grasp them thus in terms of the concept is the content of the science of right [52, §19; 57, 7:§19].

By 'rational system of the will's determination' Hegel means a social world—a set of institutions and practices that form an ongoing, self-sufficient system of cooperation—that is publicly oriented toward the social realization of practical reason, i.e., the realization of personal, moral, and social freedom. This public orientation, through socialization and educational processes in the social world that engage individuals' reason, draws allegiance to itself and leads individuals to identify with it. It also leads them to have and rationally to identify with motives it is reasonable—in light of the orientation itself—for them to have in their various circumstances. There is thus an organic relationship between the ongoing existence and reproduction of the system and the satisfaction of the drives. The latter is an organic part of the former rather than something extraneous to it.

To will the realization, maintenance and reproduction of this social world is to will the free will. In fact, in virtue of the identification of individuals with the public orientation, this social world can itself be said to be the free will that wills itself as the free will. In this way, the drives become endogenous to the will's own self-determining activity and part of its intrinsic content. They no longer are a mark of motivational estrangement. The content problem is addressed as well. The need for a social world that realizes the three kinds of practical freedom while having a stability based on reason generates adequate content, Hegel thinks, for a doctrine of right.

## 3.3   Abstract right

### 3.3.1   Personality

The first kind of freedom that Hegel examines is personal freedom, the freedom to form and pursue particular interests without interference from others. Implicit in this characterization is the idea that in being a person, I remain self-identical across possible changes in these interests. At any given time, I am conscious of myself as having a certain particularity; for example, I have certain particular desires and I am in certain particular circumstances. In that respect I am finite and determined. As a person, I am conscious of myself as determined in this way, but I am also conscious of myself as self-identical across conceivable changes in these desires and circumstances. I have a sense of myself as independent of any determinations that happen to characterize me at any given time. As independent in this way, I am infinite and free.

> It is inherent in personality that, as *this* person, I am completely determined in all respects (in my inner arbitrary will, drive, and desire, as well as in relation to my immediate external existence [*Dasein*]), and that I am finite, yet totally pure self-reference, and thus know myself in my finitude as *infinite, universal*, and *free* [52, §35; 57, 7:§35].

> Personality begins only at that point where the subject has not merely a consciousness of itself in general as concrete and in some

way determined, but a consciousness of itself as a completely abstract 'I' in which all concrete limitation and validity are negated and invalidated [52, §35R; 57, 7:§35A].

It follows that my being a person is not tied to my having any particular desires or ends or acting in any particular way. So far as my being a person is concerned, the particularity of my will is 'not present as freedom' [52, §37A; 57, 7:§37Z]:

> The *particularity* of the will is indeed a moment within the entire consciousness of the will (see §34), but it is not yet contained in the abstract personality as such. Thus, although it is present – as desire, need, drives, contingent preference, etc. – it is still different from personality, from the determination of freedom. – In formal right, therefore, it is not a question of particular interests, of my advantage or welfare, and just as little of the particular ground by which my will is determined, i.e. of my insight and intention [52, §37; 57, 7:§37].

This fact will be important when we assess the stability of social realizations of personal freedom.

### 3.3.2 Property and contract

In Hegel's view, personality, considered as an individual's self-conception, is something merely subjective, standing opposed to a nature it confronts as external. But this limitation contradicts the concept of personality as a kind of freedom—as 'infinite and universal' [52, §39; 57, 7:§39]. To actualize itself as freedom, personality must give itself an objective existence in an external sphere [52, §§39, 41; 57, 7:§§39, 41]. Property relations provide this sphere:

> The person must give himself an external *sphere of freedom* in order to have being as Idea.... The rational aspect of property is to be found not in the satisfaction of needs but in the superseding of mere subjectivity of personality. Not until he has property does the person exist as reason.... [T]he circumstance that I, as free will, am an object to myself in what I possess and only become an actual will by this means constitutes the genuine and rightful element in possession, the determination of *property* [52, §§41, 41A, 45; 57, 7:§§41, 41Z, 45].

The property relations Hegel has in mind are private property and contract. In 'Abstract Right' he defends them as necessary for social actualization of personality or personal freedom.[8]

How do private property rights contribute to the social realization of personality? Personality is fully realized when everyone is a person and respects others as persons [52, §36; 57, 7:§36]. I actualize my personality through ownership in the following way. The use rights that I acquire through ownership create socially sanctioned opportunities for me, opportunities that might otherwise remain merely abstract possibilities. As a free will I must step into determinacy. Decisions of ownership and use accomplish this step in a way that demonstrates the supremacy of my will over mere things, thereby according me the dignity of personhood. My personal freedom is given reality in an external thing [52, §41A; 57, 7:§41Z] (by means of an existing social structure). It becomes an object to me, thereby confirming my inner self-consciousness as free. Moreover, in respecting my ownership rights, others are respecting me as a person; similarly for my respect for the ownership rights of others. These attitudes of respect provide elements of recognition important to the system of property [52, §51; 57, 7:§51].

Recognition also plays an important role in relations of contract, which Hegel treats as the reciprocal transfer of property through agreement:

> Contract presupposes that the contracting parties *recognize* each other as persons and owners of property; and. . . the moment of recognition is already contained and presupposed within it [52, §71; 57, 7:§71].

Contract represents an advance in the actualization of the free will. Whereas in property as described above, the will is actualized by stepping into existence in the form of a thing (the owned object), in contract the 'aspect of existence is no longer merely a thing but contains the moment of a will (and hence the will of another person)' [52, §72; 57, 7:§72]. In other words, in contract, my will becomes objective to me not merely as an existing thing but as an existing will [52, §73; 57, 7:§73], a will posited by the contracting parties as a common will [52, §75; 57, 7:§75], a will existing in the form of an agreement. Since the contracting parties relate to each other as self-sufficient persons, this agreement, this

---

[8] See Patten [107, chap. 5] for an argument that Hegel at best shows that private property is sufficient for the development of personality, and not that it is necessary.

common will, is the product of their arbitrary wills [52, §75; 57, 7:§75]. This fact will be important below.

Hegel says that what occurs through contract is a process in which a certain contradiction 'represents and mediates itself':

> I *am* and *remain* an owner of property, having being for myself and excluding the will of another, only in so far as, in identifying my will with that of another, I *cease* to be an owner of property [52, §72; 57, 7:§72].

This remark is bound to seem somewhat mysterious until one realizes that the paradigm case of what Hegel has in mind is the *exchange of commodities*. He doesn't explicitly say that he's talking about commodities, but the resolution of the above contradiction presupposes a commodity-producing social environment. What is required is that 'each party, in accordance with his own and the other party's will, *ceases* to be an owner of property, *remains* one, and *becomes* one' [52, §74; 57, 7:§74]. The transaction Hegel is talking about is an exchange, and he claims that the problem just stated is solved by means of a two-fold form possessed by the exchanged items. Each item has a specific material form connected with its possible uses, and it has an economic value, expressible in money [52, §§63A, 77; 57, 7:§§63Z, 77]. This two-fold form is what Marx refers to as the commodity form.[9] Hegel envisages the contracting parties as completing the transaction by exchanging their items, which have different material forms, in quantities that have equal monetary value according to their estimation. Then each party (a) ceases to be an owner (of the particular bodily form of the item he is giving up), (b) remains an owner (of the value) throughout the process, and (c) becomes an owner (of a new item with a different material form). This sort of process presupposes the existence of the two-fold form and of money, both of which develop *pari passu* with the development of commodity production.[10] Hegel may not consciously think that abstract right requires commodity production, but he is committed to that claim by his depiction of the commodity form as implicated in the exercise of the rights of contract.[11]

---

[9] See the next chapter for further discussion of the commodity form.

[10] For a defense of this claim, see Chapter 2 of volume 1 of Marx's *Capital* [90; 94, vol. 23].

[11] Compare Marcuse's assertion that in Hegel's account of the contract, 'the ontological idea of reason is adjusted to the commodity-producing society and given its concrete embodiment there' [82, p. 196].

Exchange thus increases the socially available opportunities for abstraction from given circumstances. Not only can I rightfully abstract by using my property in a different way or by physically altering its form; I can also exchange it for other property. In this way exchange gives the abstract universality of personality an enhanced social realization.[12]

### 3.3.3 Wrong

Wrong is an act of personal freedom that contravenes personality itself. That wrong is possible, or worse, to be expected, raises questions about the stability of abstract right, i.e., of personal freedom realized in abstraction from moral and social freedom. A putatively free will comprising just the rights of personality might not effectively will itself as its object, contrary to the constraint set out in Hegel's Introduction and discussed in Section 3.2 above. The system of personality as we have so far characterized it (rights of private property and contract) is vulnerable on stability grounds, for two reasons:

1. Without anyone's willing against right, conflicting claims can emerge (for example, claims of ownership by two different persons over the same thing). Without an intersubjectively authoritative way of adjudicating such conflicts, they can give rise to a collision of rights in which the assertion of one requires the violation of the other, thereby leading to a breakdown of the system of right [52, §84; 57, 7:§84].
2. Since the self-conscious aspect of personality is that of the arbitrary will, it is a contingent matter whether a person's actions will in fact conform to right [52, §§81, 81R, 81A; 57, 7:§§81, 81A, 81Z]. There is no feature of the system insuring that motives will restrict actions to system-conforming ones. Self-interest might lead a person to exercise personal freedom in a way that breaks a contract or damages someone else's property, for example.

Hegel's position is that to deal adequately with these vulnerabilities requires introducing moral consciousness into the system. For example, juridical institutions could mitigate the second vulnerability, but only

---

[12] Though I know of no passage where he does so, it is possible that Hegel would argue that money, which realizes the commodity form by embodying all possibilities for commodity acquisition through exchange, is a culminating social expression of personal freedom. For Marx money and the commodity form will have quite a different social significance, as we'll see.

by imposing penalties that go beyond revenge [52, §102; 57, 7:§102] to constitute genuine punitive justice. But doing so requires the existence of a will that goes beyond freedom of choice to be a genuinely moral will, i.e., a will that judges and acts on the basis of moral consciousness or 'moral subjectivity'[13] and hence one that as a 'particular and subjective will' also wills the universal as such [52, §103; 57, 7:§103]. In the 'Morality' section of the *Philosophy of Right*, Hegel considers one way of adding this form of consciousness to the social world, one that will ultimately prove inadequate and require a transition to 'Ethical Life'.

For Hegel, any attempted realization of personal freedom that did not contain this moral element would be a realization of reason in an unreasonable form. Individuals would not be at home in this social world; for example, they wouldn't necessarily be able to endorse the rules they are subject to and that punish them if they do wrong. Rather than a realization of free practical reason, the social world would be a system of estrangement.

## 3.4   Morality

Moral freedom is the right and the ability of individuals to determine through their own reflection what is right and good and to act on that determination.

> [S]ubjective or 'moral' freedom is what a European especially calls freedom. In virtue of the right thereto a man must possess a personal knowledge of the distinction between good and evil in general: ethical and religious principles shall not merely lay their claim on him as external laws and precepts of authority to be obeyed, but have their assent, recognition, or even justification in his heart, sentiment, conscience, intelligence, etc. [58, §503; 57, 10:§503].

Moral freedom has its existence not in something external like property or contract, but in something internal, in individuals' own subjectivity. For this reason Hegel calls agents with moral freedom subjects, and not merely persons.

The basic right defining moral freedom is the right of the subjective will:

---

[13] See the next section for further discussion of moral subjectivity.

The moral point of view...takes the shape of *right of the subjective will*. In accordance with this right, the will can *recognize* something or *be* something only in so far as that thing is *its own*, and in so far as the will is present to itself in it as subjectivity [52, §107; 57, 7:§107].

The *right of the subjective will* is that whatever it is to recognize as valid should be *perceived* by it as *good*, and that it should be held responsible for an action – as its aim translated into external objectivity – as right or wrong, good or evil, legal or illegal, according to its cognizance [*Kenntnis*] of the value which that action has in this objectivity [52, §132; 57, 7:§132].

The right to recognize nothing that I do not perceive as rational is the highest right of the subject... [52, §132R; 57, 7:§132A].


Call the freedom that exists for itself as subjectivity *moral subjectivity*. Moral subjectivity is the inner self-consciousness of an individual as free. It is the inner self-consciousness of an individual will as willing the universal, i.e., as willing what is right.

Personality and moral subjectivity are essential, in Hegel's view, for the full realization of the free will. They were absent from early Greek society, where individuals immediately identified with their roles in their own particular communities: these roles gave them their respective personal interests and were not subject to reflective justification. Reflective thought, prompted by circumstances of role conflict, inevitably destabilizes this kind of social unity. But although the idea of moral subjectivity finds early expression (at least in embryo) in efforts by Socrates to get his fellow Athenians to seek reflective justification for their practices, and the idea of personal freedom achieves some social embodiment in early Roman legal practice, it is only recently, in Hegel's view, that historical struggles have yielded all the elements needed for their adequate social realization.

Yet for Hegel, personal and moral freedom cannot be realized apart from a superordinate kind of freedom, one we have been calling social freedom, which is exercised through self-conscious participation in social structures of cooperation that provide the necessary conditions for personal and moral freedom and for their (the structures') own reproduction as well. To see why Hegel holds this position, consider the social world that results merely from adding moral subjectivity to the rights of personality. Call this social world the *moral will*.

Moral subjectivity, as subjectivity, is a mere form of the will's determination, a form without intrinsic content of its own. It is compatible with differing content across persons and with unreasonable as well as reasonable content.

Because of its formal determination, insight is equally capable of being *true* and of being mere *opinion* and *error* [52, §132; 57, 7:§132].

Because of this fact, the moral will as we've specified it is incapable of solving even the problem afflicting abstract right. The function of punishment, as opposed to vengeance, is to effect a reconciliation of the wrongdoer with the requirements of the universal will. Such a reconciliation takes place through public rational certification that the will of the wrongdoer has violated its own law. To effect such certification it is not enough that the would-be 'judge' be a moral subject, or that the would-be judge and the wrongdoer be moral subjects, or that all individuals be moral subjects, or even that it be common knowledge that all individuals are moral subjects. Rather, the judge must be the *jointly recognized voice of the universal*.[14] That is to say, morality cannot remain purely inner but must attain public, external existence, recognized existence in institutional structures that embody reason's requirements.[15]

True reconciliation requires morality to attain public existence, for only as publicly existing can it provide a standard for a *practice* of reconciliation between one person and others, between the wrongdoer and the rest of society. Moreover, there must be 'universal subjectivity,' that is, intersubjective agreement on moral standards, for reconciliation to be fully effective. And finally, it is not enough that there be such agreement; the standards agreed upon must be reasonable, or as Hegel would put it, in accordance with the concept of freedom. These are three ways in which morality must attain *objectivity* if it is to perform its reconciling function [52, §§112, 112R; 57, 7:§§112, 112A].

But the moral will as we have specified it does not satisfy these requirements. Since moral subjectivity is purely inner, it lacks external existence in the moral will as we've defined it. Since it is purely formal, it has no intrinsic content and hence does not by itself insure agreement across subjects or conformity with the concept of freedom. Without

---

[14] To say precisely what constitutes such a status is a somewhat complicated matter. For entry into the issue, see Searle [135, chap. 3].

[15] It is possible I think to read Hegel as making this point in §218: 'Since property and personality have legal recognition and validity in civil society, *crime* is no longer an injury [*Verletzung*] merely to a *subjective infinite*, but to the *universal* cause [*Sache*] whose existence [*Existenz*] is inherently [*in sich*] stable and strong' [52, §218; 57, 7:§218].

objective existence its content will perforce be extrinsically determined, leading to the content estrangement discussed in Section 2.3.2.

Thus the first problem with the moral will is that it fails to be objective. A second problem is that it provides no assurance that the motivation corresponding to its requirements will be forthcoming. The minimal structure we have specified—moral subjectivity plus the rights of personal freedom—does not incorporate the 'drives' into the will's own self-determining activity, as we saw to be required in Section 3.2. It is not structured to reproduce itself and therefore fails to satisfy the requirement to will itself as the free will; it fails to have itself as its content. As a consequence, the moral will will be afflicted with the motivational estrangement discussed in connection with Kantian morality in Section 2.3.1. Failure to satisfy objectivity follows from this motivational deficiency, since the concept of the free will requires that it have itself as its content. In other words, the moral will's attaining objectivity would also solve the motivational problem.

A third problem is that since moral subjectivity in our minimal structure concerns in the first instance the morality of individual actions, rather than, say, the justice of institutions, a kind of moral individualism is in play. As a result, there are too many problems competing for individuals' attention, thereby afflicting them with burdensome and apparently intractable dilemmas.

> [T]here are always *several sorts* of good and *many kinds of duties*, the variety of which is a dialectic of one against another and brings them into *collision*. At the same time, because the good is one, they *ought* to stand in harmony; and yet each of them, though it is a particular duty, is as good and as duty absolute. It falls upon the agent to be the dialectic which, superseding this absolute claim of each, concludes such a combination of them as excludes the rest [58, §508; 57, 10:§508].

Hegel thus speaks of 'the burden [the individual] labors under as a particular subject in his moral reflections on obligation and desire'. The attainment of objectivity would also ameliorate this problem, since it would reduce the moral individualism that generates it. It would do so by in effect transforming individual-level conflicts into problems solvable at the social level through institutional design [52, §149; 57, 7:§149; 48, ¶425; 57, 3:314–315].

But can morality attain objectivity? Hegel may seem to deny that it can:

In morality, self-determination should be thought of as sheer restless activity which cannot yet arrive at something *that is* [52, §108A; 57, 7:§108Z].

Yet Hegel's position is better captured by the claim that morality can obtain objectivity, but only by transforming itself into a system of ethical life:

Only in the ethical realm does the will become identical with the concept of the will and have the latter alone as its content [52, §108A; 57, 7:§108Z].

In Rawlsian parlance, objectivity is attained through the transformation of the moral will into a social world that is stable and well-ordered by the concept of the free will.[16] But such a social world is an ethical will or a rational system of ethical life. Moral subjectivity is preserved in this social world through the intersubjectively accessible reflective acceptability of its institutions and practices.

Such a system is needed to provide not only sufficiently determinate content for personal and moral freedom, but also the social and material conditions necessary for their exercise. These conditions include forms of socialization that realize the required individual capacities and attitudes (thereby making the drives internal to the scheme's self-reproducing activity). Further, the system must make it possible for citizens to understand their individual actions in meeting their social responsibilities not only as consistent with and indeed exercises of their personal and moral freedom, but also as free cooperation with others, the exercise of a kind of social or collective freedom in the realization and maintenance of their free social world. It is only if the free will is realized as such a system that it can truly be said to have itself as its content and to give itself existence in the world. Moral subjectivity itself

---

[16] For Rawls, a society is well-ordered by a conception of justice if three conditions are satisfied: (1) everyone accepts the conception and knowledge that everyone accepts it is mutually recognized (as if citizens' acceptance were a matter of public agreement); (2) society's basic structure is publicly known (or with good reason believed) to satisfy the conception; and (3) citizens have a normally effective sense of justice—one that enables them to understand and to apply the conception and to act in accordance with it [117, pp. 8–9]. Similarly, Hegel envisages a society in which it is publicly recognized that everyone endorses the concept of freedom and knows that their society realizes it, and moreover everyone has the capacities needed to act accordingly.

is preserved and given worldly existence through the reflective, inter-subjective acceptance—the social validity—of these institutions and practices.

Moreover, individuals are released from the burden of having to solve all problems at the level of individual morality. While Kant views duties as given by the moral law through individual deliberation based on the categorical imperative, Hegel treats them as implicit in social forms that realize freedom, as requirements for actualizing and sustaining those forms as forms of life. In these ways, the system of ethical life insures that

> [o]n the one hand, [the individual] is liberated from his dependence on mere natural drives, and from the burden he labours under as a particular subject in his moral reflections on obligation and desire; and on the other hand, he is liberated from that indeterminate subjectivity which does not attain existence or the objective determinacy of action, but remains *within itself* and has no actuality [52, §149; 57, 7:§149].

For Hegel, a truly free social world must satisfy both objective conditions, on the one hand, requiring it to have a certain structure, and subjective conditions, on the other, comprised in a reflectively acceptable public conception of the social order as the substantial basis of individuals' freedom and thus as an order with which they can willingly identify. This public conception, as the self-consciousness of a free social world, completes the social realization of freedom, the actualization of the concept of the free will. The objective and subjective conditions together provide individuals with a perforce social substantiality and self-awareness that they cannot have on their own.

Hegel expresses this dependence on the social by characterizing individuals as 'accidents' of the ethical substance. He doesn't mean this characterization to imply that the ethical has its substantiality apart from its rational acceptability to the individuals it comprises. As Rawls says of Hegel's view,

> It is crucial to stress that it is only through the self-reflection of individuals, and only in their being reconciled to their (rational) social world and in their correctly seeing it as rational and living their lives accordingly, that the social world is brought to its full substantiality [116, p. 334].[17]

---

[17] In this connection, it is worth pointing out that Hegel regards the categories of substance and accident as 'determinations of reflection', where this status

Moreover, Hegel claims that while

> [i]n relation to the subject, the ethical substance and its laws and powers are on the one hand an object [*Gegenstand*], in as much as *they are*, in the supreme sense of self-sufficiency... [and] are thus an absolute authority and power... On the other hand, they are not something *alien* to the subject. On the contrary, the subject bears *spiritual witness* to them as to *its own essence*, in which it has its *self-awareness* [*Selbstgefühl*] and lives as in its element which is not distinct from itself [52, §§146–147; 57, 7:§§146–147].

Thus for Hegel ethical duties are not imposed on individuals in a way that would make them unfree in their social roles. Ethical duties do not appear to individuals in ethical life as constraints or limitations. On the contrary, Hegel says, individuals find their *liberation* in them [52, §149; 57, 7:§149]. For ethical substance is what makes their freedom possible and actualizes it.

## 3.5   Ethical life

Hegel's system of ethical life includes institutions of family life, civil society, and the political state. I will leave aside his conception of the family, consideration of which would introduce complications[18] but would not, I think, invalidate the conclusions of the following analysis. My aim is to bring out how his scheme differs from the more usual liberal treatments of civil society and the state.

Hegel thinks that in the ethical life of the city-states of Greek antiquity, individuals had no conception of themselves as persons with their own separate interests that they were entitled to pursue. Their identification with their families and with the larger social whole was thus immediate and unreflective. Though this form of life was a form of ethical substantiality, it was not a form of social practice that ran on the fully developed and articulated subjectivity essential for the full realization of the modern conception of freedom. Hence it could not withstand the force of reflection, and was destined to break down. The kinds of freedom that mark the aspirations to autonomy characteristic of modern

---

implies that neither can be realized without the other. A substance would not be actual without the accidents that manifest it. In particular, substantial freedom must realize itself through the action and consciousness of individual wills.

[18] In particular, Hegel's views about the role of women in the family would have to be taken into account.

culture—personal, moral, and political freedom—require a form of ethical substantiality that allows the most unrestrained reflection without losing its capacity for social integration, its reflective acceptability and stability.

For Hegel, civil society, an element of modern ethical life missing from Greek society, is crucial to the achievement of these forms of freedom. For it provides an arena, separate from the political state, in which individuals can act as private persons individually determining and pursuing their separate interests. As members of civil society, individuals do not take the realization and maintenance of the free will as their conscious end [52, §187; 57, 7:§187]. Yet the requirements of universality do impose themselves through the economic necessity for individuals to satisfy others' needs in order to satisfy their own. Individuals thus view the requirements of universality as necessary means for the satisfaction of their own interests. Political economy can even lead them to understand this fact and thus to see a rationale for the necessity imposed by the market. They can read Adam Smith and understand the operation of the market's 'invisible hand', which Hegel takes to be 'the reason shining through' the independently determined self-interested activities of private individuals [52, §182A; 57, 7:§182Z]. Market necessity requires particularity to develop itself in accordance with universality, while at the same time providing ethical universality with its needed content [52, §§187, 187R; 57, 7:§§187, 187R].

Nonetheless, this understanding of market necessity can only go so far in reconciling individuals to their social world; for this necessity does not present itself as freedom but only as nomological necessity that can be rationally understood. For Hegel, there must be more to civil society than an economy governed by the laws of commodity production and capital accumulation. Such an economy would be an embodiment of reason in an unreasonable form, for two reasons. One reason is formal: the necessity driving such an economy is blind rather than self-consciously rational or reasonable. Thus it doesn't even have the form of a reasonable social world (a world that realizes social freedom). The second reason has to do with content. Hegel is aware, for example, of the potential of such an economy to produce extremes of wealth and poverty, and to do so suddenly and without warning. The insecurity resulting from the risk of economic loss can subordinate all motives to those of economic gain. An impassable divide can threaten to emerge between the self-regarding motives of individuals as economic agents and the more impartial concerns required of them in moral and political deliberation and action. Competitive individualism on the market, if unchecked, can allow strategic rationality to swamp all domains, leading to a corruption of the political process, and therefore to reason in an unreasonable form. Such developments would destroy social unity and threaten the existence of all forms of practical freedom.

For these reasons Hegel incorporates certain distinctive institutional elements into his model of civil society, elements intended to support, to complement and to some degree to compensate for the effects of the private property economy (the 'system of needs'). Besides (1) the economy, Hegel envisages (2) juridical institutions charged with the administration of justice (needed for the protection of property), and (3) institutions that fill in functional gaps of these first two systems by attending to the maintenance of 'the particular interest as a *common* interest': (a) the 'police' or public authority and (b) a system of officially recognized 'corporations' [52, §188; 57, 7:§188]. These latter associations comprise people in particular industries or classes of industries, town councils, religious associations, and so on. They are not firms of the sort called corporations today; nor are they labor unions, since they include both employees and employers as members. They are rather more like professional associations and mutual aid societies. But they have legally certified status, including recognized connections with the branches of government. Their function is in part to lessen the vulnerability of their members to economic insecurity, perhaps through regulating the rate of entry into certain trades and providing support for their unemployed members. They also—we may assume—deliberate about such issues as the standards of excellence appropriate for the activity that brings them together and the kind of contribution that activity should make in the wider scheme of social cooperation. They seek to present their views about these matters in the political arena. Through these activities, Hegel thinks, they provide their members with a recognized place in the social division of labor, and thereby a determinate particular identity, something the market cannot by itself provide. And they also help to foster a concern for the common good in their members. In all of these ways, they introduce solidarity and universal concerns that prevent life in civil society from generating into an egoistic scramble for economic security, and they prepare members of civil society for their activities as citizens of the state.

Superimposed on this overall structure is an articulation of civil society into classes or 'estates': (1) one that organizes agriculture and landed property, (2) one concerned with trade and industry, and (3) the bureaucracy of civil servants. Each of these estates has a distinct presence in the political state, which is a constitutional monarchy with an executive branch and a bicameral legislature. The bureaucracy forms part of the executive branch and attains a presence in the legislature through an advisory body comprising top executive officials. The individual land owners in the agricultural estate are present as such in the upper house of the legislature. Individuals in the estate of trade and industry are represented in the lower house as members of their respective corporations. Thus the political structure is associationist: citizens are represented in the legislature through their corporations and estates rather than directly as individuals. The function of the monarch is largely ceremonial; for example, the monarch's required signature on legislative enactments, which is an action of a single person, is meant to express their character as products of a single will—the united will of the people. A central function of the legislature is to provide a public forum where citizens, through representatives of their estates and corporations, subject their claims and the claims of others to reasoned debate. In this respect the estates and corporations cooperate with the legislature to honor a right of all citizens as moral subjects to be able to recognize enacted laws and policies as justified by reasons that they can accept on reflection. The associative civil and political structure also enables citizens, Hegel thinks, to understand themselves as engaging in free cooperation and thereby realizing and maintaining their social or collective freedom.

The guiding idea is that the free will gives itself determinate content through the requirements of ethically integrated and maintained interdependent institutions that socially realize personal and moral freedom and provide for their own reproduction as well. The private concerns of individuals attain a more self-consciously ethical form through their integration into the associational concerns of their particular estates and corporations, and these in turn attain their full ethical significance through their political integration with the associational concerns of others. Throughout, deliberation is not merely formal and abstract but concrete: it takes into account agents' individual roles as participants in the collective social maintenance of their freedom.

Hegel's associative modifications to the more familiar liberal conceptions of civil society and its relation to the state are bound to raise questions. For many, they will call to mind the guilds, feudal manors, religious and aristocratic hierarchies, and so on of medieval society. As a network of such associations, medieval society tied political and personal or social status together, and the differing roles of these associations in social reproduction generated hierarchies that stood in the way of both personal freedom and political emancipation. Thus a common theme in liberal political thought supporting the political revolutions of the eighteenth century was that social progress required the free development of civil society as a domain distinct from that of the state, allowing personal freedom to flourish in the former and political equality to be achieved in the latter. And the associative remnants of medieval society seemed to stand squarely in the way of these changes.

As we'll see below, in large part Marx agrees with this analysis. He views Hegel's associations as just such remnants, incapable of playing the role that Hegel assigns them, and destined to die out. But before we look at his argument, it is important to see why Hegel holds a different view. Hegel would claim that the incorporation of abstract right and moral subjectivity are essential to a free society, and that his theoretical analysis is guided by this idea. Accordingly, individuals have many rights as individual citizens that preclude a regression to earlier forms of social unity. Among these are the rights to life, security, and private property, all of which are necessary for personal freedom. And moral freedom requires freedom of conscience and at least some degree of religious freedom, as well as the right of all citizens to participate in public reasoned debate in processes of political will formation, which concerns the structure of ethical life and the obligations it imposes on citizens.

Hegel would deny that the associationist elements of his system, including the scheme of political representation based on group membership, are at odds with these rights. He would claim that on the contrary, the associations are necessary for their maintenance and stabilization. Because he sees a serious destructive potential in the commodity market, he wants to secure some recognition for individuals that is independent of how they fare there. Even if they completely fail there, they retain their status as members of estates or corporations, and the status of citizenship, as we've characterized it above. These statuses can provide, he thinks, the appropriate social response to the Hobbesian tendencies in civil society.

## 3.6 Marx: the persistence of estrangement

There is an apparent tension in Hegel's attempted integration of civil society into ethical life that we must examine if we are to assess his attempt to overcome the estrangement he finds in Kantian morality (Section 2.3) and in the moral will more generally (Section 3.4). On the one hand, Hegel says that the members of civil society pursue their own particular interests and do not 'as such' take the realization of the free will as their conscious end:

> Individuals, as citizens of this state [i.e., of civil society], are *private persons* who have their own interest as their end... [T]he interest of the Idea... is not present in the consciousness of these members of civil society as such... [52, §187; 57, 7:§187].

On the other hand, there are several other passages where Hegel seems to contradict this assertion by claiming that

> individuals do not live as private persons merely for these particular interests without at the same time directing their will to a universal end and acting in conscious awareness of this end [52, §260; 57, 7:§260].

What are we to make of this apparent inconsistency?

One might think that the phrase 'as such' in the first passage supports the following resolution: individuals pursue their own interests as members of civil society, whereas they pursue the universal interest not as members of civil society but as citizens of the state. However, there are two problems with this interpretation. First, the second passage seems to attribute a universal interest to the members of civil society 'as such', since it states that when individuals act as private persons in pursuit of their particular interests they 'at the same time' consciously will a universal end. Second, the interpretation is problematic in that it would not secure the overcoming of moral estrangement in ethical life. If individuals had two separate roles, each with its own set of interests, namely private, independent interests in one and the general interest in the other, then there would be no assurance that they will not come into conflict. We would not have the organic synthesis of the universal and particular that the young Hegel saw as the key to overcoming moral estrangement. In accordance with that synthesis, individuals' particular pursuits must have universal significance and their universal pursuits must have particular significance. In particular, in pursuing their particular interests, individuals must be recognized—and aware of themselves—as participants in the social division of labor.

This understanding of the requirements of the synthesis is in line with Hegel's general conception of freedom. In speculative freedom, i.e., from the standpoint of absolute knowledge, self-consciousness is 'at home in its other-being as such' [48, ¶788 (translation modified); 57, 3:575].[19] Similarly, citizens are at home in their private lives as such and private individuals are at home in their political life as such. This has to be Hegel's position, if his critique of moral alienation is to be successful. Moreover, this understanding is more or less directly supported by other passages, including, for example, the following:

> [T]he universal is simultaneously the concern [*Sache*] of each [individual] as a particular [entity]. What matters most is that the law of reason should merge with the law of particular freedom, and that my particular end should become identical with the universal... [52, §265A; 57, 7:§265Z].

Finally, this understanding coheres with the interpenetration of political and economic institutions in Hegel's scheme. For example, the corporations in civil society are chartered and partially supervised by the public authority, which is part of the executive branch of the political state. The judiciary, too, belongs both to the executive branch and to civil society. Only in the absence of such interpenetration would it be possible to speak of acting, say, only in one's capacity as a member of civil society and not in one's capacity as a citizen of the state.

Is, then, the first passage quoted above—in which Hegel says that the interest of the Idea is not present in the consciousness of the members of civil society as such—an aberration, one we should count simply as an isolated misstep on Hegel's part? It is not. As Marx points out in his early confrontation with Hegel's political philosophy, there are several passages where Hegel implies that the state is separate from civil society. For example, speaking of the Estates—the houses in the legislature— Hegel says that their 'proper conceptual definition' should

> be sought in the fact that, in them, the subjective moment of universal freedom – the personal [*eigene*] insight and personal will of that sphere which has been described in this work as civil society – comes *into existence in relation* [*Beziehung*] *to the state* [52, §301R; 57, 7:§301A].

He says further that 'the proper significance of the Estates is that it is through them that the state enters into the subjective consciousness of the people, and that the people begins to participate in the state' [52, §301A; 57, 7:§301Z]. Still further, he says that 'in the *Estates*, as

---

[19] Emphasis omitted.

an element of the legislative power, the *private estate* attains a *political significance* and function' [52, §303; 57, 7:§303]. These remarks present civil society as a private sphere that is separate from the political state, because its members can act politically only through an institution external to civil society, namely the legislature. Moreover, the remarks cohere with Hegel's assertion that the position of representatives is not that of commissioned or mandated agents charged with vindicating the particular interests of the communities or corporations they represent over the universal interest, but rather that of agents working for the latter. Marx comments:

> Hegel began by regarding the representatives as representing the corporations, etc., but then introduces the further political determination to the effect that they should not vindicate the *particular interest* of the corporation, etc. He thereby nullifies his own definition, for he draws a dividing line between their *essential* determination as representatives and their *existence as part of a corporation*. Furthermore, he also cuts the corporation off from itself, from its own real content, for the corporation is supposed to elect deputies not from *its own point of view* but from the *point of view of the state*, i.e. it votes in its *non-existence as corporation* [89, pp. 192–193; 95, part 1, 2:132].

Marx recognizes the tension between Hegel's separatist and his integrationist depictions of the relation of the state to civil society, and he responds to it in two ways. First, he regards some of the integrative proposals as unsuccessful on their own terms, because they do not provide an organic synthesis or integration of universal and particular interests, but only their duality and opposition. As we've just seen, he regards Hegel's account of representation as a case in point. Another example concerns the supposed integrative role of the corporations in resolving the antithesis between private property and the higher interests of the state. To enable this role, Hegel has the officials of the corporations selected by a 'mixture of popular election by the interested parties, and confirmation and determination by a higher authority' [52, §288; 57, 7:§288]. Marx comments:

> [T]he resolution of this antithesis by means of *mixed election* is a mere *accomodation*, a disquisition on and an admission of an unresolved dualism that is itself a *dualism*, a 'mixture' [89, p. 110; 95, part 1, 2:53].

Second, Marx regards Hegel's integrationist hopes as utopian because the Hobbesian tendencies of civil society have a necessary political expression:

> Civil society is separated from the state. Hence the citizen of the state is also separated from the citizen as a member of civil society.... In order to behave as an *actual citizen of the state*, to attain political significance and effectiveness, he must step out of his civil reality, abstract from it, withdraw from this whole organization into his individuality; for the only existence he finds for his citizenship is his pure, blank *individuality*... [93, 3:77 (translation modified); 95, part 1, 2:86].

The developments in civil society that Hegel sees as realizing personal freedom require civil society's depoliticization, its separation from the state. Consequently, citizenship status must be independent of social circumstances. So a necessary political complement to the unleashing of particularity in civil society is a form of emancipation—'political emancipation'—whose fundamental tendency is to establish citizenship as a status enjoyed by everyone, regardless of particular personal and familial circumstances, economic status and associational ties. Thus, in contrast to feudal arrangements, people can no longer be restricted to a particular political status through the narrow mediation of membership in a particular estate.

> The political revolution ... *abolished* the *political character of civil society*. It broke up civil society into its simple components, on the one hand *individuals,* on the other the *material* and *spiritual elements* that constitute the vital content and civil situation of these individuals. It unfettered the political spirit, which had been, as it were, split up, partitioned, dispersed in the various cul-de-sacs of feudal society; it gathered up this spirit out of its dispersion, freed it from its intermixture with civil life and established it as the sphere of the community, the *general* concern of the people, ideally independent of those *particular* elements of civil life. A person's *distinct* activity and distinct situation in life sank to a merely individual significance. They no longer constituted the general relationship of the individual to the state as a whole. Rather, public affairs as such became the general concern of each individual and the political function his universal function.... The *establishment of the political state* and the dissolution of civil society into independent *individuals* – who are related by *law*

just as men in the estates and guilds were related by *privilege* – take place in *one and the same act* [89, pp. 232–233; 95, part 1, 2:161–162].

In making his integrationist claims, Hegel opposes this direction of social development on the grounds that it reflects an 'atomistic and abstract view' [52, §303R; 57, 7:§303A]. For Marx, the tendency has deeper roots:

> This view is certainly abstract, but it is the 'abstraction' of the political state as Hegel himself presents it.[20] It is also atomistic, but it is the atomism of society itself. The 'view' cannot be concrete when the *object* of the view is 'abstract'. The atomism into which civil society plunges in its *political act* follows necessarily from the fact that... the *political state is an abstraction* from civil society.... By expressing the *strangeness* of this phenomenon Hegel has not eliminated the *estrangement* [93, 3:79 (translation modified); 95, part 1, 2:88].

To clarify Marx's position, especially the notion of estrangement he introduces, it is useful to consider the following passage:

> Hegel describes civil law [*das Privatrecht*] as the *right of abstract personality* or as *abstract right*. And in truth it must be expounded as the *abstraction* of right and thus as the *illusory right of abstract personality*, just as the morality expounded by Hegel is the *illusory existence* [*Dasein*] *of abstract subjectivity*. Hegel expounds civil law and morality as such abstractions, from which it does not follow for him that the state, the ethical life [*Sittlichkeit*] of which they are presuppositions can be nothing but the *society* (the social life) of these illusions, but on the contrary, he concludes that they are subordinate [*subalterne*] moments of this ethical life. But what is civil law other than the law of these subjects of the state, and what is morality other than their morality? Or rather, the person of civil law and the subject of morality are the *person* and the *subject* of the state. Hegel has often been attacked for his explication of morality. He has done nothing but develop the morality of the modern state and of modern civil law.... It is... a great merit of Hegel to have assigned to modern morality its true position, though in one respect it is an unconscious achievement (since Hegel passes off [*ausgiebt*] the state whose presupposition

---

[20] 'As Hegel himself presents it': Hegel's associationist scheme, Marx thinks, contradicts Hegel's own correct account of the state as separate from civil society.

is such a morality as the realized Idea [*der Reale Idee*] of ethical life) [93, 3:108 (translation modified); 95, part1, 2:117–118].

As we have seen, in the *Philosophy of Right* Hegel presents abstract right and morality as incomplete conceptions of freedom.[21] To see either as self-sufficient, he thinks, is to be taken in by abstraction, to regard as an independent reality something that can be realized only as a subordinate aspect of a larger whole. Thus abstract right is 'the illusory right of abstract personality', and morality is 'the illusory existence of abstract subjectivity'. However, Hegel takes his system of ethical life to provide their needed completion, thereby giving them rational significance. In this larger context, then, they do not signal the absence of reason but rather play an integral role in its realization. Though they may tend to generate the false appearance of being capable of standing on their own, the system of ethical life that properly incorporates them is not merely 'the social life of these illusions'.

But as we've seen, for Marx, Hegel's integrative proposals are unworkable. Abstract right and morality do attain institutional existence and content, but not through the self-legislation of reason, though they present themselves as based on reason. Rather, modern society *is* 'the society (the social life) of these illusions'. This phrase marks an early expression of Marx's conception of alienated social forms and their supporting ideologies. It predates his conception of commodities, wage-labor, and capital as such alienated forms. Yet it is clear that he already regards the system of private rights that supposedly realizes personal freedom as in fact a system of estrangement, and the corresponding realm of moral reflection as in fact a realm of socially necessary illusion:

> Where the political state has attained its true development, man leads a double life, a heavenly life and an earthly life, not only in thought, in consciousness, but in *reality*, in *life*: life in the *political community*, where he regards himself as a *communal being*, and in *civil society*, where he is active as a *private individual*, regards other men as a means, degrades himself into a means and becomes the plaything of alien powers. The relationship of the political state to civil society is just as spiritual as the relationship of heaven to earth. The political

---

[21] As Hegel puts it, 'The course we follow is that whereby the abstract forms reveal themselves not as existing for themselves, but as untrue', and 'The sphere of right and that of morality cannot exist independently [*für sich*]; they must have the ethical as their support and foundation' [52, §§32A, 141A; 57, 7:§§32Z, 141Z).

state stands in the same opposition to civil society and overcomes it in the same way as religion overcomes the limitedness of the profane world, i.e. by likewise having to acknowledge it again, reinstate it and allow itself to be dominated by it. Man in his *immediate* reality, in civil society, is a profane being. Here, where he counts as a real individual for himself and others, he is an *illusory* phenomenon [*unwahre Erscheinung*]. In the state, on the other hand, where man counts as a species being, he is the imaginary member of an imagined sovereignty, he is deprived of his real individual life and filled with an unreal universality [93, 3:154 (translation modified); 95, part 1, 2:148–149.].

It is through the very exercise of the rights that supposedly realize their personal freedom—for example, private property and contract—that members of civil society unwittingly turn themselves into 'plaything[s] of alien powers'. That system of rights thus provides only an illusory form of freedom. Moreover, the procedures of moral reflection those individuals endorse as citizens provide only 'imagined sovereignty' and 'unreal universality', i.e., an illusory form of autonomy. In fact, abstract moral reflection is not capable of bringing reason to bear on civil society, and as a result political consciousness must 'allow itself to be dominated' by the latter. This domination is a political form of the moral estrangement—in particular, the content estrangement—that Hegel finds in Kantian morality. For Hegel, Kant's so-called pure practical reason, since it abstracts from all content of the will, must import content through a presupposed reasonableness in the background social world. We might say then that moral consciousness must 'allow itself to be dominated' by the background social world. Similarly, political consciousness, since it is an abstraction from civil society, is in the self-contradictory condition of having to import its content illicitly from the latter. As a system of estrangement, civil society is not a rationally ordered social world. Individual moral subjectivity that takes this estranged world as given, implicitly presupposing its rationality, gives only the illusion of autonomy. It thereby provides that world with ideological support rather than reflective stability based on reason.

As we'll see in the next chapter, Marx eventually refines his account by focusing on the capitalist production of commodities as a system of estrangement. He regards wage labor and capital as social projections rather than intrinsic features of production and distribution as such. They exist only in virtue of the specific way agents make their economic decisions in relation to one another. They thus owe their existence to the same economic form of agency that is expressed through the system of private property rights Hegel regards as essential to the realization of personal freedom. The systematic theory Marx develops of this economic formation enables him to advance powerful arguments that it puts all agents, but especially wage laborers, in conditions of estrangement that belie its self-presentation as a system of freedom.

# 4
# Marx: Economic Estrangement

## 4.1 Doctrinal inversion, real inversion

In Section 3.6 we examined Marx's critique of Hegel's integrationist conception of the relation between civil society and the state. We noted the implication of that critique that Hegel's proposals are incapable of overcoming the estrangement he finds in abstract right and the moral will. To appreciate how Marx develops the concept of economic estrangement, we need to note a second criticism of Hegel's political philosophy that one finds in Marx's early work, namely that Hegel's doctrine contains an 'inversion' that amounts to a mysticism of reason. My concern in this section is not to defend this criticism but to explain its role in the genesis of Marx's conception of economic estrangement.

The idea of such an inversion goes back to Ludwig Feuerbach, who studied under Hegel and became influential in the disputes among his interpreters and critics in the two decades following his death. In Feuerbach's work one can find critiques of Christianity and Hegel's philosophy that charge them with what I'll call a 'doctrinal inversion': They falsely accord, Feuerbach thinks, independence and self-subsistence to certain human ideals (under the name of 'God' or 'the Idea'), and they treat actual human existence as a form of the self-realization of these ideals. They thereby invert the true relationship: they treat the real 'subject', humanity, as a 'predicate', and the real predicates—the ideals, which are really nothing but forms of human self-consciousness—as independent subjects [32–34].

In the *Critique of Hegel's Philosophy of Right*, we can see that Marx also charges Hegel with a doctrinal inversion. The criticism especially clear in Marx's comments on Hegel's §262, which contains the following passage:

> The actual Idea is the spirit which divides itself up into the two ideal spheres of its concept – the family and civil society – as its finite mode, and thereby emerges from its ideality to become infinite and actual spirit for itself. In so doing, it allocates the material of its finite actuality, i.e. individuals as a *mass*, to these two spheres, and in such a way that, in each individual case [*am Einzelnen*], this allocation appears to be *mediated* by circumstances, by the individual's arbitrary will and personal [*eigene*] choice of vocation [*Bestimmung*]... [52, §262 (my translation); 57, 7:§262].

Marx's entire commentary on this passage is important [89, pp. 61–4; 95, part 1, 2:7–10], but I'll reproduce here just the last few lines:

> [T]he fact is that the state issues from the mass of individuals existing as members of families and of civil society; but speculative philosophy expresses this fact as an achievement of the Idea.... Thus empirical reality is taken in just as it is; it is even declared to be rational; however it is not rational because of its own reason, but because the empirical fact in its empirical existence has a meaning other than it itself. The fact, which is the starting point, is not conceived as such but rather as the mystical result. The real becomes phenomenon, but the Idea has no other content than this phenomenon. Moreover, the Idea has no purpose other than the logical one 'to be for itself infinite actual spirit.' The entire mystery of the *Philosophy of Right* and of Hegelian philosophy in general is contained in this paragraph [89, pp. 63–64 (translation modified); 95, part 1, 2:9–10].

Marx and Feuerbach saw such doctrinal inversions as inherently sophistical[1] and apologetic.[2] In this respect they distinguished themselves from many of their contemporaries on the Hegelian left, who blamed apologetic features of Hegel's writings on personal compromises with authority rather than fundamental principles of his philosophy. But even in this very early work Marx develops the notion of inversion beyond the point to which Feuerbach takes it. In particular, he treats

---

[1] For example, Marx accuses Hegel of fallaciously deducing the structure of the political constitution from the concept of organism [89, pp. 68–69; 95, part 1, 2:14].

[2] Note the above assertion that 'empirical reality is taken in just as it is; it is even declared to be rational'.

the doctrinal inversions as having a distinctive social diagnosis. They are distortions of consciousness rooted not in transsocial features of human nature and the human condition but rather in specific social forms of practice. Though they are false, they are symptomatic of something real, something itself having the character of an inversion. Underlying theoretical mysticism is a mystifying practice. Inverted consciousness reflects an underlying social and practical inversion:

> This state and this society produce religion, which is an inverted *consciousness of the world,* because they are an *inverted world* [89, 244; 95, part 1, 2:170].

Though this passage is from a portion of the *Critique* that Marx later prepared for publication, it nonetheless reflects ideas that are developed in the earlier draft. A good example is Marx's specific criticism of the institution of primogeniture (inheritance of landed property by first-born males). According to Hegel, primogeniture is a force for socio-political unity in that it insulates landed property from the fluctuations of the market and thus provides the members of the landowning class with the economic security necessary for them to act in a disinterested way in the legislature. But Marx points out that whereas property by its very meaning is supposed to be subject to the will of its owner and is alienable at will, here there is a reversal: property is not disposable at will, and in fact it is the land that inherits the owner; the owner is the serf of his own property. '[P]rivate property has become the subject of the will; the will survives only as the predicate of private property' [89, p. 168; 95, part 1, 2:110]. This criticism of primogeniture shares a form with Marx's later critique of capitalism. In a real inversion, human practices escape the control of the participants and develop their own alien dynamic, even though they exist only through human action.

Doctrinal inversions characterize certain understandings that individuals have of their own social practices. These understandings can reside in common sense as well as in the more explicitly theoretical constructions of theologians, philosophers, political economists and others. They all represent certain aspects of human life as expressive of given, self-subsistent powers or forces whose fundamental modes of realization are not susceptible to human control. These representations are 'inverted' because the represented powers are not really self-subsistent but rather exist only in virtue of certain configurations of human activity. The representations thus falsely depict something that derives from human activity as an independent determinant of that activity. But there is something true in these representations as well. They are expressions of a practice of self-alienation or self-estrangement. Individuals really are in the grip of a process with an alien dynamic; they really are the 'plaything[s] of alien powers' [89, p. 220; 95, part 1, 2:149]. Yet this alien process is nothing but their own activity in an estranged form.

For Marx, an important consequence of the fact that doctrinal inversions are rooted in such real inversions, which in turn are specific social forms of practice, is that effective criticism must go beyond pointing out the falsity or even the apologetic character of the doctrine. One must connect it up with its social basis in a mystifying practice and probe the nature of that practice for reasons agents might have for transforming it.

> Feuerbach starts out from the fact of religious self-alienation, of the doubling of the world into a religious world and a secular one. His work consists in resolving the religious world into its secular basis. But that the secular basis sets off itself from itself and establishes itself as an independent realm in the clouds is only to be explained by the cleavages and self-contradictions of this secular basis. This basis must itself, therefore, not only be understood in its contradiction but revolutionized in practice.... Feuerbach therefore does not see that 'religious sentiment' is itself a social product and that the abstract individual whom he analyzes belongs to a particular form of society.... All social life is essentially practical. All mysteries that lead theory to mysticism find their rational solution in human practice and in the comprehension of this practice [89, pp. 422–423 (translation modified); 94, 3:6–7].

In his own social investigations, Marx soon comes to see the economy as the most fundamental locus of social inversion, an arena of social practice whose most immediate conceptualization gets systematized in political economy. This means that quite early in his career, direct criticism of religion and Hegel's philosophy recedes into the background and is supplanted by criticism of political economy. His mature critique of political economy is aimed at revealing its character as a doctrinal inversion providing ideological support for an underlying economic inversion.

## 4.2 Commodity production

### 4.2.1 Social relations of commodity production

A commodity producing economy is one in which producers (or groups thereof), working independently of one another and for their own account, produce items for exchange on a market. Capitalism is a specific form of commodity production, one in which money is advanced as *capital*. That is, it is invested in the purchase, production, and sale of commodities with the aim of generating a positive net return on the investment. Since commodity production is a basic element of capitalist production, Marx begins his study of the latter in *Capital* with an analysis of commodity production considered apart from the existence of capital. He abstracts from all economic categories that presuppose the existence of capital, including wage labor. In effect he assumes an economy in which producers own their own means of production and satisfy their needs by exchanging the products of their labor on the market. He assumes in this way that individuals' own labor is their only source of income.[3] We'll follow Sweezy in referring to this economic model as 'simple commodity production' [146, p. 23].

There are two notable precedents for using abstraction in this way. The first is Hegel's consideration of abstract right and morality in abstraction from a system of ethical life. Both Hegel and Marx begin with abstract categories and then provide increasingly concrete articulations of the object of their investigation.[4] Just as Hegel claims that abstract right and morality cannot subsist on their own but require the ethical as their foundation, Marx claims that it is only with capitalism that commodity production becomes generalized and pervasive. Of course, there are also important differences. Rather than Hegel's sequential overcoming of estrangement, Marx presents an increasingly complex and mystifying structure of estrangement. Hegel lays out what he takes to be a system

---

[3] He is not very clear about these assumptions in the opening pages of *Capital*, though it is not too hard to figure out that some such assumption must be at work. However, much later in the book he says: 'Originally the rights of property seemed to us to be grounded in a man's own labor. Some such assumption was at least necessary, since only commodity owners with equal rights confronted each other, and the sole means of appropriating the commodities of others was the alienation of a man's own commodities, commodities which, however, could only be produced by labor' [90, p. 730; 94, 23:609–610]. See also his reference to a condition in which 'the product belongs to its producer, who, exchanging equivalent for equivalent, can enrich himself only by his own labor' [90, p. 733; 94, 23:613]. These passages suggest that Marx may have assumed that such an economy actually existed prior to capitalism. However, the textual evidence is mixed, and we won't assume that such a reading is correct but will treat the idea of such an economy as a useful abstraction. For a strong defense of such an interpretation or reconstruction, see Morishima and Catephores [99].

[4] The Introduction to Marx's *Grundrisse* contains an explicit comparison of the two approaches [87; 88]. Also relevant to such a comparison are some remarks by Hegel in the *Philosophy of Right* [52, §§32, 32A; 57, 7:§§32, 32Z].

of self-reproducing freedom; Marx provides what he takes to be a system of self-reproducing estrangement.

The second precedent is the tendency on the part of the classical economists to begin their studies with an analysis of the relation of exchange. Marx follows them in this regard, but in addition to the quantitative questions of exchange ratios and price determination that claim their attention, he focuses on something else that he regards as of fundamental importance. He refers to it as 'the value form' [90, p. 138; 95, part 2, 6:80], and he takes it to mark commodity production as a specific social form of production. Adam Smith, for example, does not distinguish the economic relation of exchange from other forms of the social division of labor; in fact he treats the division of labor as the result of a basic human propensity 'to truck, barter, and exchange one thing for another' [143, p. 15]. Marx, on the other hand, understands the exchange relation of commodities to arise out of a specific social form of the division of labor, a specific mode of production. He wants to characterize what he sees as a specific kind of social process that confers this property of exchangeability on the products of labor, thereby turning them into commodities.

Like all products of labor, commodities are useful objects, or 'use values'. They have that character in virtue of natural properties that render them suitable for satisfying human wants. But the fact that commodities are useful is nothing socially distinctive about them; in all forms of society the products of labor have this character. However, commodities are not merely useful objects; they are 'the material bearers of exchange value' [90, p. 126; 95, part 2, 6:70]. Exchange value initially appears as haphazard and accidental; seemingly, all there is to it are the various rates at which commodities happen to exchange on the market on various occasions. However, a closer look reveals that something more systematic is at work. The relation *is exchangeable for* orders or structures the world of commodities in certain ways. In particular, it puts them into equivalence classes. The quantities of commodities that are exchangeable for each other are thus equivalent in some respect. Exchangeability expresses or reveals equality of some kind, in much the same way that congruence of line segments expresses equality of length.

Exchange value thus manifests a property that all commodities share. Marx calls this property *value*. What kind of property is it? It can't be a natural property like weight, because any given commodity is exchangeable for any other at some rate or other, regardless of each commodity's natural properties. Rather, it is a social property; it exists only in certain forms of society. It appears as a power of 'metamorphosis', so to speak. Any commodity has the power to transform itself into any other, provided the relative quantities are right. But this power is not physical, chemical, biological, or any other kind of natural power. Rather it is social. There are forms of society in which the products of labor do not have it. The rabbits killed by a hunter in a hunting and gathering society, for example, lack it; they are not universally exchangeable for other products of labor in the society. Custom, tradition, a settled plan, or ad hoc arrangements will settle the hunter's terms of access to these products as well as how the rabbits are distributed.

What is the specific form of society in which products have the power of metamorphosis? Marx's answer is that '[o]nly the products of self-standing and mutually independent acts of private labour confront each other as commodities' [90, p. 132 (translation modified); 95, part 2, 6:75]. In all viable, reproducible economies, there must be a way in which the social division of labor is maintained and reproduced as an ongoing practice. It must be settled whether determinate activity $x$ by individual $y$ counts as participation in the economy. In some societies this might happen through established tradition, perhaps involving decisions made in advance in accordance with an established authority structure, or it might conceivably happen through free agreement establishing an authoritative production plan. But in a society in which it does not happen at the stage of production, because of the private and independent character of production decisions, it must be effected through market exchangeability of the products of labor.

The character of laboring activity as participation in the social division of labor—its character as social labor—manifests itself as the exchangeability of its product. But what manifests itself as that exchangeability is the value of the commodity. So value is social labor treated as a property of the product. Its *form*—its mode of appearance—is exchangeability, but its *substance*—what it is in essence—is participation in society's labor, or social labor. Value is social labor projected onto the commodity as a substantial property of it, a property that appears as exchangeability. This is first and foremost a *qualitative* assertion. The relation of exchangeability reflects the quality that commodities share as bearers of value.

However, with respect to quantity, appearance may not accurately represent reality: a commodity's price, its exchange ratio with some other commodity taken as standard, may diverge from the ratio of the two commodities' values. The quantity of value a commodity has is equal to the amount of labor required to produce it under standard conditions. This quantity includes not only the labor directly required in its production, but also the labor directly required to produce the means of production used up in its production, plus the labor directly required to produce the means of production used up in the production of *those* means of production, and so on. Prices may diverge from values so understood. This possibility exists for equilibrium prices (when there is no incentive for producers to switch from one line of production to another) as well as for non-equilibrium prices.

Marx was fully aware of these possibilities. Yet he proceeds throughout volumes 1 and 2 of *Capital* by treating equilibrium prices as proportional to values. We'll look into the matter in more detail later,[5] but for now we can justify this way of proceeding by attributing two successively more concrete levels of abstraction to the treatment in volume 1. The first is that of simple commodity production, which we have associated with the opening section ('Commodities and Money'). And the second is that characterized by 'equal organic compositions of capital', which requires a uniform ratio across industries of capital invested in means of production to capital invested in labor power. The first level treats commodity production in abstraction from the existence of capital, while the second treats the capital-labor relation in abstraction from certain intercapitalist relations. Under each set of conditions it is reasonable to treat (equilibrium) prices as proportional to values, as we'll see in Chapter 5. Marx thinks that by treating these more abstract levels first he highlights certain features of capitalism that tend to be obscured by its fully concrete appearance. Of course, this procedure is acceptable only if the simplifying assumptions governing the more abstract models can eventually be relaxed without destroying the significance of the more abstract analysis. Marx undertakes this more concrete part of the project in volume 3.

[5] The general claim that at equilibrium, commodities exchange in proportion to the labor required to produce them is often called the 'labor theory of value'. If we accept this label, then Marx does not subscribe to the labor theory of value. He affirms the proportionality only for certain simplified models. In Chapter 5 I argue that these affirmations are reasonable. Marx drops the simplifications in the draft materials assembled by Engels to make up volume 3. There he somewhat tentatively asserts that in general, though prices are not proportional to values, it remains true that the equilibrium rate of profit is equal to the total amount of surplus value (new value produced over and above that paid to workers in the form of wages) produced in the economy divided by the value of the total amount of capital advanced in the economy. If we think of *this* assertion as the labor theory of value, then Marx does subscribe to it. As we'll see in Chapter 5, it cannot be defended with the generality he attributes to it. We'll look into the implications of this error for the viability of his project.

We'll probe this matter in Chapter 5. In the meantime we'll follow the analysis Marx develops in volume 1.

Marx says that the substance of value is human labor in the abstract. In referring to the labor as abstract, he means that it is not this or that useful feature of the labor that makes it the substance of value, but rather its abstract general property of being a quantitative portion of the total labor of society. The exchange process, by placing all commodities into the equivalence relation *is exchangeable for*, equates them all as values and thereby equates the individual's labor qualitatively to the labor of every other commodity producer, thereby 'reducing' it to human labor in the abstract.[6] This is a form of labor certification peculiar to commodity production. In other social forms of production, an individual's labor gets certified in its concrete form; it does not have to be reduced to human labor in the abstract.

[U]nder the rural patriarchal system of production, when spinner and weaver lived under the same roof—the women of the family spinning and the men weaving, say, for the requirements of the family—yarn and linen were social products, and spinning and weaving social labor within the framework of the family. But their social character did not appear in the form of [yarn and linen's] exchanging for each other as equal and equally valid expressions of the same universal labor time. On the contrary, the product of labor bore the specific social imprint of the family relationship with its naturally evolved division of labor. Or let us take the services and dues in kind of the Middle Ages. It was the distinct labor of the individual in its original form, the particular features of his labor and not its universal aspect, that formed the social ties at that time. Or finally let us take communal labor in its spontaneously evolved form as we find it among all civilized nations at the dawn of their history. In this case the social character of labor is evidently not effected through the individual's labor's assuming the abstract form of universal labor or his product's assuming the form of a universal equivalent. The communal system on which this mode of production is based prevents the labor of an individual from becoming private labor and his product the private product of a separate individual; it causes individual labor to appear

---

[6] This 'reduction' is not something the parties involved consciously do. 'They don't know it, but they do it' [90, pp. 166–167 (translation modified); 95, part 2, 6:104–105].

rather as the direct function of a member of the social organization [86, pp. 33–34 (translation modified); 94, 13:20–21].[7]

Commodity production's mode of labor certification puts would-be producers in a peculiar position. That a person's activity is part of the social division of labor is a social fact; to be such a participant is to have a certain social status. This status is gained only through some kind of recognition of the activity as participation. But in commodity production there is no socially authoritative specification, antecedent to production, of particular products needed, particular methods of producing these products or allocation of persons to the employment of these methods. So the necessary recognition is achieved, if it is, only through exchange. It is not merely that would-be producers *do not know* at the stage of production whether they are actually participating. Rather, their actions literally *are not* productive contributions until that status is conferred on them in the exchange process. The certification, and thus the status, are necessarily retrospective.

In all production based on division of labor, each productive activity, in virtue of its concrete character, brings about a specific alteration in the form of the material worked on. In an idiom common to Spinoza and Hegel, the transformation is a specific determination or negation of the material. In modes of production where there is social settlement in advance of the products needed and the allocation of individuals to their production, each producer faces a concretely specified task to accomplish. The conditions of participation in society's productive activity are those of a particular determinate negation. In commodity production, however, the requirement each producer faces is completely formal and abstract, rather than determinate and concrete. Of course, anyone who is successful will end up having effected a specific useful determination, but there is no advance substantive indication of what this task requires, not even a menu of available options. There is only the formal, substantively empty requirement of providing an input to social consumption, that is something saleable. There is an air of paradox in the abstract requirement the producer faces.

### 4.2.2 Commodity fetishism

The substance of value is abstract human labor. Its form, however—its mode of social expression—is exchange value. The value of one commodity must be expressed in terms of some other commodity, as in '20

---

[7] There are similar passages in *Capital* [90, pp. 169–173; 95, part 2, 6:107–110].

yards of linen are worth one coat'. Some form of relative expression is necessary, for since value is a social rather than a natural property, the character of a commodity as a bearer of value is not made apparent by any of its natural properties. Those properties serve merely to express its use value. '20 yards of linen are worth 20 yards of linen' is not an expression of value. The value form of a commodity must be different from its natural form. Its value must be expressed in terms of the natural properties of another commodity.

But to express the value of linen, say, in terms of coats—that is, in terms of some other arbitrarily selected commodity as its equivalent—is inadequate. It expresses only the equivalence of linen-producing labor with coat-producing labor—weaving with tailoring. The form of value must express the linen's comparability with all other commodities if it is adequately to express the linen's value. For only such comparability establishes the comparability of linen-producing labor with all other forms of labor and thereby its character as abstract human labor. With the development of commodity production there will be a tendency for one commodity to be singled out to play the role of a universally recognized equivalent for all other commodities, making them all comparable with each other. The commodity that serves this function of a 'universal equivalent' thereby takes on the role of money. Money is not a mere convenience; it is a necessary outgrowth of the social relations of commodity production.

Marx claims that there is a kind of 'fetishism' endemic to commodity production [90, p. 165; 95, part 2, 6:103f]. In using this expression he does not mean to refer to an excessive concern for material comforts or to the idea that a person's worth is determined by his possessions. On one meaning of the term, to turn something into a fetish is to invest it with powers it does not have on its own, while nonetheless treating these powers as intrinsic to it. It is this phenomenon that is Marx's concern. Commodity production invests commodities with powers they do not have as natural objects. As we've seen, in commodity production, the social character of producers' labor takes the form of a property of their products. The labor of the individual producer is established as part of the labor of society through the product's establishing itself as a member of the world of mutually exchangeable commodities. It does so by finding an expression of its value in terms of the bodily form of some other commodity—ultimately money, the universal equivalent. Since this amounts to finding an expression of its value in terms of natural properties, value takes on the appearance of something natural or transsocial rather than the socially specific property it is.

Commodity production contains no antecedent social orientation to use value, whether in the form of authoritative tradition or a freely adopted social plan. Therefore the establishment of an individual's labor as activity of this or that concrete sort will not establish its social character. That character can only be established through its reduction to human labor in the abstract. This reduction is at the root of the fetish character of commodities. It is a real social process, effected by the economic institutions of commodity production. This social process has its own dynamic; it operates 'behind the backs' of economic agents, outside the scope of their control; that is why there can be such things as economic laws or tendencies that can be the subject of a social science like economics. In Marx's view, agents in commodity production become 'the plaything of alien powers' (as he describes the members of civil society in 'On the Jewish Question' [89, p. 220; 95, part 1, 2:149]). They unwittingly put *themselves* in this condition. The alien powers exist and work their effects only in virtue of the specific way individuals exercise their powers of agency—their rational powers—in relation to one another. In making their economic decisions, producers cannot decide the state of the economy; rather, they must anticipate it and react to it. They may be able to do so quite rationally. But nonetheless the passage of the economy through its various states is a blind function of the economic actions they take and are willing to take. Their own use of reason has an unreasonable social form. It is they, therefore, who turn their own powers of agency over to the world of commodities, which takes the form of a 'second nature' with its own laws. 'Their own social movement has for them the form of a movement of things controlling them instead of being controlled by them' [90, p. 167–168; 95, part 2, 6:105]. What we may presume is rational agency on the part of individuals assumes the form of an alien power, restricting their freedom. It is reason in an unreasonable form.

This estrangement, reification, or social inversion, in which products rule the producers, gets reflected in corresponding doctrinal inversions in political economy that take the fetish character of commodities at face value and in effect treat value as a nature-imposed necessity rather than a contingent social property. A critical analysis of fetishism can thus form part of a critique of political economy for its ideological aspects. Marx distinguishes different economic theories according to degrees to which they are infected by the distortions of commodity fetishism. 'Vulgar economy' gets fully taken in by appearances and treats value as intrinsic to things. Marx quotes a remark by Samuel Bailey as an example and offers a comment:

> 'Riches (use-value) are the attribute of man, value is the attribute of commodities. A man or a community is rich, a pearl or a diamond is valuable... A pearl or a diamond is valuable as a pearl or diamond'. So far no chemist has ever discovered exchange-value in either a pearl or a diamond [90, p. 177 (translation modified); 95, part 2, 6:113].

'Classical political economy', the economics of Smith and Ricardo, for example, sees the connection of exchange-value with labor, but it fails to take into account the social specificity of the representation of labor by exchange-value.

> Political economy has indeed analysed value and its magnitude, how-ever incompletely, and has uncovered the content concealed within these forms. But it has never once asked the question why this con-tent has assumed that particular form, that is to say, why labour is expressed in value, and why the measurement of labour by its duration is expressed in the magnitude of the value of the product. These formulas, which bear the unmistakable stamp of belonging to a social formation in which the process of production has mastery over man, instead of the opposite, appear to the political economists' bourgeois consciousness to be as much a self-evident and nature-imposed necessity as productive labor itself [90, pp. 173–175; 95, part 2, 6:110–111].

Marx elaborates in a footnote:

> It is one of the chief failings of classical political economy that it has never succeeded, by means of its analysis of commodities, and in par-ticular of their value, in discovering the form of value which in fact turns value into exchange-value. Even its best representatives, Adam Smith and Ricardo, treat the form of value as something of indif-ference, something external to the nature of the commodity itself. The explanation for this is not simply that their attention is entirely absorbed by the analysis of the magnitude of value. It lies deeper. The value-form of the product of labour is the most abstract, but also the most universal form of the bourgeois mode of production; by that fact it stamps the bourgeois mode of production as a particular

kind of social production of a historical and transitory character. If then we make the mistake of treating it as the eternal natural form of social production, we necessarily overlook the specificity of the value-form, and consequently of the commodity-form together with its further developments, the money form, the capital form, etc. [90, p. 174n34; 95, part 2, 6:111n32].

## 4.3 Capital

For Marx, the circulation of commodities is the starting point of capital. Capital has its modern history, he says, beginning with the sixteenth century, when commodity circulation developed to the point of world trade. The ultimate product of commodity circulation, its culminating economic form, is money, and money is the first form in which capital appears.

The simple circulation of commodities has the form:

$$C - M - C'$$

This is the form of 'selling in order to buy'. Its point is the appropriation of use-value. This rationale requires a qualitative difference between the extremes $C$ and $C'$. In this form of circulation, money functions simply as money. However, circulation, the buying and selling of commodities, allows the development of a different form, one in which money circulates as capital:

$$M - C - M'$$

This is 'buying in order to sell'. Again, for the process to have any meaning, the extremes must differ from each other. But here the extremes are qualitatively identical. Hence only a quantitative difference gives the process any meaning. The money is advanced as value that grows and returns to its owner in increased quantity:

$$M' = M + \Delta M$$

where $\Delta M$ is an increment in value that Marx calls 'surplus value'.

> The value originally advanced, therefore, not only sustains itself [*erhält sich*] while in circulation, but alters its magnitude, adds to itself a surplus-value, or realizes itself [*verwerthet sich*]. And this movement converts it into capital [90, p. 252 (translation modified); 95, part 2, 6:169].

There are both real and doctrinal inversions associated with this appearance of capital in the sphere of circulation:

> The independent forms, the money forms, that the value of commodities assumes in simple circulation, mediate only their exchange and vanish in the end result of the movement. In the circulation $M - C - M$, on the other hand, both money and commodities function only as modes of the existence of value itself, money as its general, the commodity as its particular, so to speak merely disguised mode of existence. It constantly changes from one form into the other without becoming lost in this movement, and thus it is transformed into an automatic subject.... [V]alue becomes here the subject of a process in which, under constant change of form between money and commodities, it changes its own magnitude, throws off itself as surplus value from itself as original value, realizes itself [*sich selbst verwerthet*]. For the movement in which it adds surplus value is its own movement, its realization therefore self-realization. It has acquired the occult quality of positing (*setzen*) value because it is value.... If in simple circulation, the value of commodities attained at most a form independent of their use values, the form of money, now value suddenly presents itself as a processing, self-moving substance, for which commodities and money are mere forms. [90, p. 255 (translation modified); 95, part 2, 6:171–172].

There are two aspects to a real inversion: (1) the estrangement or reification, whereby agents split off a part of their agency and convert it into a process with an independent dynamic, and (2) the flow of that reified process itself and its effects on the agents caught up in it. This passage deals most directly with the second aspect. But there is also an indirect reference to the first: there is a note of irony in Marx's reference to 'occult' powers. He is criticizing the doctrinal inversion that would not see the reification (aspect (1)) as the source of capital's power of self-expansion, treating that power as something totally independent of human activity. As we've seen, Marx sees political economy as guilty of such a doctrinal inversion, which in its content is just a development of commodity fetishism.

An adequate account of the possibility of capital must respect the following constraints:

1. Surplus value cannot originate in circulation. One would-be capitalist could make a profit by buying below value or selling above value

(buying cheap and selling dear), but not all can. To conclude otherwise would involve the fallacy of composition. To put it another way, what needs explaining is an absolute increase in value and not the mere redistribution of a constant sum.

2. But surplus value cannot originate entirely apart from circulation. The would be capitalist must be able to buy and sell, though at value, and still end up with more value than he started with.

Marx's solution, in brief, is this: The capitalist must be able to buy on the market a commodity whose consumption is a process of value creation. Since labor is the substance of value, this commodity can only be labor power, the capacity to provide labor. Under certain technological conditions this commodity can be used to produce not only value, but more value than it itself has. This extra value is the surplus value appropriated by the capitalist. The value of labor power is given by the number of worker-hours necessary to produce a partly culturally determined subsistence basket, consumption of which replenishes the worker's labor power. Provided that the productivity of labor is high enough and the working day long enough, the working day will contain more worker-hours than necessary to produce the subsistence basket. In these circumstances, more value is created than is paid to the workers in the form of wages, and surplus value is produced.

What about the means of production used up in the production process? By definition of value as the sum of direct and indirect labor requirements, their value reappears, unchanged in quantity, as part of the value of the product. They also play a causal role in making the production of surplus value possible by helping to make the productivity of labor high enough.

## 4.4   The real subjection of labor to capital

The capitalist advances a certain sum of value as capital. Through purchases and hirings he transforms this sum into two forms: means of production and labor power. The portion of capital that takes the form of means of production Marx calls *constant capital*, to indicate that the value of means of production is simply transferred to the product. That portion of the advanced capital does not undergo any alteration in value. On the other hand, Marx calls the portion of capital that is turned into labor power *variable capital* because that portion of the capital does undergo an alteration in value. 'It both reproduces the equivalent of its own value and produces an excess, a surplus-value, which may itself vary, and be more or less according to circumstances' [90, p. 317; 95, part 2, 6:219–220]. The ratio of surplus value to variable capital is called the *rate of surplus value*. Call the time necessary to reproduce the value of labor power *necessary labor time*. Call the difference between the length of the working day and the necessary labor time *surplus labor time*. The ratio of surplus labor time to necessary labor time is the *rate of exploitation*. Surplus value produced could be increased either through an increase in the length of the working day or through a decrease in the necessary labor time. To capture this difference Marx makes a distinction between 'absolute surplus-value' and 'relative surplus-value':

> I call that surplus-value which is produced by the lengthening of the working day, *absolute surplus-value*. In contrast to this, I call that surplus-value which arises from the curtailment of the necessary labor-time, and from the corresponding alteration in the respective lengths of the two components of the working day, *relative surplus-value* [90, p. 432; 95, part 2, 6:313–314].

Any change that causes a decline in the value of labor power will generate relative surplus value. Here are some examples:

1. Productivity increases in industries supplying direct or indirect inputs into wage goods. In lowering the value of wage goods, such increases will lower the value of labor power.
2. Intensification of labor. The value of a commodity is defined as the labor time socially necessary to produce it. This is the time it takes workers working at 'normal' or 'average' intensity to produce the commodity. If a worker works at twice that intensity, then one hour of his labor creates twice as much value as an hour of labor working at normal intensity. However, if there is a general increase in the intensity of labor, then though all workers are working more intensely and producing more products per hour, they do not create any more value per hour than before, because there is a new average intensity that defines the standard or normal level, and they are all working at this level. The effect is the same as an increase in productivity of labor of constant intensity: the value of a unit of output goes down. With general intensification of labor, the value of the wage basket will decrease, and thus the value of labor power will decrease, and relative surplus value will be generated. This effect is hindered to the extent that intensification wears out a worker's labor power more quickly, creating a need for more wage goods to reproduce it.

3. Deskilling of the work process. A decrease in the level of skill required in the labor process will decrease the time needed to acquire and maintain that level, thereby lowering the value of labor power.
4. A decrease in the standard of living culturally accepted as minimally adequate for a worker (say through effective ideological campaigns).

For each of these ways of generating relative surplus value, we must be able to find sufficient individual incentive to motivate the necessary actions on the part of capitalists. That a development is in the interest of capital doesn't by itself guarantee that it will happen. The individual incentives for items 2–4 are fairly clear. It is item 1 that needs some explaining. Marx's account goes as follows: Every capitalist has an incentive to modify his production process so as to lower the amount of labor time it takes to produce a unit of his product (say, by increasing the productivity of his own workers). For doing so will lower his costs and thereby win him extra profits until competitors catch up with him by introducing the new technique themselves. If the industries in which such new techniques are introduced supply direct or indirect inputs for the production of wage goods, these changes will eventually lower the value of labor power, thereby reducing the necessary labor time and generating relative surplus value.[8]

Marx distinguishes between the 'formal' and the 'real' subjection of labor to capital (or subsumption of labor under capital) [90, pp. 645–646, 1019–1038; 95, part 2, 4(1):91–108, 6:479–480]. Labor is formally subjected to capital as soon as relations of production are capitalist: the economy is a system of commodity production, labor-power is a commodity, and society is class divided, with a class of owners of the means of production and a class of workers who have no commodity to sell but their labor power. With the real subjection of labor to capital, capitalist relations of production are anchored and reinforced by material and technical features of the labor process and of the forces of production. The process of real subjection coincides with and is realized through the development of various modes of relative surplus value generation: (1) cooperatively organized labor, (2) the manufacturing division of labor, and (3) the supplanting of handicraft production by mechanized production and large-scale industrial techniques. This development in turn was spurred and accelerated by legal limitations of the length of the working day, which placed constraints on absolute surplus value generation.

---

[8] See Marx's illustration [90, pp. 433ff; 95, part 2, 6:315ff].

These forms of the real subjection of labor to capital are forms of estrangement, and as such they are outgrowths of the estrangement that characterizes commodity production. As we have noted, producers in commodity production face an abstract demand when deciding on their hopefully productive activities: they must engage in abstract human labor. They face no more concretely specified demand at the stage of production. This abstract requirement remains in place under the more specific conditions of the capitalist production of commodities. There are two sides to this phenomenon. On the one hand, the producers must make their production decisions on the basis of their projections of the state of the economy, which has an independent dynamic even though it is a function of what they do and what they are willing to do. To that extent, they become estranged from their own agency. On the other hand, there is the apparently liberating aspect that they are not tied down to a particular concrete mode of action in production. Any action will do, so long as its product meets with success on the market. This second side of the phenomenon, though it may seem to be a liberation at the level of individual action, is shaped by the independent dynamic, which operates 'behind the backs' of individuals, as a kind of malevolent form of Smith's invisible hand, so as to lead to the distinctive forms of cooperation, division of labor, and mechanized production that constitute the real subjection of labor to capital. By no means should these forms be understood as cooperation, division of labor, and mechanized production 'as such'. Set free by the abstraction characteristic of commodity production and taking place in a capitalist economic environment, these activities assume specific forms conducive to capital expansion.

### Cooperation

Cooperation takes place when many workers work together side by side in the same or in connected processes. It is important to understand that their actions are coordinated and that coordination requires a directing authority, at least if the cooperation is on a sufficiently large scale. Cooperation can increase productivity in many ways, even without increased division of labor:

1. It makes possible economies in the use of means of production. For example:

   A room where twenty weavers work at twenty looms must be larger than the room of a single weaver with two assistants. But it costs less labor to build one workshop for twenty persons than to build ten to accommodate two weavers each; thus the value of the means of production concentrated for use in common on a large scale does not increase in direct proportion to their extent and useful effect. When consumed in common, they give up a smaller part of their value to each single product... [90, p. 442; 95, part 2, 6:322].

2. It can fuse many forces into one (think of many people cooperating to move a heavy boulder):

    In such cases the effect of the combined labour could either not be produced at all by isolated individual labour, or it could be produced only by a great expenditure of time, or on a very dwarf-like scale. Not only do we have here an increase in the productive power of the individual, by means of co-operation, but the creation of a new productive power, which is intrinsically a collective one [90, p. 443; 95, part 2, 6:323].

3. Through social contact, it leads to emulation and the stimulation of 'animal spirits' (ibid.).

4. It makes possible the 'bucket brigade' phenomenon [90, pp. 444–445; 95, part 2, 6:324].

5. It allows critical periods to be accommodated (e.g., harvests, sheep shearing, barn building, and so on) [90, p. 445; 95, part 2, 6:325].

With cooperation the real subjection of labor to capital begins:

[A]t first, the subjection of labour to capital was only a formal result of the fact that the worker, instead of working for himself, works for, and consequently under, the capitalist. Through the co-operation of numerous wage labourers, the command of capital develops into a requirement for carrying on the labour process itself, into a real condition of production. That a capitalist should command in the field of production is now as indispensable as that a general should command on the field of battle [90, p. 448; 95, part 2, 6:327].

Marx's point here is that the technique of production has changed: it is not one that can be engaged in by individual laborers working on their own. Such laborers could of course stick to old techniques; but they could not successfully compete with cooperatively organized production, given the higher productivity of the latter. And given that the economy is a capitalist one, the only way to engage in cooperative labor is by working for a capitalist. The relations of production still play a role in binding workers to capitalists, but this dependence is technologically reinforced. Before cooperation, it was just the fact that workers did not own means of production that required them to work for someone else. But now there is another factor as well: they do not have the ability, as individuals, to execute the production process.

Another point is important in connection with the real subjection effected by cooperation. All cooperation on a large scale requires a directing authority: 'A single violin player is his own conductor: an orchestra requires a separate one' [90, pp. 448–449; 95, part 2, 6:327]. In capitalism, this directing authority must be a representative of capital (though not necessarily a capitalist [90, p. 450; 95, part 2, 6:328–329]), because the direction needs to ensure that surplus value is produced. The directing authority performs two functions: it implements the coordination or control necessary in any cooperative endeavor, and it ensures the extraction of surplus value. It does the latter *through* doing the former, or through the specific way it does the former.

This real subjection of labor to capital thus estranges individuals from their collective productive powers, the powers of socially organized labor. The social capacities they deploy in cooperative labor confront them in the form of the productive powers of capital. The application of reason in the organization of production is pressed into the service of an alien power. It is therefore reason in an unreasonable form. Moreover, this subjection creates more developed forms of mystification or fetishism than the more general forms due simply to commodity production as such. Because the productive power of labor due to cooperation costs capital nothing, and because workers do not realize this power until they have been employed by capital, it appears to be a power inherent in capital, a power by nature capitalistic, just as gold seems inherently and by its very nature a measure of value, or money [90, p. 451; 95, part 2, 6:330].

*Manufacturing division of labor*

Marx defines manufacture as division of labor based on handicraft production. Workers here are working with tools (as opposed to large machines). Division of labor brings about increases in productivity and reduction of skills required in production, and these effects serve to increase relative surplus value. The process Marx describes is in fact the defeat of the guild system based on skilled handicrafts.

The real subjection of labor to capital and the accompanying fetish character are further advanced and developed through the manufacturing division of labor. Cooperation is now a technical as well as an economic necessity: the worker lacks even the skills necessary to produce a complete commodity. His technical dependence on the capitalist's workshop is thus increased.

> If the worker originally sells his labor power to capital because he lacks the material means of producing a commodity, now his individual labor power itself refuses its services unless it has been sold to capital. It functions only in a context that exists only after the sale, in the workshop of the capitalist. Rendered incapable by nature to make anything that stands on its own [*etwas Selbstständiges zu machen*], the manufacturing worker develops productive activity as a mere appendage of the capitalist's workshop [90, p. 482 (my translation); 95, part 2, 6:355].

The effective application of intelligence and skill in the production process is no longer mediated through the individual worker's consciousness; human intelligence and skill are present only at the collective level and are pressed into the service of capital, in a hostile relation to the individual worker. Workers are further alienated from their social powers, which appear to them in the form of the powers of capital. It appears that workers are productive only in virtue of their incorporation into capital, whereas in reality capital is productive only through its realization in the labor process.

*Machinery and large-scale industry*

The key variable distinguishing capitalist production by machinery from manufacture is not complexity or source of power, but the seizure of the workers' tools from their hands and their incorporation into a mechanism. Workers become mere attendants to an alien process, living appendages to automatic systems of machinery. They become technically and even physically dominated by the products of their own labor:

> It is common to all capitalist production, in so far as it is not only a labour process but at the same time the realization process [*Verwerthungsproceß*] of capital, that it is not the worker who employs the conditions of work, but inversely, the conditions of work that employ the worker. However, it is only with the coming of machinery that this inversion first acquires a technical and palpable reality. Through its conversion into an automaton, the instrument of labour confronts the worker during the labour process itself as capital, as dead labour that dominates and pumps dry living labour-power [90, p. 548 (my translation); 95, part 2, 6:410].

Marx attributes the problem not to machinery per se but rather to the specific way it is designed and used within capitalism. Some of these specific factors are the wedding of the worker to one mindless detail operation, long working hours, separation of the worker from knowledge of the overall process and the principles that underlie it, and the failure to mechanize certain routine jobs.

There is a further alienation of social powers, since with the development of machinery and modern industrial techniques, science, a social accomplishment, not only gets embodied in the production process only at the level of the 'collective worker' and not at the level of the individual worker, but as so embodied bears a hostile and dominating relationship to the individual worker. There is a further development of fetishism as well, since

> machinery is an instance of the way in which the visible products of labour take on the appearance of its masters. The same transformation may be observed in the forces of nature and science, the products of the general development of history in its abstract quintessence. They too confront the workers as the *powers* of capital. They become separated effectively from the skill and the knowledge of the individual worker; and even though ultimately they are themselves the products of labour, they appear as an *integral* part of capital wherever they intervene in the labour process [90, p. 1055; 95, part 2, 4.1:122].

## 4.5   Reproduction and accumulation

### 4.5.1   Simple reproduction

The process of production in society cannot be a one-shot affair; it must repeatedly go through the same phases. Since people cannot stop consuming, they cannot stop producing. For production to be a continuing process, it must satisfy certain constraints; used up means of production must be replaced, for example, as must the consumption items necessary for replenishing labor power. The conditions of production must also be those of reproduction.

This requirement extends beyond the reproduction of material or technical conditions to the reproduction of social conditions. If production is capitalist in form, so must be reproduction. Capitalist social relations must be reproduced if capitalist production is to be something ongoing. The social conditions of capitalist production include fundamentally a capitalist class with capital to invest and a working class willing to sell its labor power to capital, on terms that permit the production of surplus value.

Conceptually, reproduction is possible without any technical change or expansion of production over time. This is the case of 'simple reproduction', as opposed to 'expanded reproduction' or 'accumulation'. On the material side, the same things, in the same quantities, are produced and consumed, year after year. On the social side, the value advanced as capital is recouped by the capitalist, through the sale of his commodities, ready to be advanced again. The surplus value produced each year has the form of a stream of revenue, which each year replenishes a fund used by the capitalist for his own consumption. Workers receive as income their wages, which they spend on items whose consumption reproduces their labor power, making them able to sell it to capital again, and willing to sell it, because, having spent their wages on consumption (and dependent materially on capital in ways Marx has described in his treatment of the real subjection of labor to capital), they have no other means of making a living.

While simple reproduction is a hypothetical state, it is worth considering for the insight it yields. To study reproduction, whether simple or not, we must leave the perspective of the participants in an individual enterprise and adopt a point of view from which we can consider the economy as a whole, as an ongoing, self-reproducing system. Marx claims that this shift brings at least four facts of significance to light.

First, variable capital loses its character as a value advanced out of the capitalist's funds and comes to light as the money form of products of workers' labor: it is the workers' own labor, realized in products, that is advanced to them by the capitalist.

> Variable capital is therefore only a particular historical form of appearance of the fund for providing the means of subsistence, or the labour-fund, which the worker requires for his own maintenance and reproduction, and which, in all systems of social production, he must himself produce and reproduce. If the labour-fund constantly flows to him in the form of money that pays for his labour, it is because his own product constantly moves away from him in the form of capital. But this form of appearance of the labour-fund makes no difference to the fact that it is the worker's own objectified labour which is advanced to him by the capitalist [90, p. 713; 95, part 2, 6:524–525].

To illustrate this claim, Marx considers a feudal arrangement in which a peasant produces his own means of subsistence on his own land and then does compulsory surplus labor on his lord's domain. He then describes a hypothetical transformation of this arrangement into a capitalist one: The lord appropriates all the land and means of production and then hires the peasant as a wage laborer. *Materially, nothing changes*: the worker does exactly the same thing in terms of production as before, and he consumes the same things as well. The only thing that has changed is the economic form: the worker's entire labor appears as paid labor, and he buys his consumption goods from the capitalist with his wages.

Now Marx claims that what is true about this transformed relationship between peasant and lord is true about the relationship between the working class as a whole and the capitalist class as a whole. Wages are just a special economic form of something required in all systems of production: the labor fund, the products required for the maintenance and reproduction of labor.

> The capitalist class is constantly giving to the working class drafts, in the form of money, on a portion of the product produced by the latter and appropriated by the former. The workers give these drafts back just as constantly to the capitalists, and thereby withdraw from the latter their allotted share of their own product. The transaction is veiled by the commodity-form of the product and the money-form of the commodity [90, p. 713; 95, part 2, 6:524].

The critical side of Marx's project comes out strikingly here. He launches his investigation in *Capital* with an analysis of the commodity form. Here he asserts that that form, when viewed in connection with social and economic reproduction, displays its true character as a misleading form of appearance of an exploitative class relationship.

The second important fact that an examination of reproduction reveals is that even constant capital sooner or later consists of the workers' own labor confronting them in an alien form. For simple reproduction sooner or later converts all capital into accumulated capital or capitalized surplus value, even if we assume that the initial value advanced as capital was acquired by the capitalist through selling the products of his own labor and not through any appropriation of the unpaid labor of others. The contrary claim would be like the claim of someone still to own his property when he has put the property up to secure a loan that is now due, and he has spent the loan on goods he has consumed. Though he legally may still hold the title, it is clear that 'his property represents nothing but the sum total of his debts. And so it is with the capitalist; when he has consumed the equivalent of his original capital, the value of his present capital represents nothing but the total amount of surplus-value appropriated by him without payment. Not a single atom of the value of his old capital continues to exist' [90, p. 715; 94, 23:595].

Third, the class division that is a specific social prerequisite of capitalism is not only the starting point but also the continually reproduced result of capitalist production itself. The 'worker himself constantly produces objective wealth, in the form of capital, an alien power that dominates and exploits him; and the capitalist just as constantly produces labour-power, in the form of a subjective source of wealth which is abstract, exists merely in the physical body of the worker, and is separated from its own means of objectification and realization; in short, the capitalist produces the worker as a wage-labourer' [90, p. 716; 95, part 2, 6:527].

Fourth, from a social point of view the working class is an appendage of capital; the worker's individual consumption is a phase in the the process of production, just as, say, feeding the horse that pulls the plow is part of the farmer's process of production [90, pp. 717–719; 95, part 2, 6:528–529].

In the following passage, Marx draws on these points and returns to the theme of the commodity form as veil:

> In reality, the worker belongs to capital before he has sold himself to the capitalist. His economic bondage is at once mediated through, and concealed by, the periodic renewal of the act by which he sells himself, his change of masters, and the oscillations in the market price of his labour [90, pp. 723–724; 95, part 2, 6:533–534].

### 4.5.2 Conversion of surplus value into capital

When all or part of the surplus value is invested as additional capital, we have reproduction on an expanded scale, or the accumulation of capital. Here again the point of view appropriate to looking at reproduction brings things to light that are not seen as long as we focus on individual transactions. A crucial case in point is 'the inversion which converts the property laws of commodity production into laws of capitalist appropriation' [90, p. 725; 95, part 2, 6:534]. Marx's discussion of this phenomenon is important for understanding his attitude toward Proudhon and other social reformers who labeled the exploitative aspects of capitalism as injustices that resulted from an adulteration or violation of the property rights corresponding to commodity production. There was a tendency among reformers to think that commodity production embodied the principle that legitimate property rights are based on labor. Hence they were concerned to make things right for the worker by somehow implementing an 'unadulterated' form of commodity production.

Marx is concerned to refute such schemes. He claims that wage labor and the appropriation of surplus value, even on an expanded scale, by no means violate the property rights corresponding to commodity production. This is one reason why he assumes that prices are proportional to values when he traces the origin of capital to the appropriation of surplus labor time of the workers. But the most important result of Marx's analysis has a significance that goes beyond this dispute with the social reformers. It is that the fundamental issue does not concern rates of exchange at all, because from a social point of view

> [t]he relation of exchange between capitalist and worker becomes a mere semblance belonging only to the process of circulation; it becomes a mere form, which is alien to the content of the transaction itself, and merely mystifies it. . . . [P]roperty turns out to be the right, on the part of the capitalist, to appropriate the unpaid labour of others or its product, and the impossibility, on the part of the worker, of appropriating his own product. The separation of property from labour thus becomes the necessary consequence of a law that apparently originated in their identity [90, pp. 729–730; 95, part 2, 6:538].

As we'll see below (Section 4.6.3), this analysis contains an implicit critique of Hegel's view of private property and exchange as social realizations of freedom.

### 4.5.3   Unemployment and poverty

Marx defines 'accumulation' as the investment of surplus value as capital. He regards accumulation as a crisis-ridden process, with boom periods that lead to recessions bringing about unemployment and poverty, which in turn produce conditions favorable to further accumulation. In this way, the class relationship between capital and labor is reproduced.

Accumulation and technical change are interdependent phenomena. To grasp them in their interrelation, Marx employs several concepts of the 'composition' of capital. The *technical* composition is a material or physical specification of the relative quantities of the various means of production and the labor expended in the production of a commodity. The *value* composition is the ratio of the value of the constant capital advanced to the value of the variable capital advanced in the production of a commodity. The *organic* composition is the value composition of capital 'insofar as it is determined by its technical composition and mirrors changes of the latter' [90, p. 762; 94, 23:640]. Marx doesn't elaborate, and his meaning is obscure. Morishima offers a seemingly plausible suggestion:

> A change in a physical-input coefficient... or the labour-input coefficient... due to a technological improvement causes a change in the technical composition of capital. But it also brings about changes in the values [of the various commodities] as well... so the value-composition reflects not only the change in technical composition but also the induced changes in the value structure. There are, however, cases in which we may ignore the latter and where the value composition 'mirrors the changes in the technical composition'. For instance, a proportional decrease in the labour-input coefficients of all industries... gives rise to a proportional decrease in the absolute values of all commodities; in this case... the effects of the changes in absolute values are offset in the formula for the value composition.... When Marx discussed the effects and consequences of technical improvements by using the concept of the 'organic composition of capital', he assumed them to be neutral, in the sense that they had no effects on relative values (or absolute values) [98, p. 35].

However, Marx does not use the term 'organic composition' consistently in this way; often he uses it merely to refer to the value composition. Fortunately, we will not have occasion to make any distinction.[9]

For Marx, capitalism has a tendency to produce an 'industrial reserve army' of unemployed workers in sufficient numbers to insure reproduction of the class relationship. His reasoning is as follows: If the organic composition of capital remains constant, then accumulation reproduces the capital-labor relation on an expanded scale, thereby increasing the demand for labor. These circumstances are the most favorable for the workers, but they do not signal the end of the system. If demand for workers leads to too high an increase in wages, an economic

---

[9] For a careful discussion and reconstruction of several categories used by Marx, see Wolff [152, appendix B].

slowdown will automatically occur, leading to unemployment and consequent downward pressure on wages, and thereby restoring conditions favorable to capital expansion.

Capitalists might try to respond to increases in wages by increasing the productivity of labor. To accomplish such increases they must change the technical composition of capital, for example by replacing workers with machines. The resulting higher productivity itself causes a change in the technical composition, by increasing the amount of raw materials a worker processes in a given length of time. These changes in the technical composition tend to cause increases in the organic composition. With an increase in the organic composition a given sum of capital will typically employ fewer workers. Once again the effect is to set free workers and thereby to produce downward pressure on wages. These effects lead to impoverishment of the unemployed workers and even of portions of the employed population.

## 4.6  Hegel revisited

In this section I wish to bring out some criticisms of Hegel's account of freedom that are latent in Marx's account of economic estrangement as presented in this chapter.

### 4.6.1  Commodity production

We've seen (Section 3.4) that for Hegel, moral subjectivity must attain public existence for moral freedom to be actualized. This process of actualization thus requires the establishment of certain rights, among which are the rights of intention and objectivity:

> The *right of intention* is that the *universal* quality of the action shall have being not only *in itself*, but shall be *known* by the agent and thus have been present all along in his subjective will; and conversely, what we may call the right of the *objectivity* of the action is the right of the action to assert itself as known and willed by the subject as a *thinking agent* [52, §120; 57, 7:§120].

For Hegel, moral freedom cannot be realized unless it attains social existence and objectivity, which require social structures of cooperation that realize and maintain a reasonable social world. Such structures constitute a society well-ordered by the concept of freedom, and it is self-conscious participation in such structures that realizes social freedom (see Section 3.4). When Hegel refers to the 'universal quality' of an action in the above passage, I take him to be referring to its character as such participation, and when he says that this universal quality must be known by agents and present all along in their subjective wills, I take him to be pointing to the necessarily self-conscious character of such participation. Further, when he refers to the right of objectivity, the right of the action to assert itself as known and willed by the subject as a thinking agent, I take him to be pointing to the feature of a society well-ordered by the concept of freedom whereby an individual's actions are able to reflect and express the reasonableness and rationality of that individual in performing those actions.

In particular, in the economy, agents must be able correctly to affirm their producing activities, including labor allocation and product distribution, as reasonable and rational with respect to the division of labor. And they must be able to make this affirmation not just retrospectively, via successful exchange, but prospectively, at the time of decision and action. For otherwise their activity will not be self-conscious participation in the realization and reproduction of the free will as its own object, and they will not attain social freedom, without which they cannot be personally or morally free. It follows that if Marx is right, then contrary to what Hegel affirms, there is no room for commodity production in a free social world as he conceives of it. For the estrangement Marx sees as inherent to commodity production precludes advance certification of producing activities as part of the social division of labor.

### 4.6.2  Division of labor and machinery

We've seen that in Marx's view, there is a connection between the estrangement characteristic of commodity production and the real subjection of labor to capital through specific forms of cooperation, division of labor, and production based on machinery. The estrangement has its roots in the abstract demand faced by commodity producers when they are making their production decisions. They face an abstract demand because there is no concrete specification available at the stage of production of what they should produce or how they should go about producing it. The only requirement is that the product sell, thereby confirming its membership in the world of commodities. The added structure of capital makes this demand more specific, but it does not change its abstract character: any form of action is acceptable, so long as it is surplus-value producing labor, labor that produces and realizes a profit. Capitalists are thus reduced to treating the economy as something independent of them whose behavior they have to anticipate in making their decisions, and this very treatment actually gives the economy an independent dynamic, one that has a determining influence on what they do. They are not tied down to any particular concrete mode of action in production; they are 'free' to tailor their production process, and their means of production, to their view of the requirements of profitability. This 'freedom' may seem to be a liberation at the level of individual action, but at the economy-wide level, the requirements of surplus value extraction hold sway, giving rise to the distinctive forms of cooperation, division of labor, and mechanized production that mark the real subjection of labor to capital, with all of its debilitating and alienating aspects.

In his discussion of division of labor and machinery in the *Philosophy of Right*, Hegel seems oblivious to these developments. There is a cryptic reference to 'abstraction' as leading to the division of labor and simplification of work, but even so, one could plausibly read Hegel as reporting nothing but positive developments:

> The universal and objective aspect of work consists... in that [process of] *abstraction* which confers a specific character on means and needs and hence also on production, so giving rise to the *division of labour*. Through this division, the work of the individual [*des Einzelnen*] becomes *simpler*, so that his skill at his abstract work becomes greater, as does the volume of his output. At the same time, this abstraction of skill and means makes the *dependence* and *reciprocity* of human beings in the satisfaction of their other needs complete and entirely necessary. Furthermore, the abstraction of production makes work increasingly *mechanical*, so that the human being is eventually able to step aside and let a *machine* take his place [52, §198; 57, 7:§198].

This reticence is puzzling, because in prior writings Hegel seems to show more insight. In Jena, during the period 1803–1806, Hegel gave two sets of lectures on the philosophy of spirit [49; 56, vol. 6; 50; 56, vol. 8]. Drawing on his readings of Smith and another classical economist, James Steuart, he significantly anticipates some elements of Marx's account of economic estrangement, even to the point of using some of the same language.[10] For example, he notes that since the worker does not directly address his own concrete needs or those of any other particular individual in his productive activity, his direct participation

[10] Avineri [5, p. 98] points out that Marx had no acquaintance with these texts.

is abstract and he only meets his concrete needs through an exchange process mediated by money (which expresses the abstract equality of commodities as items of value):

> The labor that is concerned with the need of a single [agent] becomes in public life a) the [labor] of a single agent, but b) even [though it] is only motivated by his need it is a universal.... In other words his labor, qua laboring of a single [laborer] for his own needs, is at the same time a universal and ideal [factor of public life]; he satisfies his needs by it certainly, but not with the determinate thing that he worked on; in order that that may satisfy his needs, it must rather become something other than it is; man no longer works up what he uses himself, or he uses no longer what he has worked up himself; that becomes only the possibility of his satisfaction instead of the actual satisfaction of his needs; his labor becomes a formally abstract universal.... His labor is for need [in general], it is for the abstraction of a need as universally suffered, not for his need; and the satisfaction of the totality of his needs is a *labor of everyone*.... *This manifold* laboring at needs as things must likewise realize their concept, their abstraction; their universal concept must become a thing like them, but one which, qua universal, represents all needs; *money* is this materially existing concept, the form of unity, or of the possibility of all things needed [49, pp. 246–249].

Hegel is also cognizant to some extent here of the debilitation of individual workers resulting from the process of abstraction through its impact on the division of labor within the workshop and the incorporation of machinery. Here is a sample passage on the division of labor:

> [T]he *division of labor* increases *the mass* of manufactured [objects].... But in the same ratio that the number produced rises, the value of the labor falls...the labor becomes that much deader, it becomes machine work, the skill of the single laborer is infinitely limited, and the consciousness of the factory laborer is impoverished to the last extreme of dullness... [49, p. 248].

And here is one on machinery:

> When [man] lets nature be worked over by a variety of machines, he does not cancel the necessity of his own laboring but only postpones it, and makes it more distant from nature; and his living labor is not directed on nature as alive, but this negative vitality evaporates

from it, and the laboring that remains to man becomes itself *more machinelike*; man *diminishes* labor only for the whole, not for the single [laborer]; for him it is increased rather; for the more machinelike labor becomes, the less it is worth, and the more one must work in that mode [49, p. 247].

With respect to both developments together he says:

In the individual's skill is the possibility of sustaining his existence. This is subject to all the tangled and complex contingency in the [social] whole. Thus a vast number of people are condemned to a labor that is totally stupefying, unhealthy and unsafe—in workshops, factories, mines, etc.—shrinking their skills. And entire branches of industry, which supported a large class of people, go dry all at once because of [changes in] fashion or a fall in prices due to inventions in other countries, etc.—and this huge population is thrown into helpless poverty.... This inequality between wealth and poverty, this need and necessity, lead to the utmost dismemberment of the will, to inner indignation and hatred [50, pp. 139–140].

Of course Hegel must regard freedom as incompatible with a 'dismemberment of the will', so the account he provides clearly concerns a form of estrangement. He also shows cognizance of the independent dynamic of this estrangement:

Need and labor, elevated into this universality, then form on their own account a monstrous system of community and mutual interdependence in a great people; a life of the dead body, that moves itself within itself, one which ebbs and flows in its motion blindly, like the elements, and which requires continual strict dominance and taming like a wild beast [49, p. 249].

The significance of the 'dominance and taming' referred to here should not be exaggerated, for Hegel's considered view is that there are systemic limitations to the amelioration of the deleterious developments and tendencies he discusses:

[I]nterference should be as inconspicuous as possible, since commerce is the field of arbitrariness. The appearance of force must be avoided, and one must not attempt to salvage what cannot be saved, but rather employ the suffering classes in other ways.... Commerce is certainly left to its own devices—but with the sacrifice of this generation and the proliferation of poverty, poor-taxes and institutions [50, p. 140].

The reference to the necessary sacrifice of a generation may signal an incipient belief on Hegel's part that the ills he discusses are only temporary. He openly expresses this belief in his 1917–1918 Heidelberg lectures:

> [In a factory] the work becomes abstract, uniform, and thus easier, since there is only one skill the individual subject learns, only one routine he practices, and so he can acquire more readiness at this single operation.... This is why factory workers become deadened [*stumpf*] and tied to their factory and dependent on it, since with this single aptitude they cannot earn a living anywhere else.... But once factory work has reached a certain degree of perfection, of simplification, mechanical human labor can be replaced by the work of machines, and this is what usually comes about in factories. In this way, through the consummation of this mechanical progress, human freedom is restored.... Human beings are accordingly first sacrificed, after which they emerge through the more highly mechanized condition as free once more [53, §101].

Shortly thereafter in the *Philosophy of Right*, as we've seen, the reference to the sacrifice of a generation is omitted, and only a reference to a liberating automation remains. But Hegel cannot plausibly have thought that anything had changed with respect to the alienation described in the earlier works. He had been drawing his various accounts from his knowledge of English society as presented in the works of classical political economy, and those works do not develop a rosy picture of the kind he provides. And he cannot consistently be read as acknowledging the alienation but offering a prediction of a future automation that would remove it, since his explicitly stated view in the *Philosophy of Right* is that the *existing* social world, in its fundamentals, is an adequate realization of freedom.

But even if the earlier views more adequately capture the reality of the civil society that is Hegel's concern, they are nonetheless not beyond criticism from Marx's point of view. Though Hegel shows a sensitivity to the abstraction Marx discusses, he does not trace that abstraction to a specific social form of the division of labor. For Marx, commodity production is social production by private individuals and is thus only one possible social form of the division of labor. He would say that Hegel, like the classical economists, too closely associates the division of labor with the development of commodity exchange. One sign of this is his repeated comparison of the division of labor in commodity production to autarkic production, in which an individual produces determinate products for his own use. Another sign is his assertion that the 'blind dependence' of the producer on the disruption-ridden dynamic of the economy is due to the *complexity* of the division of labor, the fact that the 'coherence of the singular kind of labor with the whole infinite mass of needs is quite unsurveyable' [49, p. 248] rather than the fact of the private and independent character of production decisions. If the deleterious phenomena Hegel describes are ineradicable, without there being foreseeable circumstances in which they could be eliminated, then perhaps individuals could be reconciled to them. But Hegel's account, Marx would say, forecloses inquiry into that possibility.

### 4.6.3    The commodity form as a semblance of freedom

For Hegel, the exchange of commodities, as a jointly willed, reciprocal transfer of private property between mutually recognized owners, is an expression and social realization of freedom. We've already identified as latent in Marx's work one criticism of this claim: commodity production precludes the self-conscious participation in social reproduction required for the existence of freedom (Section 4.6.1). However, there is another criticism implicit in Marx's account of reproduction and accumulation. Hegel includes as a realization of freedom the hiring transaction between the capitalist and the wage laborer [52, §67; 57, 7:§67]. But Marx argues that this transaction is a deceptive, localized manifestation of a systemic, self-reproducing process of exploitation. Though it appears in its immediate setting as a free, bilateral exchange between equals, when one considers its more system-wide context, especially its connection with production in the ongoing reproduction of the entire economic system, it shows its character as a false appearance of a compulsory, continuous, self-reproducing, unilateral transfer from one class to another (see Section 4.5, especially 4.5.2). If Marx is right, then a capitalist economy cannot form part of a social world that satisfies Hegel's requirement that it constitute 'the free will that wills itself as the free will'. For capital reproduces itself as a system of exploitation. Driven by individually rational decisions, it is nonetheless a realization of reason in an unreasonable form.

### 4.6.4 Poverty and Hegel's rabble

Hegel recognizes that the economy has a systematic tendency to produce poverty, along with its characteristic disposition, an 'inward rebellion against the rich, against society, the government, etc.' He even suggests that this disposition is *warranted*: 'No one can assert a right against nature, but within the conditions of society hardship at once assumes the form of a wrong inflicted on this or that class'. Poverty can produce this attitude among the poor, thereby generating a 'rabble', a class of persons alienated from their social world [52, §§241, 243, 244A; 57, 7:§§241, 243, 244Z]. Moreover, extremes of wealth and poverty can produce a corresponding attitude among the rich:

> On the one hand, poverty is the ground of the rabble-mentality, the non-recognition of right; on the other hand, the rabble disposition also appears where there is wealth. The rich man thinks that he can buy anything, because he knows himself as the power of the particularity of self-consciousness. Thus wealth can lead to the same mockery and shamelessness that we find in the poor rabble. The disposition of the master over the slave is the same as that of the slave.... These two sides, poverty and wealth, thus constitute the corruption of civil society [52, p. 454; 59, pp. 194–196].

Hegel's own description here clearly indicates a radical breakdown of social unity, and thus the absence of a society well-ordered by the concept of freedom. Moreover, he seems to despair of a social solution:

> If the direct burden [of support] were to fall on the wealthier class, or if direct means were available in other public institutions (such as wealthy hospitals, foundations, or monasteries) to maintain the increasingly impoverished mass at its normal standard of living, the livelihood of the needy would be ensured without the mediation of work; this would be contrary to the principle of civil society.... Alternatively, their livelihood might be mediated by work (i.e. by the opportunity to work) which would increase the volume of production; but it is precisely in overproduction and the lack of a proportionate number of consumers who are themselves productive that the evil [*Übel*] consists [*besteht*] and this is merely exacerbated by the two expedients in question. This shows that, despite an *excess of wealth*, civil society is *not wealthy enough* – i.e. its own distinct

resources are not sufficient – to prevent an excess of poverty and the formation of a rabble [52, §245; 57, 7:§245].

It is true that at one point Hegel indicates a possible role for corporations in the amelioration of poverty [52, §253R; 57, 7:§253A], but he cannot consistently appeal to the corporations as an adequate solution. Corporations might attempt to prevent their members, who are skilled at a craft, trade or profession, from falling into poverty, though how successful they could be is debatable, given their capitalist economic environment, in which, as he had earlier recognized [50, pp. 139–140], 'entire branches of industry...go dry all at once' [153, p. 242; 61, pp. 75ff]. However, the bulk of the vulnerable are unskilled workers, whose specified relation to corporations he leaves ambiguous at best.[11]

What does Marx add to this analysis? While Hegel correctly treats workers as vulnerable to unemployment and poverty in virtue of the economic insecurity generated by the contingencies of competition and technical change, Marx goes further by tracing these phenomena to a specific social form of the division of labor, i.e., to the specific social relations that constitute the capital-labor relationship and by displaying their systematic and recurring role in the automatic reproduction of this relationship.

[11]  Here I agree with Avineri [5, pp. 117–118].

# 5
# Marx: Prices and the Rate of Profit

## 5.1 Introduction

In volume 1 of *Capital* Marx assumes that equilibrium prices are proportional to values (in his sense of 'value', according to which the value of a commodity is the labor socially necessary to produce it). Not all of the claims about estrangement and ideology surveyed in the last chapter rest on this assumption. Among those that don't is the claim that commodity production is a system of estrangement because in it, economic agents' 'own social movement has for them the form of a movement of things controlling them instead of being controlled by them' [90, pp. 167–168 (my translation); 95, part 2, 6:105]. Even the related doctrine of commodity fetishism is easily stated as the claim that the power of exchangeability that commodities possess takes on the guise of a power they have as natural objects rather than one they possess in virtue of certain specific relations of production.

But the same cannot be said of several other important claims. Marx appeals to the assumption that prices are proportional to values in order to identify the profit realized in an enterprise with the surplus value produced in the enterprise, and hence to identify the sum of profits across the economy with the sum of surplus values. He uses these claims in turn to warrant the assertion that profit is an expression of alienated surplus labor. He then appeals to this antagonistic class relationship in explanations of struggles over the length of the working day and of technological changes that subjugate workers materially (technically) to the requirements of capitalist production. Then, appealing to an economy-wide perspective on capitalist production as an ongoing, self-reproducing system, he displays the wage transaction, though it appears to the individual participants as a free exchange of equivalents, as an episode in an ongoing, unilateral transfer from one class to another, a process in which workers create the very capital that exploits them, so that in confronting capital, workers are actually confronting their own labor in an alien form. Directly or indirectly, all these results of Marx's analysis in volume 1 rest on an appeal to the proposition that prices are proportional to values.

Yet as Marx was fully aware—before the publication of volume 1[1]—this proposition is true only in certain special circumstances. He nonetheless treats it as true, in order to illuminate the exploitation and estrangement phenomena just mentioned. He works with simplified models that abstract from certain features of capitalism that he thinks obscure these phenomena. This procedure is justifiable only if two conditions can be satisfied. First, it must be reasonable to claim that prices are proportional to values in the abstract models. And second, when the simplifying assumptions are relaxed, thereby removing the abstractions, it must be possible to sustain the main thrust of the conclusions of the earlier analysis. In this chapter, I argue that these two conditions can be met, though the second one can be met only in a form that corrects an error in his volume 3 analysis and hence in a form that he did not anticipate.

With regard to the first condition, I argue that the two abstractions that Marx makes—the first from capital, in order to consider simple commodity production, and the second from differences in organic compositions of capital, in order to get a clear view of the exploitative and alienating relationship between capital and labor—supply appropriate conditions for assuming that prices are proportional to values.

With regard to the second condition, Marx began to investigate the consequences of relaxing the simplifying assumptions in the draft materials that Engels used to assemble volume 3 of *Capital*. These materials develop some preliminary results but leave the investigation in an incomplete and inadequate state. I discuss the implications of a more adequate account below. In doing so I have a limited aim: to determine the extent to which the earlier account of economic estrangement can survive the transition to a more general setting. Given that prices are not

---

[1] The issue is discussed in draft materials for volume 3 that were written prior to the publication of volume 1. There is also a confirming footnote in volume 1 [90, p. 269n24; 93, part 2, 6:183n37].

in general proportional to Marx's values, is there nonetheless a determinate relationship between them that will underwrite the basic thrust of his earlier analysis? In particular, does support remain for the claims (1) that profits are an expression of surplus value and hence an alienation of workers' laboring activities, (2) that capital is workers' own labor in an alien form, and (3) that capital has a tendency to subjugate workers materially and not merely formally, thereby estranging them from their own social productive powers? I argue that the answer to these questions is yes.

## 5.2   Marx's view of values and prices

Call any quantity defined defined in terms of value magnitudes (in Marx's sense of 'value', according to which the value of a commodity is the amount of labor socially necessary for its production) part of the *system of value accounting*, and any quantity defined in terms of prices (rates of exchange with money) part of the *system of price accounting*. Our goal is to determine whether and how these systems can be translated into one another, what systematic relation (if any) holds between them. We'll work with a model that reflects Marx's typical assumptions:[2]

1. The economy produces $n$ commodities by means of those same commodities and labor.
2. In each industry there is a single efficient technique of production (no 'choice of techniques').
3. Each industry produces a single product (no 'joint production').
4. There are no non-produced means of production yielding rent to their owners.
5. All labor is reducible to unskilled labor.
6. All commodities have the same period of production.
7. All means of production have the same span of life, equal to a single production period (no problems of 'fixed capital').
8. Inputs are made at the beginning of the production period and outputs are obtained at the end of the period.

In volume 3 Marx argues that if organic compositions are not uniform across the economy, then equilibrium prices cannot be proportional to

---

[2] Largely following Morishima [98, p. 12]. For studies at the same or a higher level of generality, see Abraham-Frois and Berrebi [1], Medio [97], Morishima [98], Pasinetti [106], Roemer [125], and Wolff [152].

values. One way of rendering his reasoning is as follows: Suppose that the economic system is in equilibrium: there is a uniform profit rate across sectors of the economy, so that there is no incentive for capital to move from one sector to another. There is a nonnegative rate of profit $\pi$ such that if $\pi_i$ is the rate of profit in sector $i$, then for each sector $i$,

$$\pi_i = \pi. \tag{5.1}$$

Suppose further that prices are proportional to values. That is, there is an $\alpha > 0$ such that for all $i$,

$$p_i = \alpha \lambda_i \tag{5.2}$$

where $p_i$ and $\lambda_i$ are respectively the price and value of a unit of commodity $i$. Then from 5.2, for each $i$,

$$\pi_i = \frac{\alpha S_i}{\alpha C_i + \alpha V_i} = \frac{S_i}{C_i + V_i} = \frac{\frac{S_i}{V_i}}{\frac{C_i}{V_i} + 1} \tag{5.3}$$

where $C_i$ is the value of the constant capital advanced in industry $i$, $V_i$ is the value of the variable capital advanced in industry $i$, and $S_i$ is the surplus value produced in industry $i$. Now we may take as a premise that the rate of surplus value $S_i/V_i$ is uniform across industries. That is, for each $i$ and $j$,

$$\frac{S_i}{V_i} = \frac{S_j}{V_j}. \tag{5.4}$$

Assumptions that would justify this premise are (1) that the length of the working day is uniform across industries and (2) that each worker's labor power has the same value. From 5.1, 5.3, and 5.4, there is a uniform organic composition of capital $C_i/V_i$ across industries. That is, for all $i$ and $j$,

$$\frac{C_i}{V_i} = \frac{C_j}{V_j}. \tag{5.5}$$

So if at equilibrium prices are proportional to values, then organic compositions must be uniform. Therefore, if organic compositions are *not* uniform, then equilibrium prices are not proportional to values.

Marx thus shows awareness that disproportionality of prices and values follows from differences in organic composition. But given this awareness, and given that the general case should countenance possible differences in organic composition, why does Marx treat prices as proportional to values in volume 1? The answer lies in Marx's systematic use of abstractions. We've already seen that in part 1 of volume 1 Marx considers commodity production in abstraction from capital. The rest of volume 1, as a general rule, deliberately considers capital in abstraction from differences in organic composition.

Is the assumption that prices are proportional to values appropriate in these abstractions? To answer this question we have to delve into the systems of value accounting and price accounting. These systems are captured by systems of equations. Values are given in the following system:

$$\Lambda = \Lambda A + L. \tag{5.6}$$

Here $\Lambda$ is the $1 \times n$ vector $(\lambda_1, \ldots, \lambda_n)$, where $\lambda_j$ is the value per unit of commodity $j$, for $j = 1, \ldots n$; $A$ is the $n \times n$ matrix $[a_{ij}]$, where $a_{ij}$ is the amount of commodity $i$ needed to produce a unit of commodity $j$; and $L$ is the $1 \times n$ vector $(l_1, \ldots, l_n)$, where $l_j$ is the amount of labor directly required to produce a unity of commodity $j$. Equation 5.6 asserts in matrix notation that for each $j$, the value of a unit of commodity $j$—the labor required to produce it—is given by the labor required to produce the means of its production plus the labor directly expended in its production:

$$\lambda_j = \sum_i \lambda_i a_{ij} + l_j.^3$$

And the price accounting is partly determined[4] by the following system:

$$p = (1 + \pi)(pA + wL) \tag{5.7}$$

where $p$ is the row vector $(p_1, \ldots, p_n)$ of commodity prices, $\pi$ is the equilibrium rate of profit, and $w$ is the wage rate. This equation says that gross product prices must be just sufficient to cover the initial outlay for means of production (at going prices) and wages (paid at a uniform rate) plus profit as determined by a uniform rate of return on that outlay. In other words, for each $j = 1, \ldots, n$,

$$p_j = (1 + \pi)(\sum_i p_i a_{ij} + wl_j).$$

---

[3] Thus, for example, if $n = 2$, then $\lambda_1 = \lambda_1 a_{11} + \lambda_2 a_{21} + l_1$ and $\lambda_2 = \lambda_1 a_{12} + \lambda_2 a_{22} + l_2$.

[4] I say partly determined because 5.7 is a system of $n$ equations and $n + 2$ unknowns: the $n$ prices $p_1 \ldots p_n$, the rate of profit $\pi$, and the wage rate $w$. For a complete set of equations, see Equations A.6–A.8 in the appendix to this chapter.

Now since the essence of capital realization is investment of money in the purchase, production, and sale of commodities in order to make more money, setting $\pi = 0$ in this system should give us one view of commodity production in abstraction from capital:

$$p = pA + wL.$$

This equation system may be rewritten as follows:

$$p(I - A) = wL \tag{5.8}$$

$$p = wL(I - A)^{-1}. \tag{5.9}$$

And our value system 5.6 may be rewritten as follows:

$$\Lambda(I - A) = L \tag{5.10}$$

$$\Lambda = L(I - A)^{-1}. \tag{5.11}$$

It follows from 5.9 and 5.11 that

$$p = w\Lambda. \tag{5.12}$$

The first abstraction implies that prices are proportional to values, with factor of proportionality $w$.

The second abstraction is from differences in organic composition across industries. Suppose organic compositions are equal: There is a $q > 0$ such that for $i, j = 1, \ldots, n$,

$$\frac{C_i}{V_i} = \frac{C_j}{V_j} = q.$$

Assume further that rates of surplus value are equal across the economy: There is a $\sigma > 0$ such that for $i = 1, \ldots, n$,

$$\frac{S_i}{V_i} = \sigma.$$

Then prices that are proportional to values will equilibrate the system, by establishing an economy-wide rate of profit: There is an $\alpha > 0$ such that for $i = 1, \ldots, n$,

$$\pi_i = \frac{\alpha S_i}{\alpha C_i + \alpha V_i} = \frac{S_i}{C_i + V_i} = \frac{\frac{S_i}{V_i}}{\frac{C_i}{V_i} + 1} = \frac{\sigma}{q + 1} = \pi. \tag{5.13}$$

Therefore, since equilibrium prices are unique,[5] they will be proportional to values. The assumption of proportionality is appropriate to the second abstraction as well.

Given that the two abstractions work the way Marx claims they do, why does he avail himself of them? There are at least two reasons. First, using these models allows him to support, in an easily understandable way, some claims about the inner workings of capitalism, especially with regard to its impact on workers in the production process. In particular, he wants to provide a clear depiction of the dependence of the profits of capital on the appropriation of surplus labor and of capital itself as a projection of social labor as an independent property of its products, one that confers on them an alien dynamic with respect to their movement through the various stages of economic processing—production, circulation, distribution, growth, and so on. Second, the models allow him to give a clear critique of contemporary claims that the origin of profits lies in the non-coincidence of prices and values, and thus that the existence of capital depends on a violation of the economic laws of commodity production and thereby on a violation of workers' property rights. As we have seen in Chapter 4, Marx's view is that on the contrary, though profits depend on the appropriation of surplus labor, they do so in a manner entirely consistent with the economic laws and property rights that define commodity production.

Of course, Marx cannot properly rest content with the results obtained with these simplified models. He must investigate the extent to which the results can survive a transition to a more general setting. With respect to some issues the answer is clear without further theoretical investigation. If for example profit is possible when prices are proportional to values, then its basis cannot lie in their non-proportionality. But defense of other claims will require further theoretical development. He takes on this task in the discussion of prices and profits in volume 3.

We can illuminate Marx's theoretical strategy by situating it with respect to the tradition of classical political economy, as represented in particular by the work of Adam Smith [143] and David Ricardo [124]. The main concern of that tradition is to develop a theory that relates the origin, distribution, and disposition of the social product to the processes of economic growth and stagnation. The theory of value

---

[5] The uniqueness of equilibrium prices (up to a scaling factor) follows from an application of the Perron-Frobenius theorem provided in Section A.2 to the matrix $A^+$ discussed in Section A.3. In this application the price vector $p$ is determined as the uniquely positive eigenvector shown to exist by the theorem.

is developed as a tool in this endeavor. Since in the type of society under investigation economic processes are mediated by price-guided exchange, the need arises for a theory relating price determination to the processes of production and distribution.

Ricardo's central concern is distribution of the national product among the three major social classes: workers, capitalists, and landlords. This process is not a matter of direct transfer of products but rather is mediated by price-guided exchange: each class gets as income a sum of money that it then uses to purchase, at going prices, its share of the national product. Workers receive wages as income, capitalists receive profits, and landlords, rents. These income categories are 'price-defined' in the sense that they are sums of money, the universal commodity-equivalent for purposes of price-guided exchange. Also price-defined are various categories derivative from these, such as the rate of profit and the wage rate. Ricardo wants to formulate laws of distribution—principles that determine alternative possible distributions of the national product—in terms of price-defined categories. For example, he wants to know what would happen as a result of a general increase in wages. Would profits go down or would they stay the same because prices would go up? However, he fails to reconcile this aim with his conviction that distributive shares, specified in physical terms, have an appropriate non-price-defined measure, namely their 'real cost of production', what has to be 'given up'—not to other persons in exchange, but rather 'to nature', as it were—in order to bring the commodities into existence in the first place. This is their 'real' or 'absolute' value, as opposed to their 'exchangeable' value or price. And since everything is 'originally purchased' by labor, real value is given by labor requirements: the value of a commodity is the labor directly and indirectly required to produce it [120, p. 397].

But for value conceived in this way to provide a theoretically appropriate measure of distributive shares, there must be a determinate relation between values and prices, in virtue of the price-mediated character of distribution. Values must be expressed in a determinate way in the system of price accounting. Ricardo opts—without really seeing any alternative—for the most direct relation: prices, he asserts, are proportional to values [122, pp. 1–2; 120, p. 398]. This relation would provide a transparent, non-distorted representation, in terms of price-defined categories, of the process of distribution. However, Ricardo now runs up against the difficulty that two of his claims, namely

(1) prices are proportional to values

and

(2) values are given by labor requirements

together imply the generally false assertion

(3) prices are proportional to labor requirements.

Ricardo is aware of this problem, but it creates a theoretical impasse for him. Not being willing to give up either claim, he never resolves the difficulty, though he tries to salvage general empirical and practical relevance for his theory by claiming approximate validity for it [121, p. 279; 123, p. 66; 124, pp. 43–46].[6]

Marx agrees that it is theoretically appropriate to measure distributive shares by reference to labor requirements, so he holds on to claim 2. He gets out of the impasse by denying claim 1, Ricardo's seemingly obvious assumption that prices are proportional to values. As we've seen, he provides an argument against the claim. But he cannot rest content with that, for then his theory would be left without any assertion about how values are expressed in the system of price accounting. He must supply a connection, and he must offer a conception of capitalism that makes it plausible.

The connection he affirms is the following: At competitive equilibrium, there is a uniform rate of profit $\pi$ (a price-defined notion) across the entire economic system, given by the ratio of two value quantities: the total amount of surplus value produced in the various sectors and the value of the total amount of capital (constant plus variable) advanced in those sectors:

$$\pi = \frac{\sum_i S_i}{\sum_i (C_i + V_i)} = \frac{S}{C + V}. \tag{5.14}$$

If organic compositions are not uniform but nonetheless prices are proportional to values, then the system is out of equilibrium, since profit rates will vary across industries. In such circumstances, competition will bring about movement of capital from lower profit-rate industries to higher profit-rate industries and consequent changes in prices until

---

[6] For more discussion of Ricardo's efforts to formulate an adequate theory of value, see Wolff [152, chap. 3] and Sensat [138; 139]. For efforts to situate both Ricardo and Marx with respect to the classical tradition and to that of input-output analysis, in both of which they played significant roles, see Kurz et al. [74] and Baumol and ten Raa [8].

uniform profit rates (and hence equilibrium) are restored. Marx understands this process as in essence a redistribution of all the surplus value produced in the economy to the various capitalists in proportion to their respective shares of the total amount of capital invested in the economy. Even though the amount of surplus value *produced* in an enterprise remains proportional to the number of workers employed in that enterprise, the amount of surplus value *appropriated* in that enterprise does not. Rather, it becomes proportional to the total amount of capital (constant plus variable) invested in that enterprise. As a result, while the sectoral ratios of surplus value produced to value of capital advanced may depart from the uniform rate of profit, at the level of the economy as a whole the two ratios are equal. In Marx's view, this necessary connection between the price and value systems confirms that the profits appropriated by the capitalist class depend on the surplus labor performed by the working class.

The conception of capitalism that Marx supplies in support of this claim is that of an economic system that provides distorted and misleading appearances of itself to its participating agents. The value-price relation proposed by Ricardo would have provided a maximally transparent representation in the system of price accounting of the alternative possible distributions of the social product. The relation proposed by Marx requires transparency only at the level of certain social aggregates—the distributive share going to the capitalist class, for example. At the level of individual agents and more micro-denominated sectors of the economy it leaves room for the sorts of mystification that Marx finds endemic to commodity production and capitalism. For him, the appearance of profits as an expression of a power that capital has independently of its degree of incorporation into labor is just one more example of the fetishism characteristic of commodities and capital.

## 5.3   Critical analysis of Marx's proposal

Marx's proposal is not acceptable without qualification. The problem is not simply a matter of the incompleteness of his analysis. While his proposal opens up a way to get beyond Ricardo's impasse, it cannot be reconciled with another Ricardian claim that is on a sounder—albeit not fully worked out—theoretical footing. This claim concerns the relation between the equilibrium rate of profit and technical conditions in the production of luxury commodities. In his *Principles* Ricardo maintains that these conditions have no bearing on the equilibrium rate of profit:

> It has been my endeavor to shew throughout this work, that the rate of profits can never be increased but by a fall in wages, and that there can be no permanent fall of wages but in consequence of a fall of the necessaries on which wages are expended. If, therefore... by improvements in machinery, the food and necessaries of the laborer can be brought to market at a reduced price, profits will rise.... [B]ut if the commodities obtained at a cheaper rate... by the improvements of machinery... be exclusively the commodities consumed by the rich, no alteration will take place in the rate of profits. The rate of wages would not be affected, although wine, velvets, silks, and other expensive commodities should fall 50 per cent, and consequently profits would continue unaltered [124, p. 132].

Marx comments:

> Even in the case of luxury articles, such improvements can raise the general rate of profit, since the rate of profit in these spheres of production, as in all others, bears a share in the leveling out of all particular rates of profit into the average rate of profit. If in such cases, as a result of the above-mentioned influences, the value of the constant capital falls proportionately to the variable, or the period of turnover is reduced... then the rate of profit rises [85, p. 423].

It is easy to see why Marx says what he does, since the conditions of production of luxuries manifestly do affect the value of $\pi$ as it is given in Equation 5.14. Ricardo's position is in direct opposition to Marx's view. Yet if one suspends judgment on that view, it is not hard to see that Ricardo's position has something going for it. If all profits were reinvested as additional capital, then at equilibrium the economy would be growing at a maximal rate, in fact at a rate identical to the rate of profit. This reflection suggests that the rate of profit reflects the growth potential of the economy, as determined by the requirements of worker subsistence and production technology in sectors directly or indirectly contributing to the satisfaction of those requirements. By definition, these sectors do not include luxuries. So the conditions of luxury production are irrelevant to determining the growth potential of the economy and thus also irrelevant to determining the rate of profit, which is a reflection of that potential.

*Table 5.1* System E

| | Iron | Corn | Labor | → | Iron | Corn | Whiskey | Labor power |
|---|---|---|---|---|---|---|---|---|
| Iron industry | 36,000 | | 6,000 | | 42,000 | | | |
| Corn industry | 3,000 | 6,000 | 15,000 | | | 15,000 | | |
| Whiskey industry | 3,000 | 3,000 | 3,000 | | | | 3,000 | |
| Labor power | | 6,000 | | | | | | 3,000 |
| Totals | 42,000 | 15,000 | 24,000 | | 42,000 | 15,000 | 3,000 | 3,000 |

For an illustration and confirmation of this line of thought, consider a hypothetical three-commodity economy ($n = 3$). Call it system E. Commodity 1 is iron, which serves as means of production. Commodity 2 is corn, which serves both as means of production and as the sole worker-subsistence good. Commodity 3 is whiskey, a luxury good. Let $d$ be the length of the working day in hours, and suppose that $d = 8$. This implies that a unit of labor power—the labor power of one worker for a day—can supply eight worker-hours of labor. Suppose that the economy is operating at the activity levels indicated in Table 5.1. Inputs are given to the left of the arrow; outputs, to the right. For example the first line says that in one production cycle in the iron industry, the expenditure of 6,000 units of labor uses up 36,000 units of iron in the production of 42,000 units of iron. The fourth line tells us that 6,000 units of corn support 3,000 units of labor power (worker-days), which supply the 24,000 units of labor (worker-hours) expended in a production cycle.

To do the value accounting for the system, we first determine the value of each commodity $i$, $\lambda_i$, and the value of labor-power, $\lambda_{lp}$, from the following equations:

$$42,000\lambda_1 = 36,000\lambda_1 + 6,000, \tag{5.15}$$

$$15,000\lambda_2 = 3,000\lambda_1 + 6,000\lambda_2 + 15,000, \tag{5.16}$$

$$3,000\lambda_3 = 3,000\lambda_1 + 3,000\lambda_2 + 3,000, \tag{5.17}$$

$$3,000\lambda_{lp} = 6,000\lambda_2. \tag{5.18}$$

We can solve these to get:

$$\{\lambda_1 = 1, \lambda_2 = 2, \lambda_3 = 4, \lambda_{lp} = 4\}. \tag{5.19}$$

*Table 5.2* Value magnitudes: system E

|  | $C_i$ | $V_i$ | $e$ | $S_i$ | $\frac{C_i}{V_i}$ | $\frac{S_i}{C_i + V_i}$ |
|---|---|---|---|---|---|---|
| Iron industry | 36,000 | 3,000 | 1 | 3,000 | 12 | $\frac{1}{13}$ |
| Corn industry | 15,000 | 7,500 | 1 | 7,500 | 2 | $\frac{1}{3}$ |
| Whiskey industry | 9,000 | 1,500 | 1 | 1,500 | 6 | $\frac{1}{7}$ |
| Economy | 60000 | 12,000 | 1 | 12,000 | 5 | $\frac{1}{6}$ |

Using these results and the entries in Table 5.1, we can compute the value magnitudes in Table 5.2. Notice the variation across sectors in the organic composition of capital $C_i/V_i$. The aggregated (that is, economy-wide) magnitudes are given on the last line.[7] The rate of exploitation, $e$, is computed as the fraction $(d - \lambda_{\mathrm{lp}})/\lambda_{\mathrm{lp}}$. It is the ratio of the portion of the working day in excess of the portion workers spend reproducing the value of their labor power to that latter portion. It is the ratio of the time workers spend producing surplus value to the time they spend reproducing the value of their labor power.

For the price accounting, we can use the following equations:

$$42,000p_1 = (1 + \pi)(36,000p_1 + 6,000w), \tag{5.20}$$

$$15,000p_2 = (1 + \pi)(3,000p_1 + 6,000p_2 + 15,000w), \tag{5.21}$$

$$3,000p_3 = (1 + \pi)(3,000p_1 + 3,000p_2 + 3,000w), \tag{5.22}$$

$$24,000w = 6,000p_2, \tag{5.23}$$

$$p_1 = 1. \tag{5.24}$$

Equations 5.20, 5.21, and 5.22 express the requirement that at equilibrium there is a uniform rate of profit $\pi$ throughout the economy and in each industry the monetary value of the gross output is equal to $(1 + \pi)$ times the monetary cost of the inputs. Equation 5.23 states that money wages just enable each worker to purchase the real wage basket. Equation 5.24 reflects an assumption that iron is the money commodity. It does not have any implications concerning whether prices are

---

[7] In terms of our notation, these would be the (non-subscripted) magnitudes $C$, $V$, $S$, and others built up out of them.

proportional to values; the answer to that question is independent of a choice of numeraire for prices. We can solve this system to get:

$$\{p_1 = 1, p_2 = .84299, p_3 = 2.3147, w = .21075, \pi = .12708\}. \qquad (5.25)$$

Comparing these price solutions with the value solutions in 5.19, and comparing this solution for $\pi$ with that for (economy-wide) $S/(C+V)$ in the lower right-hand corner of Table 5.2, we can see that not only are prices not proportional to values—a result that according to Marx we should expect—but there is also a divergence of the rate of profit from the ratio of aggregate surplus value to aggregate value of advanced capital. This result is contrary to Marx's theory as we've stated it.

The cause of the discrepancy has to do with the fact that system E contains a luxury sector (whiskey). By definition, luxuries are not needed as means of production or wage goods for the production of any commodities except possibly themselves. There is no input column for whiskey in Table 5.1, and $p_3$ does not enter any of our price-determination equations except for 5.22, the one for industry 3 (whiskey) itself. We could therefore strike that equation from our list and still solve for the other unknowns. Hence the equilibrium rate of profit does not depend on conditions of production in sector 3. But in Marx's Equation 5.14, that rate does depend on those conditions, since they determine the value of the capital advanced and the surplus value produced in that sector.

On this particular issue Ricardo is correct and Marx mistaken. What are the implications of this fact? Ladislaus von Bortkiewicz, an early sympathetic critic of Marx and defender of Ricardo on this issue [10–15], claimed that correction of the error could actually bolster Marx's position, since the exclusion of the conditions of production of luxuries precludes any dependence of profits on the productive power of capital, while their dependence on how cheaply the working class can be reproduced coheres with their dependence on surplus labor:

If it is indeed true that the level of the rate of profit in no way depends on the conditions of production of those goods which do not enter into real wages, then the origin of profit must clearly be sought in the wage-relationship and not in the ability of capital to increase production. For if this ability were relevant here, then it would be inexplicable why certain spheres of production should become irrelevant for the question of the level of profit [15, p. 33; 13, pp. 446–447].[8]

In any case, the story is not over at this point. Ricardo's account leaves unanswered our original question of the relation between value accounting and price accounting. As we'll see, however, his insight leads to the development of further ideas that can provide an answer to this question.

Consider a hypothetical economy E* obtained from economy E by eliminating its luxury sector (whiskey) and reallocating its labor to the other two sectors so as to allow the system to sustain a maximal rate of balanced growth.[9] Call this rate of growth R. In E*, (1) iron output equals $(1+R)$ times total iron input to the economy, (2) corn output equals $(1+R)$ times total corn input (whether as means of production or wage good), and (3) the total labor input is all the labor expended in system E. It is not hard to see that Marx's Equation 5.14 holds in E*. Because of facts (1) and (2) just stated, the vector specifying the physical surplus of iron and corn is a scalar multiple of the vector of total inputs of these two commodities, that scalar being precisely R:

(net iron output, net corn output)
$= R \times$ (total iron input, total corn input).

In more general terms, the vector of commodities constituting the physical surplus is equal to R times the vector of commodities constituting the aggregate physical input to production (as means of production or wage goods). Hence no matter how the different commodities are reduced to a common measure, and in particular, *whether it is done through prices or Marxian values*, the resulting ratio of surplus output to aggregate input will be equal to R. Moreover, since the ratio specified in price terms is precisely the rate of profit, this equality confirms Marx's Equation 5.14.

This result does not depend on any specific features of E, the system on the basis of which we constructed E*. It simply depends on the assumption that E* is in a configuration of maximal balanced growth. So Equation 5.14 holds of any system in maximal balanced growth. One might claim that this fact completely vindicates Marx's theory, on the

---

[8] See also Bortkiewicz [14, p. 209].
[9] For details concerning the construction of E* from E, and for an illustration of the central claim of this and the next paragraph that Marx's Equation 5.14 holds in models of maximal balanced growth, see Section A.1.

grounds that economies in maximal balanced growth conform to Marx's conception of capitalism as aimed not at satisfying the capitalist's consumption needs but rather at the maximal realization of capital as self-expanding value. However, there are two considerations that make this claim at best premature. The first concerns the fact's *explanatory* significance. The ratio of physical surplus to aggregate physical input is indifferent to their reduction to a common measure: *any* semi-positive measure, such as commodity volume, for example, will yield the same ratio. Consequently, where $x$ is any semi-positive measure for commodities, the counterpart of Equation 5.14 obtained by substituting $x$ for value will *also* hold. Moreover, the value of $R$ itself does not immediately depend on any system of valuation. Rather, it is a function of the constituents of the real wage and of the production technology in the sectors participating directly or indirectly in the production of those constituents. These are the factors that determine the possibilities for balanced growth. Marx takes Equation 5.14 to be an expression of the determination of the rate of profit through the sharing among enterprises of the total amount of surplus value produced in the economy in proportion to the value of the capital advanced in those enterprises. Yet $R$'s independence of any system of valuation and the arbitrariness of the measures for which Equation 5.14 and its counterparts hold suggest that proportional sharing of surplus value is not causally determinative but instead, all these equations hold as a byproduct of the price mechanism's ability to sustain a configuration that fully realizes the growth potential of the economy.

However, though Marx may have thought that proportional sharing of surplus value is causally determinative, such a claim goes beyond what we have characterized as the main task, namely the establishment of a determinate relationship between price accounting and value accounting. And Equation 5.14 establishes just such a relationship for balanced growth economies.

However, the second consideration casting doubt on the claim that this result vindicates Marx's theory is simply that his theory should be able to tell us something significant—as he thought it did—about capitalist economies that lie off the path of maximal balanced growth, which include all real-world capitalist economies. I believe it is reasonable to impose this condition on the theory, and hence that its correct results for balanced-growth economies are not enough to vindicate it.

Yet I think that it can meet this condition. Every viable economy has associated with it a hypothetical economy in maximal balanced growth, one constructible through the procedure we described for constructing system E* from the elements of system E. System E* realizes the growth potential of system E, and in system E* the rate of growth is equal to the rate of profit in system E. E's rate of profit reveals its growth potential. All this we can know from within the system of price accounting. What doing the value accounting and connecting it up with the price accounting add to this knowledge is that to maximize economic growth it is necessary to make the ratio $S/(C + V)$ equal to that rate of profit. If the rate of profit in E is $\pi$, then for E to become a pure capitalist system (E*), it must appropriate and reinvest surplus labor at the rate of $\pi$. Relating the two systems of accounting thus tells us something significant about the actual system, if there are dynamics in it pushing it toward maximal growth. We learn something about how that system treats workers in the processes of production and distribution.

Of course Marx thinks you get a better idea of this treatment by considering the rate of exploitation (rather than the ratio $S/(C + V)$) and its connection with the system of price accounting. He thinks that positive profits are an indicator of exploitation (the performance and alien appropriation of surplus labor). This relation goes beyond what is asserted in the last paragraph. Can it survive a correction of Marx's theory of price and profit determination? It turns out that the answer to this question is yes. It is possible to establish the following results:

1. The rate of profit is positive if and only if the rate of exploitation is positive. This result has been called the 'Fundamental Marxian Theorem' (Okishio [103]).
2. Changes in the rate of profit and the rate of exploitation are inversely related in the following sense: An increase in the rate of exploitation, which must occur either through a decrease in a material element of constant capital or the real wage basket or in direct labor requirements, or through an increase in the length of the working day, will increase the rate of profit, other things equal.[10] Conversely, an increase in the rate of profit, which must occur either through a decrease in a material element of constant capital or the real wage basket or in direct labor requirements, or through an increase in the length of the working day, will increase the rate of exploitation, other things equal. Similarly, a decrease in the rate of exploitation will decrease the rate of profit, other things equal, and conversely.

[10] By 'other things equal' I mean that the changes referred to in constant capital, real wages, direct labor requirements, and the length of the working day are not accompanied by changes in those factors in the opposite direction.

For proofs of these results, see Sections A.2 and A.3. Item 2 specifies certain elementary dynamic[11] relationships among price-level variables, value-level variables, and material variables. These relationships figure importantly in the volume 1 accounts of struggles over the length of the working day, of the real subjection of labor to capital, and of the reproduction of the capital-labor relationship. In virtue of item 2, they retain their relevance in the more general setting that is the focus of volume 3. Combined with the Fundamental Marxian Theorem, they make it possible to extend Marx's account of profits as an expression of surplus labor and of capital as estranged labor to the case of unequal organic compositions of capital.

---

[11] Strictly speaking, comparative-static.

# 6
# Strategic Estrangement

## 6.1 Introduction

We've seen that Marx applies the charge of doctrinal inversion in novel and surprising ways (Section 4.1). It was natural for Feuerbach to extend his critique of religion to Hegel's philosophy, since the latter claims to be a conceptually adequate account of the same content that religion captures in images, narratives and metaphors. Feuerbach could trace both projections to the same psychological need for reconciliation. But Marx finds a doctrinal inversion in the unlikely doctrine of political economy, which aspires to be an empirical theory of economic mechanisms rather than something akin to a theodicy. Economic value (as manifested in monetary or exchange value) is for Marx a social projection rather than something intrinsic to commodities as natural objects: value only exists in virtue of the specific and contingent way the economy is organized. But political economy, he claims, ignores this fact by explaining the workings of the economy as a social response to certain immutable natural laws of value. In this way, it mischaracterizes not only value but capital—self-expanding value—through a doctrinal inversion. They depend on a certain configuration of human activities for their existence, but political economy treats them as an independent determinant of those activities. Such representations of the economy thus have an inherently apologetic character, because they treat socially variable features of it as fixed in the nature of things. They in effect treat value and capital—and thus capitalism—as always with us, as something whose forces can be channeled, perhaps, but not eliminated. On this view, trying to get rid of capitalism is as foolish as trying to get rid of gravitation.

But what is really distinctive and striking about Marx's critique is not that it is an unusual charge of doctrinal inversion, but rather that it traces that inversion to a real social inversion (Section 4.1). That is, it treats the doctrinal inversion as an aspect and symptom of a social practice in which individuals unwittingly convert their own actions into a process whose dynamic lies outside their control and is an important underlying determinant of what they do. In this inverted social world, individuals confront aspects of their own agency in the alien or 'reified' form of a given, determining reality, a 'second nature', as it were. The doctrinal inversion, then, though it is false, nonetheless reflects a real inversion.[1] If it is true that an initial investment of a given sum of value yields a net return only through a propitious configuration of human activities (of purchase, production and sale of commodities), it is nonetheless true that this realization of value as capital is value's own self-realization process, in which it displays its 'occult quality of positing value because it is value' [90, p. 255 (translation modified); 95, part 2, 6:171]. What the doctrinal inversion gets wrong is the nature of this occult property, treating it as nonsocial when it—and indeed value and capital themselves—have a purely social objectivity, owing their existence and power to certain alterable forms of economic organization.

Marx's stunningly original idea that society is an inverted world, that an inversion in practice underlies all the inversions in theory, is what marks the significance of his work for classical German philosophy. It is in fact the key to a correct interpretation of his entire doctrine. Moreover, it represents his most distinctive and important potential contribution to modern society's efforts at self-understanding. For as I will try to make clear below, it offers a new perspective for social criticism and a new potential source of progressive and egalitarian motivation. Unfortunately, it remains the least recognized and least understood element of his doctrine.

---

[1] In the *Grundrisse*, Marx speaks of a condition in which 'the monstrous objective power which social labour itself erected opposite itself as one of its moments' and he says that '[t]o the extent that, from the standpoint of capital and wage labour, the objective body of labour happens in antithesis to the immediate labour capacity... this twisting and inversion [*Verdrehung und Verkehrung*] is a *real* [*phenomenon*], not a merely *supposed one* existing merely in the imagination of the workers and the capitalists' [87, p. 831; 88, part 2, 1(2):698]. As we'll see below, in another location he calls the objectivity of the real inversion 'imaginary'. I hope to make clear in this chapter how both claims can be true.

Part of the problem is that he leaves unclear precisely how the process of reification or real inversion gains and maintains its hold on the agents caught up in it. He tells us that the objectivity of commodities, money and capital is 'ghostly [*gespenstige*]', 'imaginary [*eingebildete*]', and 'purely social' [83, p. 171; 90, pp. 128, 138–139; 95, part 2, 3.2:457, 6:72, 80]. How can there be a kind of objectivity that is mediated by the imagination? What kind of objectivity is purely social, and how does it depend on the attitudes of economic agents? What is the nature of the 'occult' power that value has 'to posit value, because it is value'? More generally, what is the nature of the forces at work in an inverted world? In what sense can agents invest their own actions with an alien dynamic? It is clear that Marx regards these questions as having scientifically respectable answers.[2] But he leaves them sufficiently unresolved that he is often interpreted as falling victim to precisely the kind of doctrinal inversion he finds in others, by hypostatizing capital, for example, just as Hegel supposedly hypostatizes the Idea.[3] As a result, the distinctive features of his doctrine are occluded, and their significance for today remains unexplored.

What is needed is a defensible account, suitably generalized, of the kind of process Marx was grappling with, one that can clarify not only how a real inversion exerts and maintains its hold on agents, but also under what conditions it is possible to eliminate it, and what sorts of reasons agents might have for doing so. It should be an account that can engage present-day concerns in philosophy and the social sciences. Though even sympathetic interpreters have doubted the possibility of such an account,[4] I believe that one can be fashioned from the following ideas: a conception of rationality as deliberative control, a distinction between independent and collective agency as socially specific ways of realizing this conception, and a notion of extrinsic information deriving from treatments of extrinsic uncertainty in general equilibrium theory and from efforts to integrate game theory and decision theory.

---

[2] This is clear from remarks in the preface to the first edition of *Capital*, for example [90, pp. 89–93; 95, part 2, 5:11–15].

[3] See Elster [30], for example.

[4] Colletti, for example, states: 'I am perfectly conscious that the notion of an upside-down reality appears to jar with the precepts of any science. Marx was convinced of the validity of this notion. I do not say that he was necessarily right. I cannot yet state whether the idea of an inverted reality is compatible with a social science' [26, p. 19].

My main purpose in this chapter is to sketch an account of what I call 'strategic estrangement' as a more general form of Marx's social inversion. In developing the account I have several aims: (1) to clarify the puzzling features that Marx attributes to value and capital, (2) to show that the idea of social inversion is applicable to other domains besides the narrowly economic (gender relations, for example), (3) to show how what I call independent agency provides fertile ground for the development of estrangement, (4) to illustrate how estrangement can generate for itself a supporting ideology, and (5) to clarify the ways in which estrangement may be subject to criticism.

## 6.2  Rationality

The following analysis conceives of rationality as deliberative control. This conception takes rational action to issue from a reflectively acceptable practical orientation, and it requires rational deliberation to accommodate a concern to identify and to adopt such an orientation. It is not a merely instrumental conception, since it refers to the active adoption of beliefs and values and not merely the identification of best prospects relative to given beliefs and values. It is pragmatic, however, in its focus on beliefs and values to serve as a basis for action. Assigning a higher value to a clean water supply than to a new baseball stadium requires being willing to choose it over the stadium, should those be the only two options. And fixing beliefs in hypotheses requires determining one's willingness to let items of value ride on them in various hypothetical situations. A practical orientation may be represented by a choice function or a preference relation, and the relevant beliefs and values are those one would be prepared on due reflection to make implicit in such a representation.

Two important formal criteria for the acceptability of an orientation are coherence and determinacy. Coherence protects the possibility of acting on well-defined beliefs and values. We can think of it as the requirement that the orientation have at least one expected-utility representation.[5] Determinacy constrains the orientation to provide sufficient direction for the case at hand. It requires all expected-utility

---

[5] Roughly, if we think of an orientation as given by a set of preferences, then an expected-utility representation is an assignment of utilities to possible outcomes of action and probabilities to possible states of the world, such that one action is preferred to another if and only if its expected utility is higher. The

representations to agree in their designations of best prospects in the given set of feasible actions.[6]

In addition to being coherent and determinate, a reflectively acceptable orientation must acceptable in light of due consideration of alternatives. Rather than go into what due consideration requires, I will simply assume that there are feasible deliberative procedures that are more or less responsive to this demand and are thereby more or less rational, ceteris paribus.

The formulation of a decision problem requires a specification of decision variables, ranging over feasible alternative courses of action, consequence variables, ranging over relevant possible consequences of action, and environmental or state variables, ranging over aspects of the decision situation that are beyond influence and that together with the values of the decision variables determine the values of the consequence variables.

The ideal of deliberative control has implications for the formulation as well as for the solution of decision problems.[7] For example, the consequence variables should capture the possibilities for all features of outcomes that on due reflection would be deemed important to take into account. An important standard of problem formulation is deliberative responsiveness of action: problems should be set up so that chosen action can be a fully deliberative response to genuinely unalterable environmental conditions. For example, decision variables should range over an exhaustive set of genuine alternatives. And the problem formulation should avoid other ways of representing as fixed independently of deliberation factors that in reality can be controlled or influenced through deliberation. As we shall see, social inversions can run afoul of this constraint.

## 6.3 Social form

Sociality introduces an additional degree of freedom into the idea of regulation of deliberation and action by a conception of rationality. Deliberation typically takes place in multi-agent, multi-deliberator situations, and to at least some extent agents can take this fact into account

expected utility of an action is a weighted average of the utilities of its possible outcomes, with the weights given by the probabilities of the states that determine those outcomes. For a more precise definition see Sensat [140].

[6] For formal definitions of coherence and determinacy, see Sensat [140].

[7] For further detail, see Sensat [140].

in the formulation and solution of their decision problems. Application of the same conception of rationality can thereby assume a variety of social forms, reflecting the different ways agents might set up and solve decision problems arising from common or overlapping settings. For example, consider *independent agency* as a social mode of deliberation and action. Jack and Jill[8] exercise independent agency with respect to each other when they each formulate their own separate decision problems. The feasible set for Jack's problem contains only his own available actions, and Jill's feasible set likewise contains only hers. Jack views Jill's action as an environmental variable rather than a decision variable, a matter of uncertainty his deliberation has to address, but not a matter he is to take part in deciding. And similarly for Jill's view of Jack's action. For each individual, both problem formulation and problem solution are constrained at the most basic level by reflective acceptability to that individual alone. Jill views herself as accountable to herself alone, and similarly for Jack.

In *collective agency*, by contrast, the agents treat the setting as posing a problem for the group. They view the feasible set as containing joint actions that they can perform together, by each agent's performing some individual action. To solve the problem, they aim their deliberation at the construction of a joint orientation, one mutually acceptable to all as a basis of joint action. They thus embrace the possibility of reasoned consensus as a constraint on deliberation. Were Jack and Jill to engage in collective agency, Jack would view himself as accountable not only to himself but also to Jill, where he understands Jill as similarly accountable to him. And Jill would have the corresponding self-conception.[9]

In fully realized collective agency, the foregoing facts are common knowledge among the participating agents. It is not only true but common knowledge that each agent acts under a collective intention—an intention to act jointly with the others by performing his or her individual action. Moreover, it is common knowledge that these intentions have as a common object the performance of the entire profile of individual actions. For example, the action pair $(x, y)$ would be a common object of collective intention if agent 1 had the intention of jointly

---

[8] I ask the reader not to presume that Jack and Jill are acting jointly, as the nursery rhyme may seem to suggest.

[9] In taking deliberation about joint action to stand under a requirement of interpersonal justifiability that does not constrain independent-agent deliberation, I am in agreement with Sellars [137, chap. 7] and Gilbert [40; 41].

performing $(x,y)$ with agent 2 by performing $x$, while agent 2 had the intention of jointly performing $(x,y)$ with agent 1 by performing $y$.[10] In acting on these intentions they would assume it to be common knowledge that the pair is such a common object of collective intention. In fully realized collective agency, this assumption would be correct. Social inversion is a phenomenon associated with independent agency, and collective agency can sometimes provide a way out.

## 6.4 Information

Information can be first order or higher order. For example, my information that you are rational is first order. Your information that I am informed that you are rational is second order. Information is full when it is common knowledge: everyone is in possession of this information, everyone knows that everyone is in possession of it, everyone in turn knows that everyone knows *that*, and so on. There are two kinds of information agents in a common decision situation typically have. *Intrinsic information* concerns the following:

1. Feasibility conditions: the actions available to each agent and the outcomes the various action combinations would have.
2. Valuational conditions: how the agents value the different possible outcomes.
3. Rationality conditions: whether or not the various agents are rational.

Information that is not intrinsic is *extrinsic*. For example, information about sunspots would be extrinsic to an economy on the assumption that sunspot activity does not affect production possibilities, the feasibility or value to consumers of consumption activities, or the rationality of economic agents. Also extrinsic would be certain information about the behavior of the economy itself, for example as reflected in histories of price fluctuations.[11]

---

[10] In treating a collective intention as an intention to act jointly with others by performing an individual action, I am in agreement with Searle [134; 135]. I would be inclined to endorse the refinement of Searle's analysis by Bardsley [7], however.

[11] I borrow these labels, as well as the example in Section 6.6 of the sun as a possible randomizing device in an information system, from the literature on extrinsic uncertainty and sunspot equilibria in general equilibrium theory,

### 6.4.1 Extrinsic information and independent agency

Extrinsic information can play a role in independent agency because coherence and consistency with intrinsic information may fail to insure determinacy. The coherent orientations consistent with intrinsic information may not all certify the same set of actions as expected-utility maximizing, even when all parties are rational and intrinsic information is full—i.e., feasibility, valuational and rationality conditions are common knowledge.

For example, consider the formal class of games of complete information. In these situations, feasibility conditions are given by sets of available actions or strategies (one set for each player), an outcome space, and a function from action profiles to outcomes. Valuational conditions are given by (von Neumann–Morgenstern) utility functions on outcomes (one function for each player, specifying that player's valuation of each possible outcome).[12] These parameters are assumed to be common knowledge among the players. Game theory also assumes common knowledge of rationality, in whatever sense of 'rationality' turns out to be appropriate for game situations. Players in these games thus possess full intrinsic information.

Assume that their conception of rationality is that of Section 6.2. This conception is 'Bayesian' in requiring them to adopt a practical orientation representable by a set of pairs of probability and utility functions, with each pair certifying the same subset of feasible actions as expected-utility maximizing. Typically, then, they must find some way to rule out many abstractly possible pairs. One thing they can do is to insist on consistency with their intrinsic information. For example, they can rule out positive probability assignments to the strongly dominated actions[13] of any player as inconsistent with their information that all players maximize expected utility. Once these actions are eliminated from consideration, new actions may become strongly dominated, with common knowledge of rationality licensing a second round of eliminations. And further rounds may be possible. In some cases this iterative procedure will pare down admissible expectations enough to determine a set of

---

which I read as getting at basically the same idea with different theoretical tools. For entry into this literature, see Shell [142].

[12] I am sketching here, somewhat roughly, the normal or strategic form of representation, which suppresses dynamic structure.

[13] An action is strongly dominated for a player if that player has available another action that has better results for that player no matter how the other players act.

*Table 6.1* A game of chicken

| | |
|---|---|
| (6,2) | (0,0) |
| (5,5) | (2,6) |

expected-utility maximizing actions. But often there will be a number of ways a player can assign probabilities to the choices of others without contradicting intrinsic information, with these different assignments giving contradictory advice on how to maximize expected utility.[14] In these cases, there is room for extrinsic information to play a role in rational expectation determination.

Consider, for example, the game specified in Table 6.1, which has the well-known 'chicken' structure. The game is played between 'row chooser', who chooses a row of the table, and 'column chooser', who chooses a column. As usual, the first number in each pair represents row chooser's valuation of the corresponding outcome, and the second number, column chooser's valuation.[15]

Suppose that row chooser (call her 'Jill') and column chooser (call him 'Jack') have common knowledge of each other's rationality and of the feasibility and valuational conditions specified in the matrix. They thus have full intrinsic information. There are expectations consistent with this information relative to which a choice of *top* maximizes Jill's expected utility while a choice of *bottom* does not. She could expect (with certainty, say, or with sufficiently high probability) Jack to choose *left*. She could reconcile this expectation with her knowledge of Jack's rationality by expecting him to expect *her* to choose *top* (since this second-order expectation attributes an expectation to Jack relative to which a choice of *left* maximizes *his* expected utility). She could in

[14] Call a player's strategy *rationalizable* if it would maximize his expected utility relative to expectations consistent with his information about the defining parameters of the game together with his information that Bayesian rationality is common knowledge. Although the point in the text may seem fairly obvious, its foundations have only relatively recently been clarified by studies that identify rationalizability as the solution concept implied by the basic decision-theoretic analysis of a game and display its connection with iterated deletion of dominated strategies. For a brief overview, see Brandenburger and Dekel [17, secs. 1, 3; 16].

[15] The lore: Row chooser and column chooser are driving toward each other on a collision course. Row chooser 'swerves' by choosing *bottom*; column chooser, by choosing *left*.

turn respect her knowledge of his knowledge of *her* rationality by adopting the third-order expectation that Jack expects her to expect him to choose *left*. She could construct a hierarchy of expectations along these lines that would respect her intrinsic information and would require choice of *top* and rejection of *bottom*. But she could equally well respect that information with a hierarchy requiring choice of *bottom* and rejection of *top*. And Jack is in a similar condition. For each player there is no action that is maximal relative to all expectations consistent with that player's intrinsic information.

The point is not that their problems are unsolvable, but only that their intrinsic information is not logically strong enough to imply a solution. Consequently, there is room for their extrinsic information to come into play. For example, it might be common knowledge between them that on numerous past occasions they have encountered each other in games of chicken, and in each one Jill has yielded to Jack; that is, the profile of chosen actions has been the counterpart of (*bottom, right*) in the current game. This information could support expectations underwriting those choices this time as well. Bayesian rationality does not rule out their using it.

Of course, it is conceivable that an alternative conception of rationality, for instance one obtained through refinement of Bayesian rationality with supplementary principles, could trump the use of extrinsic information. This idea in fact provides a useful way of looking at much game-theoretic research.[16] I cannot argue against this possibility here.[17] The fact remains that fairly standard decision-theoretic principles leave room for extrinsic information to play a role in independent agency.

We can explore this potential with the concept of an *extrinsic information system* for a given multi-agent decision situation.[18] Such a system is composed of the following elements:

---

[16] The aim of securing determinacy of expectations on the basis of intrinsic information through refinement of Bayesian rationality is fairly explicit in Harsanyi and Selten [46]. However it is implicit in many other attempts to arrive at adequate solution concepts for games through refinements of Nash equilibrium, since full intrinsic information corresponding to unrefined Bayesian rationality does not guarantee Nash equilibrium. For further details, see Sensat [141].

[17] I do so however in Sensat [141].

[18] The notion was developed by Aumann in studies aimed at integrating decision theory and game theory [2–4]. He does not use the label 'extrinsic'.

1. A 'randomizing device' with a finite state space $\Omega$ whose states do not enter the determination of feasibility, valuational or rationality conditions.
2. For each agent, an assignment of prior probabilities to the states in $\Omega$.
3. For each agent, an information partition of $\Omega$.[19]
4. For each agent, a function that makes that agent's chosen action depend on the state of the device in a manner consistent with that agent's information.[20]

Such a system plays an effective role in a setting of independent agency when agents succeed in making use of information about the state of the randomizing device and how the actions of others correlate with these states in order to form expectations determinate enough to solve their respective decision problems. Each agent is prepared to make a determinate probability assignment to the possible states of the device, prior to receiving any information about its actual state. Hence the set of priors. These can differ across agents. The agents receive private information—possibly partial and differential—about the device. The partitions characterize this information: if the true state of the device is $\omega$ and $\omega \in h$ where $h$ is an element of an agent's partition, then that agent is informed that the true state is an element of $h$, but not which element it is. The behavior of the device influences action through the mediation of this information. The functions from states to actions characterize this influence. The priors, partitions and functions are all common knowledge. That these matters are common knowledge is extrinsic information, but it nonetheless provides the agents with a basis for certifying their respective choices as expected-utility maximizing. Given the expectations that their information enables them to form about the actions of the other agents, they maximize expected utility by choosing the actions indicated by their respective functions.[21]

[19] $H$ is an information partition of $\Omega$ if $H$ is a set of nonempty subsets of $\Omega$ such that every element of $\Omega$ is an element of exactly one element of $H$.

[20] In formal terms, for each agent $i$ with set of available actions $A_i$ and partition $H_i$, there is an $H_i$-measurable function $f_i : \Omega \to A_i$. (To say that $f_i$ is $H_i$-measurable is to say that for every $h \in H_i$ and every $x \in \Omega$ and $y \in \Omega$, if $x, y \in h$, then $f(x) = f(y)$.)

[21] Thus for a system to work effectively, it must satisfy an equilibrium condition. In the context of games of complete information, the appropriate condition is that of a posteriori equilibrium [4; 16]. It requires that the priors, partitions and functions be such that each agent, given his private information as determined by his partition, maximizes conditional expected utility by choosing in accordance with his function, on the assumption that the others choose in

Here are two examples, each of which could work for the above variant of Chicken:

*System 1:*

1. $\Omega = \{\omega_1, \omega_2\}$
2. Prior probability assignments:
   Jill: .5 to $\omega_1$, .5 to $\omega_2$
   Jack: same as Jill
3. Partitions:
   Jill: $\{\{\omega_1\}, \{\omega_2\}\}$
   Jack: same as Jill
4. Functions from states to actions:
   Jill: $\omega_1 \to top$, $\omega_2 \to bottom$
   Jack: $\omega_1 \to left$, $\omega_2 \to right$

In this system, which might be implemented with a coin each agent thought was fair, each agent is informed of the actual state of the device. Let $\omega_1$ be heads and $\omega_2$ tails. The agents both observe a single toss of the coin and choose as required by their functions. Heads thereby leads to (*top, left*) and tails to (*bottom, right*).

The next example illustrates differential and partial information.

*System 2:*

1. $\Omega = \{\omega_1, \omega_2, \omega_3, \omega_4\}$
2. Prior probability assignments:
   Jill: $\frac{1}{3}$ to $\omega_1$, $\frac{1}{9}$ to $\omega_2$, $\frac{1}{18}$ to $\omega_3$, $\frac{1}{2}$ to $\omega_4$
   Jack: same as Jill
3. Partitions:
   Jill: $\{\{\omega_1, \omega_2\}, \{\omega_3, \omega_4\}\}$
   Jack: $\{\{\omega_1, \omega_3\}, \{\omega_2, \omega_4\}\}$
4. Functions from states to actions:
   Jill: $\omega_1 \to top$, $\omega_2 \to top$, $\omega_3 \to bottom$, $\omega_4 \to bottom$
   Jack: $\omega_1 \to left$, $\omega_2 \to right$, $\omega_3 \to left$, $\omega_4 \to right$

Suppose that the randomizing device for this system is a ball-selecting machine of the kind used in various lotteries, set up to select one

accordance with their functions. For a more thorough discussion, see Sensat [140]. For development of the relevant equilibrium concepts, see Aumann [2; 4] and Brandenburger and Dekel [16].

ball from several balls marked '1', '2', '3', or '4' and augmented by an information processor that would transmit information about the selected ball through two channels, one in accordance with each of the partitions.

To see how the system would work, suppose that the actual state is $\omega_2$ (a 2-ball has been selected). Hence Jill is informed that the true state is in $\{\omega_1, \omega_2\}$. She accordingly updates her prior and assigns a probability of $\frac{3}{4}$ to $\omega_1$ and $\frac{1}{4}$ to $\omega_2$. Referring to Jack's function, she then assigns $\frac{3}{4}$ to his choosing *left* and $\frac{1}{4}$ to his choosing *right*. Against these probabilities she maximizes expected utility by choosing *top*. Jack, on the other hand, is informed that the true state is in $\{\omega_2, \omega_4\}$. Updating his prior, he assigns $\frac{2}{11}$ to $\omega_2$ and $\frac{9}{11}$ to $\omega_4$. Referring to Jill's function, he assigns $\frac{2}{11}$ and $\frac{9}{11}$ to her options *top* and *bottom* respectively. Against these probabilities he maximizes expected utility by choosing *right*. For each state in $\Omega$ there is a similar set of calculations that will lead to a unique outcome in the game.

The foregoing treatment does not fully chart the potential role of extrinsic information in independent agency. We have focused on games of complete information because of their relative simplicity and in order to stress that even when intrinsic information is full, there may still be room for extrinsic information to play a role.

### 6.4.2 Extrinsic information and collective agency

The potential role of extrinsic information in collective agency is quite different from its potential role in independent agency. Given common knowledge of feasibility, valuational and rationality conditions, only a plurality of best options could generate any uncertainty for rational co-agents about each other's action. The deliberative determination of a unique best option settles expectations without recourse to extrinsic information. For example, if Jack and Jill treat their situation as presenting them with a collective decision problem, they might settle on (*bottom*, *left*) as their single best option; that decision itself would obviate any need to rely on extrinsic information.[22]

To forestall an objection as well as to clarify the difference between independent and collective agency, it is important to note that the rationality of collectively deciding on and conforming with (*bottom*, *left*)

---

[22] Thus the decision settles expectations rather than the reverse. Expectations are epiphenomenal to successful reasoning from a first-person plural perspective [144, p. 87; 7, pp. 149–150].

is not precluded by its not being an equilibrium in the independent-agent matrix.[23] That matrix represents independent-agent reasons and motivations, not collective-agent ones. It is also important to note that determining (*bottom, left*) as a unique best option is just one possibility; it is not required by the 'logic of decision' for collective agency.

Certain qualifications aside, when collective deliberation yields a set of several best options, additional coordination of individual actions is necessary to ensure that the realized profile falls inside that set.[24] There is room here for an extrinsic information system to play a role. But which system is used could itself be an object of collective decision—think of a collectively adopted system of traffic lights, for example.

A breakdown of collective agency can also create space for extrinsic information. A collective decision is made to hold a meeting, but the person delegated to make the arrangements inadvertently leaves the location off the announcement, and time doesn't permit collective resolution of the problem. This situation is perhaps best analyzed as generating a problem of independent-agent coordination, in which the individuals involved must form expectations about each other's action in order to make a decision. Extrinsic information about where meetings have been held in the past could play a role in making these expectations sufficiently determinate.

## 6.5  Inversion

### 6.5.1  A definition

Suppose the members of population $N$ use agency of type $A$ in settings of type $S$. Then we can speak of population $N$ as realizing a *system of type-A agency* (in type-$S$ settings). For example, if $A$ is independent agency, they realize a system of independent agency, and if $A$ is collective agency, they realize a system of collective agency. If extrinsic information plays a certain kind of role in supporting the persistence or stability of such a system—a role specified below—then the system has the key marks

---

23  That is, by the fact that in the independent-agent matrix, at (*bottom, left*) some agent (in this case each one) has a better response to the other's action.

24  If the best options are 'interchangeable' profiles—that is, they form the Cartesian product of each agent's set of component actions in those profiles—then there is no need for further coordination. For no matter which component each agent performs, the resulting profile will be a best option.

of social inversion. The behavior of the system, as characterized by certain variables reflecting what agents do in type-$S$ situations, is governed by laws and tendencies that are outside the scope of deliberative control, even though that behavior is constituted by the deliberation and action of the agents in the system. Moreover, the agents respond to these laws and tendencies in their deliberation and action, through the mediation of their beliefs and information about the system. They thus realize through their agency an autonomous, non-deliberative process that is itself an important underlying determinant of what they do. In this way they are caught up in what Sections 4.1 and 6.1 refer to as a real inversion.

Extrinsic information can contribute to the persistence and stability of systems of agency because the way agents rely on extrinsic information in a given setting can influence how they rely on extrinsic information in future, relevantly similar settings. Call a setting that takes the form of a game of chicken in systems of independent agency a *proto-chicken* situation. Suppose Jack and Jill are members of a large population whose members process proto-chicken situations as independent agents, and it is common knowledge across this population that the randomizing device specified in Section 6.4.1 has found pervasive past use in such situations. Jack and Jill are thus members of a population who realize a system of independent agency through reliance on the device. Their common knowledge of this fact could lead them to rely on the device in their current situation. And their current reliance could contribute to a background of information that would support similar reliance in the future, thereby contributing to the persistence of the system of agency.

Information-based inversion depends on this potential of extrinsic information, but in the most thoroughgoing cases there is another factor involved. In the above example, agents rely on information about a randomizing device whose behavior is exogenous to the system of agency: the decisions and actions of agents have no effect on the behavior of the device. However, in other cases the variables characterizing the relevant extrinsic events in the information system might be partly or fully endogenous to the system of agency. The system of agency might even serve as its own randomizing device. In this case agents would be basing their decisions on information and expectations about the state of their own system of agency. It is this kind of reliance on extrinsic information that figures in in the most thoroughgoing and most mystifying cases of inversion.

To sum up, we might characterize the phenomenon of interest with the following definition: A system of agency $(N, A, S)$ is an *inverted world* with respect to a set $\Omega$ of its own states if:

1. The states in $\Omega$ are extrinsic to settings of type $S$.
2. The agents in $N$ rely on an information system with state space $\Omega$ in settings of type $S$.
3. The behavior of the system of agency $(N, A, S)$ with respect to $\Omega$ is a function of what agents do in $S$-situations.
4. That behavior, however, lies outside the scope of $A$-agency control.

Though not fully general, this definition will serve for purposes of understanding the following example, which once again makes use of games of complete information.

### 6.5.2 An example

Consider a hypothetical system of independent agency with respect to certain proto-chicken situations between men and women. Assume that intrinsic information is full so that these situations, in the context of the system of agency, have the character of games of complete information. For each situation, think of the woman as row chooser and the man as column chooser, and label outcomes as indicated in Table 6.2. Assume also that valuations are those given in Table 6.3.

Temporally partition the behavior of the system into periods $1, 2, \ldots$. Assume that no more than $m$ interactions can occur in a single period, and for each period $j$, let $X_j$ be the number of interactions occurring during period $j$. Assume that for each $j$, $X_j$ is an independent random variable uniformly distributed over $\{1, 2, \ldots, m\}$. For any positive integer

*Table 6.2* Outcomes

| $o_1$ | $o_2$ |
|-------|-------|
| $o_3$ | $o_4$ |

*Table 6.3* Valuations

| $(6, 2)$ | $(0, 0)$ |
|----------|----------|
| $(5, 5)$ | $(2, 6)$ |

$n$, let $S_n = \sum_{j=1}^{n} X_j$. For $i \in \{1, 2, 3, 4\}$ and $j$ a positive integer, let:

$a_{ij}$ = the number of occurrences of $o_i$ in period $j$

$$b_{ij} = \begin{cases} 0 & \text{if } j = 1 \\ \frac{\sum_{k=1}^{j-1} a_{ik}}{S_{j-1}} & \text{if } j > 1 \end{cases} \quad \left( \frac{o_i\text{'s before } j}{\text{interactions before } j} \right)$$

$$c_{ij} = \begin{cases} \frac{1}{3} - b_{ij} & \text{if } i = 1 \\ \frac{1}{9} - b_{ij} & \text{if } i = 2 \\ \frac{1}{18} - b_{ij} & \text{if } i = 3 \\ \frac{1}{2} - b_{ij} & \text{if } i = 4 \end{cases}$$

$$s(j) = \omega_l \text{ if } l = \min_{k=1}^{4} \left\{ k \mid c_{kj} = \max_{i=1}^{4} \{c_{ij}\} \right\}.$$

The function $s$ takes values in the set $\Omega = \{\omega_1, \omega_2, \omega_3, \omega_4\}$, which provides a state space for the system of agency: $s(j)$ is the state of the system in period $j$. This fact makes it possible for the system of agency itself to serve as a randomizing device for information system 2 specified in Section 6.4.1. In fact, the system works in precisely this way. Each time a man and a woman find themselves in the specified type of chicken situation, they make use of the specified information system, using their own system of agency as the randomizing device. For each $i = 1, ..., 4$, the system moves into state $\omega_i$ when $\max_k \{c_{kj}\} = c_{ij}$ (with ties being broken by favoring the minimum index). Moreover, if the system is in state $\omega_i$ in period $t$ (i.e., $s(t) = \omega_i$), then the information transmitted through the partitions to the agents leads them to choose actions that together have outcome $o_i$. Consequently, in period $t + 1$, past occurrences of $o_i$ as a fraction of past occurrences of all outcomes will be higher than in period $t$. That is, $b_{i(t+1)}$ will be greater than $b_{it}$, and thus $c_{i(t+1)}$ will be less than $c_{it}$. Changes in these directions will eventually move the system out of state $i$ and into some other state. The overall effect is a probabilistic convergence of $b_{ij}$, the relative frequency over time of outcome $o_i$ (as well as a convergence of the relative frequency of realizations of state $\omega_i$) to the common prior assigned to state $\omega_i$ by each agent. This convergence lends stability to the system by helping to reproduce the priors over time.

If the same number of interactions occurred each period, then the succession of states would follow a quite regular pattern, and information about past states could be used to ascertain the present state. Such information could thus lead agents away from assigning the priors specified in the information system. The assumption that $X_j$ is a uniformly distributed random variable blocks this source of instability.

Other factors might undermine persistent use of the information system. For example, one or more women might depart from their specified functions and choose *top* in several encounters in an effort to turn expectations to their advantage by establishing the appropriate reputation. A similar possibility applies to men. However, there are conceivable circumstances without such sources of instability. The contemplated strategy requires reformulating a sequence of encounters as parts of a single, more complex decision problem, and working effectively with such a reformulation might exceed agents' deliberative capacities. Apart from that possibility, staying with the prevailing system might provide a better prospect, given high costs of failing to refocus expectations and a low probability of future encounters with others whose expectations have been successfully diverted.

Persistence of the differing partitions for men and women might rest on differing modes of socialization or even biological differences that give men and women different capacities or opportunities of cognitive access to information about their society. Such assumptions might be unrealistic, but they are coherent enough to enable the model to illustrate the nature of inversion.

Suppose the agents understand their practice as follows: Women's private information conveys the strength of the yin, or female force. The element $\{\omega_1, \omega_2\}$ of their partition indicates strong yin; the element $\{\omega_3, \omega_4\}$, weak yin. Similarly, men's information conveys the strength of the yang, or male force: $\{\omega_1, \omega_3\}$ indicates weak yang and $\{\omega_2, \omega_4\}$, strong yang. The agents thus understand their practice as responsive to and expressive of certain natural or quasinatural forces. They have a common theory about these forces. Strong yin and weak yang works best for women (outcome $o_1$) and the reverse works best for men (outcome $o_4$). Strong yin and strong yang together yield disaster for both (outcome $o_2$), while if both forces are weak then both men and women fare pretty well (outcome $o_3$). Moreover, there are laws or tendencies of coexistence for these forces. Very rarely are they both weak (hence the prior of $\frac{1}{18}$). Only somewhat less rarely are they strong together (hence the prior of $\frac{1}{9}$). They tend to combine either in strengths that favor men or in strengths that favor women, and there is more of a tendency to favor men ($\frac{1}{2}$ compared to $\frac{1}{3}$). If the yin is weak then the yang is almost certainly strong (conditionalization of $\{\omega_2, \omega_4\}$ relative to $\{\omega_3, \omega_4\}$ yields $\frac{9}{10}$). And so on. There is even an academic discipline, political sexology, devoted to a systematic study of these laws. Many professors of this discipline warn that it would be foolish to try to eliminate the gender oppositions and inequalities of social life; the forces of gender cannot be done away with, they say, any more than can gravitation. In the face of attempts at political regulation, these forces would only assert themselves in novel ways, to the detriment of everyone, including women. These agents are caught up in a double inversion, a doctrinal one and a social one. The objectivity of the forces of gender is purely social; it supervenes on the agency of the individuals in society. These forces are those of a self-reproducing system of expectations. Taking away those expectations and their basis in independent agency would break the hold of the forces. Yet the agents involved view the forces as fixed in the nature of things. This is the doctrinal inversion. Individuals mistake a socially based aspect of their agency for a quasi-natural force that their actions respond to and express. The social inversion, on the other hand, is what actually creates and confers (social) objectivity on the forces of gender: in setting up their decision problems, agents treat the regularities of gender-structured agency as characteristics of their decision environment, and this way of making decisions actually gives that aspect of their agency an independent dynamic, thereby turning it into a fixed, given reality with its own nomological necessity.

Theoretically, the social inversion could exist without the doctrinal one. Moreover, given the existence of both, merely seeing the falsity of the doctrinal one would not free an individual from the social one. The two are distinct, though it is easy to see how the social could give rise to the doctrinal, which could in turn help to sustain it. A Marx of gender would want to criticize the doctrinal inversion, perhaps in a work entitled *Gender: A Critique of Political Sexology*, since it would play the same role with respect to the inversion that *Capital: A Critique of Political Economy* does with respect to the fetishism of commodities and capital. The aim of the work would be not only to establish the falsity of the doctrinal inversion but also to display the social inversion as its underlying basis and to probe the latter for its susceptibility to criticism as a social practice.

### 6.5.3 Inversion and reason

But to what could such a critique appeal? It might seem that it could gain no foothold in the reason of the agents caught up in it, precisely because it arises and reproduces itself through their rational deliberation and action. They hold themselves accountable to the conception of rationality as deliberative control. By relying on extrinsic information about the way their system of agency works, they achieve solutions to their respective decision problems, solutions that are rational according to this conception.

It is true that a social inversion involves the realization of each agent's reason in this way. Nonetheless, it constricts deliberative control, and its realizations of reason are stunted realizations. In addition, under some circumstances the agents caught up in it can be faulted for mistakes in problem formulation.

Suppose I am considering whether to embark on a career in philosophy or a career in business. Philosophy would be my choice were I certain I would persist in doing it properly, which in my view inevitably raises more questions than it answers and turns one into 'Socrates unsatisfied'. However, I am worried that I have a character flaw that would divert me from this path and into competitive jockeying for professional status and influence and monetary rewards. Such jockeying would turn me into a 'fool satisfied', a less desirable condition than being Socrates unsatisfied. If I were certain I had the flaw, I would choose to go into business, where instead of the largely trivial games of academia there are plays for real money and power (I am confident in my wiles in either situation, but the rewards in business would be more satisfying). However, I am not certain I have the flaw, and a career in business without it would leave me a frustrated intellectual. So I set up my decision problem and assign utilities to the consequences as indicated in Table 6.4.

With the indicated valuations, it is rational for me to go into philosophy only if the probability I'm willing to assign to having the flaw does not exceed 0.5. Since I deem it more likely than not that I have the flaw, I decide to go into business.

Is there anything wrong with this analysis? Kant would say so. For him, when we take up the practical point of view, we must act under the idea of freedom. We must conduct our deliberations on the assumption that our judgments will depend only on reasons we assess by our own principles and that we can accept and act upon whatever conclusions we reach. We must represent to ourselves our reason, and thus our agency, as having an absolute spontaneity incompatible with the determination of our actions by past conditions and psychological laws, such as those that produce the character flaw. We must view our character

*Table 6.4* Philosophy or business?

|  | Flaw | No flaw |
| --- | --- | --- |
| Go into philosophy: | fool satisfied (0) | Socrates unsatisfied (10) |
| Go into business: | fool more satisfied (7) | frustrated intellectual (3) |

as itself something of which we are the author, something within our free power of choice, something 'up to us'. So I should deliberate about going into philosophy under the assumption that I am capable of staying the course, should the balance of reasons favor it. I should not put the possibility of psychological determination to the contrary into the state-space. Rather, I should represent as available options both (1) going into philosophy and staying the course and (2) going into philosophy and turning to one-upmanship at some point. These sequences are within the scope of my powers of agency. They need not be settled by psychological laws rather than rational deliberation. For Kant then it would never be appropriate to formulate a problem with a state variable representing the possibility that one's character will determine one to act in a certain way in certain circumstances. For him, the satisfaction of deliberative responsiveness requires an assumption of absolute spontaneity.

But does it? A more compatibilist line would not oppose practical reason and psychological determinism in this way. It would not take the practical point of view as ruling out the external determination of our reason, but only the determination of our choice among options by something other than a deliberative procedure that tracks reflective acceptability. So I cannot deliberate about a set of options containing (1) and (2) except under the assumption that they fall within the scope of my deliberative control. Nonetheless, impairment of or interference with that control is always an abstract possibility. And I may have good reason in this case to regard it as a serious possibility or even a practical certainty. If so, then my problem formulation should represent it as such and restrict the feasible set accordingly.

The idea behind deliberative responsiveness as a constraint on problem formulation is that problems should be set up to give as much play as possible to 'the force of reason'. In particular, the formulation should represent factors within the reach of deliberative control by decision variables. Sometimes, however, non-reflective dispositions to act do enter into possible states of the decision environment. Such states would bind action to circumstance in a way that fails to track reflective acceptability. It is the problematic dispositions themselves, and not the problem formulation, that block the force of reason. A problem formulation that acknowledges this fact does not violate the deliberative responsiveness requirement. It merely faces up to a deficiency in deliberative control which, albeit itself a deficiency in rationality, cannot be effectively brought within the scope of decision variables.

However, such a problem formulation would become faulty should it become possible to supplant non-reflective by reflective determination. For example, suppose I come to realize that my tendency to lapse into gamesmanship is fueled by an unreasonable fear of failure or of the consequences of failure. It might be possible for me to hold on to this insight and thereby to rid myself of the impairment. If so, then I should list (1) and (2) as feasible options.

Social inversion is an impairment in the capacity for rational agency that has much in common with the foregoing example. It is not a psychological impairment but a social one. Nonetheless, it is a constriction of the capacity for deliberative control that occurs when non-deliberative tendencies of action become genuine aspects of the decision environment. Sometimes there is no way of preventing it, and agents cannot be faulted for subjecting themselves to it. However, sometimes there is a way out, and to persist is to violate the requirement of deliberative responsiveness.

Consider the formulation in Table 6.5 of the decision problem that confronts women in the system of inversion. So long as the agents in the system have no alternative to independent agency as a way of processing their proto-chicken situations, the states marked here are legitimately viewed as possible states of the decision environment. And the laws that relate these states to one another and that mark the developmental tendencies of the system of agency are legitimately viewed as features of that environment. Yet these states and laws supervene non-reflectively on the agency of the individuals in the system. They connect action and circumstance in ways that do not track reflective acceptability. They are thus agency-produced constrictions in the capacity for rational agency, just as the psychological impairments are.

There is an important difference from the psychological example. There the impairment resulted from an inability to follow through on what would be the rational solution to a problem (we supposed that I would be unable to stay the course were I to go into philosophy, even though that is what reflective acceptability would require). But

*Table 6.5  Top or bottom?*

|  | $\omega_1$ | $\omega_2$ | $\omega_3$ | $\omega_4$ |
|---|---|---|---|---|
| Choose *top*: | $o_1$ (6) | $o_2$ (0) | $o_1$ (6) | $o_2$ (0) |
| Choose *bottom*: | $o_3$ (5) | $o_4$ (2) | $o_3$ (5) | $o_4$ (2) |

here there need be no individual disposition to irrationality; all individuals could be fully rational in the formulation and solution of their respective decision problems. Yet potentially important features of their actions are escaping the reach of decision variables. Moreover, that they are doing so is due to the social form of agency. The system of agency is thus a realization of reason in an unreasonable form. There is a form of unfreedom here, similar to the one that Hegel found in Kant's moral individualism (Section 2.3.3).

However, were there available a deliberative procedure responsive to the requirements of joint deliberative control, collective agency would provide a way for the agents to dissolve the 'second nature' their own agency is generating. They might collectively decide that in the problematic proto-chicken situations, outcome $o_3$ is the unique best outcome, thereby giving women and men reason to choose *bottom* and *left*, respectively, in those situations. Instead, they might decide that given the currently disadvantaged position of women with respect to resources, $o_1$ and thus (*top*, *left*) represent the rational course of action for the time being. Or they might decide that the most desirable course of action will depend on other, more variable circumstances not represented in the independent-agent matrix.[25] Some of these possibilities for collective decision would not involve any reliance on extrinsic information at all. Others might incorporate some randomization based on extrinsic events, as a way of incorporating certain elements of fairness, for example. There would then be reliance on extrinsic information, but it would be under deliberative control. In all these cases the values of the function $s$ would still exist, mathematically speaking, but they would have no non-deliberative social force; in particular, they would not reflect the forces of gender that hold sway in the system of inversion.

When such collective deliberation is available, to exclude the second nature from the scope of decision variables unnecessarily limits the scope of agency, thereby violating the deliberative-responsiveness constraint on problem formulation.

---

[25] The utility functions defining a game, though they carry cardinal significance, are not per se interpersonally comparable with respect to levels or units of any resource or good accorded the different agents by the outcome of the game; this is one reason why the agents may want to take additional information into account in deciding how to characterize the situations of concern to them.

## 6.6    Marx revisited

The case is strong that Marx was grappling with an inverted world of the sort we've displayed. Four points of similarity are important to notice. First, Marx himself stresses the importance of independent agency as a factor in inversion:

> [In commodity production, individuals] exist only materially [*sachlich*] for one another, [a mode of existence] that is only further developed in the money relation, where their communal life itself appears as an external and therefore accidental thing in relation to all of them. That the social context arising through the collision of independent individuals appears at the same time as material necessity and also as an external bond in relation to them represents precisely their independence, for which social existence is to be sure a necessity, but only a means, and thus appears to the individuals themselves as something external, in money even as a palpable thing. They produce in and for society, as social, but at the same time this appears as pure means to objectify their individuality. Since they neither are subsumed under an indigenous [*naturwüchsig*] community nor on the other side subsume their communal life under themselves as consciously social beings, in relation to them as independent subjects it must exist opposite them as something likewise independent, external, accidental, material. This is precisely the condition for their standing as independent private persons in a social context [88, pp. 908–9 (my translation)].

Second, Marx advocates as a remedy a change in the social form of production, to what is plausibly construed as a system of collective agency. He refers to a community of free individuals, regulating their production in accordance with a common social plan, thereby realizing a different social form of the same rationality that Robinson Crusoe takes with him to his island from the world of commodity production [90, pp. 171–172; 95, part 2, 6:109]. Third, as the example in Section 6.5.2 makes clear, an information-based real inversion can give rise to a corresponding doctrinal inversion, just as Marx asserts about the inverted world of commodities and capital. And fourth, though Marx of course does not explicitly formulate or use the concept of extrinsic information, he does describe and attribute importance to the formation of expectations about the economic system itself. In commodity production, the economic success of each producing unit depends importantly on the activities of all. But because of their independence, commodity producers do not confront a given division of labor in which they have an assigned place; nor do they establish labor and resource allocation and product division in advance through the construction of an intersubjectively authoritative social plan. As a result, these important relational aspects of their activities are settled through the mediation of marketability relations among their products—factors such as prices, interest rates, the profitability of various lines of investment, and so on. Producers thus have to base their economic decisions on expectations about the state of the market, a variable they don't control even though it is a function of what they do and what they are prepared to do as economic agents.

Studies have confirmed that extrinsic information can indeed play a role in the determination of such expectations. Intrinsic information in this context would cover 'economic fundamentals', such as technology,[26] resources, endowments, labor-consumption possibilities, consumer preferences, and so on, as well as information about whether or not agents in the economy are rational. Such information is of course relevant to expectation determination. However, there is room for other factors to play a role as well. Suppose that sunspots do not enter into the determination of economic fundamentals. They do not work through the weather, for example, to affect agricultural productivity or the relative desirability of commodities. Even so, they can affect prices, through the mediation of beliefs that they do and information about them. General-equilibrium economic models have been constructed with equilibria depending on such factors. Such 'sunspot equilibria' can be 'rational-expectations' equilibria; they need not depend on systematic forecasting errors by economic agents. The beliefs involved can amount to self-fulfilling prophecies [6; 18; 19; 142]. These models clearly indicate that the sun (as depicted) can serve as a randomizing device in an extrinsic information system that helps to generate price expectations.

However, the randomizing device need not be exogenous to the economic system. Agents quite often do in fact make economic decisions on the basis of expectations formed in light of information about prices themselves and their beliefs about how the economy works. In such cases, the economy itself is serving as their randomizing device. In basing their decisions on their estimations of the course of evolution of

---

[26] I would include here the 'technology' of exchange—feasible moves in bargaining or contracting processes and how they result in exchange transactions.

the economy, these agents are simultaneously treating economic matters as having an independent dynamic and thereby giving them such a dynamic through their deliberation and action. Our account can thus explain how in reifying value and capital economic agents actually give their own actions an alien dynamic.

The account also suggests plausible answers to the other puzzling questions raised in Section 6.1. How does the inverted world of commodities and capital exert and maintain its hold on agents? Answer: through its effects on the informational background of decision. For example, capital realization requires that workers perform surplus labor. What causes negotiations between workers and capitalists to arrive at terms of employment requiring surplus labor? Our account directs us to look for a self-reproducing system of expectations. Some prominent elements in this system would be workers' expectations that competing workers are willing to accept such terms of employment and capitalists' expectations that competing capitalists will hold out for such terms. Other elements would be higher level, for example workers' and capitalists' expectations that workers and capitalists have the foregoing expectations. Such a nested hierarchy can lead capitalists and workers to settle on the required terms, thereby helping to reproduce an informational environment that will support the same hierarchy of expectations and the required terms once again. The bias against workers in this system is analogous to the bias toward outcomes unfavorable to women built into the model of gender-structured agency.

Marx points to a number of other factors that play an important role in the reproduction of the capital-labor relationship. The informational factors work in a mutually reinforcing way with these others. With what Marx calls the 'real' as opposed to the merely 'formal' subjection of labor to capital (see Section 4.4), the dependence of labor on capital and the exploitation of the former by the latter acquire a material and technical aspect, rooted in feasibility conditions and their determinants in individual abilities, production possibilities and the technical and even physical characteristics of means of production. For example, because of the division of labor that developed within the workshop during the period of manufacture, workers came to lack the skills (and not just the economic means) to produce a complete commodity, and as the factory system of modern industry developed they were forced to adapt their movements to those of an automatic system of machinery. The inverted world of capital maintains itself and works its effects through material and technical channels as well as the channels of information. Even so, the informational factors play a key role. Self-reproducing expectations about the necessity of profitability for economic survival and about terms of employment that workers and capitalists will accept are even important explanatory factors behind the contributions of both capitalists and workers to the path of evolution of the feasibility environment.[27]

How can the objectivity of value and capital be purely social, ghostly, and imaginary? It is purely social because it can arise only in a system of independent agency, which is a specific social form of agency. It is ghostly and imaginary because it is not the objectivity of physical, chemical or any other mind-independent processes; the existence and reproduction of specific human attitudes are essential.

What is wrong with the inverted world of commodities and capital? Perhaps many things, but as a system of inversion it is an agency-induced social impairment in the capacity for rational agency. Under what conditions can it be eliminated? When consensual regulation of economic affairs provides a genuine alternative. What kinds of reasons do agents have for wanting to be free of it? Perhaps several, but at least those reasons sketched in Section 6.5.3 deriving from the deliberative-control conception of rationality. It is a realization of reason in an unreasonable social form, and therefore it is incompatible with the realization of a free social world.

One might object that there is nothing intrinsically wrong with inversion, because it might be the case that from a collective point of view the behavior of the inverted social world is perfectly acceptable—even optimal. Let us concede the possibility of such an eventuality for the sake of argument. There would still be a problem as far as freedom is concerned, if the situation had not been collectively evaluated. As far as independent agents are concerned, non-deliberative tendencies of action would still form part of the decision environment. Freedom needs to be self-conscious, and self-consciousness is lacking here. However, suppose that the tendencies of action had been evaluated in a public co-deliberation and found acceptable. Then individuals could at some level regard themselves as acting collectively, as participating in the realization and maintenance of their free social world. This social unity is

---

[27] Some people take Marx's account to focus on the social inducement and repro-duction of values and preferences (for example, Roemer [126, p. 153]). While this idea is is by and large off the mark as an interpretation of Marx, there is room within the framework of this chapter to develop a conception of inver-sion as working through valuational as well as informational and feasibility conditions.

necessary for the estrangement to be overcome. If it is beyond reach, because collective agency is not a real possibility, then there would remain an agency-induced restriction of the scope of rational agency, even though in this case it just happens to be comparatively harmless with respect to the outcomes of the non-deliberative tendencies of action. If it is within reach, then society should take responsibility for the non-deliberative tendencies and either approve of them, in which case they would no longer be non-deliberative, or dissolve them in favor of some other course of action.

# 7
# Rawls: Toward a Well-Ordered Society

## 7.1 Introduction

I begin this chapter with general remarks about the potential relevance of conceptions of estrangement for the critical interpretation and assessment of John Rawls's political philosophy. Then I consider several specific issues within this area.

The following statement of Rawls's principles of justice will suffice for our purposes [117, §§13, 49.1–49.3]:

1. Each person has the same indefeasible claim to a fully adequate scheme of equal basic liberties, which scheme is compatible with the same scheme of liberties for all.
2. Social and economic inequalities are to satisfy two conditions: first, they are to be attached to offices and positions open to all under conditions of fair equality of opportunity; and second, they are to be to the greatest benefit of the least advantaged members of society (the difference principle).

In the first principle, the basic liberties include not only civil liberties but also political liberties, which are required to have a fair value for all. The first principle is prior to the second, and in the second, fair equality of opportunity is prior to the difference principle. These priorities mean that a given principle is to be applied only when prior principles are fully satisfied. In the first principle, a 'fully adequate scheme' is one that allows for the development of the moral powers of free and equal persons to a point that enables their full and effective exercise in judging the justice of society's basic structure and forming, revising, and rationally pursuing a conception of the good. These moral powers are those of moral personality, understood as capacities for rationality and reasonableness, or, in other terms, the capacities for a conception of the good and a sense of justice [117, §§7, 13]. Finally, the difference principle should be consistent with a principle of just savings, which provides a schedule that specifies a level of required real savings for each level of social wealth. Rawls believes that these principles would be chosen over major alternatives in the philosophical tradition, in particular alternatives that incorporate a utilitarian element, in his 'original position', which is a hypothetical agreement situation set up so that the parties to the agreement are placed in fair circumstances for coming to agreement on principles of justice [117, §6]. The parties represent citizens (one representative for each citizen) and are concerned to protect their respective client citizens' fundamental interests in the development and exercise of the two moral powers. They come to an agreement under a 'veil of ignorance' that precludes their making use of information about the social position, natural endowment, or conception of the good of the citizens they represent.

## 7.2    Rawls as a philosopher of estrangement

Notwithstanding Rawls's conception of a purely political liberalism, with its idea of sidestepping important philosophical controversies, his writings evince strong affinities with elements of Kant's and Hegel's philosophical projects and also, at least occasionally, a sense of the importance of engagement with Marx's ideas. These connections implicitly make a concern with estrangement important to his project.

First, there is a specific affinity to Kant's critique of reason. At the most general level, Kant's critical project aspires to be a self-examination by reason through which it removes itself from a state of self-incurred disunity, by working out for itself how all of its various interests, theoretical and practical, are to be ordered or weighed in relation to one another. This effort to work out a 'constitution of reason' makes Kant a philosopher of estrangement, for it is an attempt to put reason into reasonable form. Rawls follows Kant in this effort insofar as his project is aimed at bringing political reason into coherence and situating it with respect to non-political reasons of all kinds. In particular, his effort to reconcile democratic social unity with reasonable pluralism aims at overcoming a form of reason's self-estrangement. Pluralism without social unity is reason in an unreasonable form, as is social unity that rules out pluralism.

Second, Rawls's idea of democratic social unity echoes similar conceptions from the earlier thinkers we've studied: Kant's realm of ends, Hegel's rationally ordered system of ethical life, even Marx's notion of 'an association of free persons who work with means of production held in common and self-consciously expend their various individual laboring capacities as a unified social labor force' [90, p. 173 (my translation); 95, part 2, 6:109]. Each of these social worlds is, in the mind of its author, a realization of freedom. This commonality suggests looking at Rawls's writings in light of the idea of estrangement, an idea shared and developed by the earlier thinkers and signifying a barrier to the social realization of freedom. As we've seen, they take estrangement to be a social condition in which reason is at odds with itself and thereby blocks its own full and free realization.

Third, in spite of some major differences between the social worlds deemed reasonable by Rawls and Hegel, there are some striking similarities.[1] We've already characterized Hegel's 'free will that wills the free will' as a society well-ordered by the concept of freedom, in part because it maintains and reproduces itself as free over time. Similarly, Rawls's well-ordered society is one that through its reasonableness generates its own support and thereby reproduces itself as reasonable. All citizens—for example, the most advantaged as well as the least advantaged—must be able to find the well-ordered society acceptable on the basis of good reasons. Rawls here echoes Hegel's concern to avoid a 'rabble mentality' among both the rich and the poor, a mentality that reflects a state of estrangement, as we've seen. Both Rawls and Hegel recognize a right of moral subjectivity and thereby are concerned with a social world in which its members can be 'at home'.

Rawls's conception of justice aims at fully realizing for all citizens their fundamental interests in developing and exercising their two moral powers. These two powers—the capacity for a conception of the good and the capacity for a sense of justice—correspond respectively to the personal freedom and the moral freedom that Hegel claims to be essential to a free society. Moreover, just as Hegel thinks that these two freedoms require social freedom, through which individuals participate in the collective realization and reproduction of their reasonable social world, Rawls conceives of the citizens of his well-ordered society as able

---

[1] See Schwarzenbach [132; 133] and Bercuson [9] for related discussion. These authors stress affinities between Hegel's and Rawls's projects, though their accounts differ somewhat from the comparison to follow.

to regard themselves as engaged in a collective project of giving each other justice and thereby reproducing their just political society.

Fourth, Rawls shares with these earlier thinkers the view that philosophy (or critical social theory, in Marx's case) plays an important social role. Rawls begins a book on his theory of justice with a consideration of the possible role of political philosophy 'as part of a society's public political culture' [117, p. 1]. The discussion may seem inconsequential, but it signals features of Rawls's project that shape it in fundamental ways. For one might wonder why the discipline of political philosophy, in working out a conception of justice, should proceed in light of any envisaged social role for itself. Why isn't the soundness of its arguments all that matters? Why can't it work out what justice requires without worrying about whether the doctrine that answers this question is capable of filling some pre-assigned social role? Rejecting such a 'Platonic' conception of political philosophy [119, p. 3], Rawls's project proceeds in a self-reflective way, aiming at a conception of justice that could play an organizing role in a well-ordered society and be the focus of an overlapping consensus.

It is true that Rawls would restrict this task to a limited domain, that of the political relationship characteristic of a modern constitutional democracy. Seeking to apply the principle of toleration to philosophy itself, he would reject Hegel's aspiration to unify the social world on the basis of a single comprehensive philosophical doctrine, i.e., one that addresses all aspects of life. For citizens in a democracy cannot reasonably expect agreement on such a doctrine. Rather, we must, he thinks, seek social unity on the basis of ideas rooted in the public political culture of a democratic society, the ideas of toleration and civic respect, for example. Richard Rorty [127] once said that this constraint accords a priority to democracy over philosophy that fundamentally separates Rawls's project from those of Hegel and his forbears. Yet it is precisely the idea of democratic social unity based on a perforce philosophical conception of justice that *connects* Rawls with this tradition. For it is through its elaborated idea of democratic social unity that philosophy plays its educative role in defense of reason. Ideas such as those of toleration and civic respect for persons as free and equal citizens are no less *philosophical* for being *political*. When philosophy assumes its legitimate social role in sustaining democratic social unity, it doesn't simply disappear without a trace; rather, it and democracy come together.

Hegel sees estrangement as a historical development arising in the form of social antinomies growing out of role conflict in the ancient world and depicted most dramatically in the tragedies of Sophocles. It is an objective social condition insofar as existing institutions or practices provide a stunted, distorted or otherwise inadequate embodiment of reason's requirements. However, Hegel views his own social world as one in which roughly speaking[2] all the social conditions necessary for the realization of freedom are present except for the element of cultural explicitness and self-consciousness, which is to be provided in its most adequate form by philosophy. Accordingly, we might call the estrangement he takes himself to be addressing merely subjective. However, there would be something misleading if not inaccurate in this assertion. It is true that Hegel takes the task of philosophy in his historical situation to be that of making explicit the reasonableness of the social world, thereby supplying the missing social self-understanding. But in so doing, on his account, philosophy would effect a change in the social world itself. That world is fully reasonable only when it provides its citizens with the capacity and the resources to comprehend its reasonableness and to act accordingly. In supplying this missing element, philosophy reconciles individuals to their social world and thereby completes the social realization of freedom.

Rawls's ideal of a well-ordered constitutional democracy requires a liberal conception of justice to play an educative role similar to the one Hegel envisages for philosophy.[3] Unlike Hegel, Rawls does not believe that but for the element of self-consciousness, our current social world is fully reasonable. Nonetheless, he assigns to political philosophy important tasks of reconciliation [117, pp. 3–4]. For example, he hopes that a political conception of justice can reconcile us to 'the fact of reasonable pluralism', which is

> the fact of profound and irreconcilable differences in citizens' reasonable comprehensive religious and philosophical conceptions of the world, and in their views of the moral and aesthetic values to be sought in human life [117, p. 3].

He also says that an important task of reconciliation is to extend the scope of real political possibility by elaborating social conceptions that, while utopian in specifying an ideal, are nonetheless realistic in reflecting actual social tendencies.

---

[2] I say 'roughly speaking' because even though all the institutional components that Hegel thought essential to freedom had attained some measure of contemporary realization, there was no single political society that incorporated them all.

[3] See Bercuson [9, chap. 2] for a related discussion.

The idea of realistic utopia reconciles us to our social world by showing us that a reasonably just constitutional democracy existing as a member of a reasonably just Society of Peoples is *possible*. . . . [This] possibility is not a mere logical possibility, but one that connects with the deep tendencies and inclinations of the social world. For so long as we believe for good reasons that a self-sustaining and reasonably just political and social order both at home and abroad is possible, we can reasonably hope that we or others will someday, somewhere, achieve it; and we can then do something toward this achievement. This alone, quite apart from our success or failure, suffices to banish the dangers of resignation and cynicism [and] gives meaning to what we can do today [114, pp. 127–128].[4]

Fifth, and finally, Rawls draws a connection with Marx in cautioning us against pitfalls facing projects of reconciliation:

The idea of political philosophy as reconciliation must be invoked with care. For political philosophy is always in danger of being used corruptly as a defense of an unjust and unworthy status quo, and thus of being ideological in Marx's sense. From time to time we must ask whether justice as fairness, or any other view, is ideological in this way; and if not, why not? Are the very basic ideas it uses ideological? How can we show they are not [117, p. 4n]?

Rawls credits Marx with identifying ideological distortion as a threat to projects of reconciliation. Yet Rawls's work contains very little by way of explicit, systematic exploration of the questions he raises in this passage. Such an investigation would quickly take us to the idea of estrangement, precisely because a society to which its members are (with good reason) reconciled is a society without estrangement.

It can easily happen that the conceptions of a practice of estrangement held by its participants don't properly reflect its underlying realities but rather distort or obscure them and thereby provide the practice with ideological support. In the language of Chapter 6, a real inversion can easily find support in a corresponding doctrinal inversion, which thereby provides a false reconciliation. As we've seen above

---

[4] Note however that this example seems to imply that one can be reconciled to a social world that contains estrangement. Perhaps the task described here is better characterized as a task of orientation rather than reconciliation [117, p. 3]. However, the task of orientation is embraced by Hegel, Marx, and the critical theory tradition as well.

(Section 4.5.2), for example, in Marx's account of capitalism, the participants in individual wage transactions between workers and employers may conceive of them as marking free, bilateral exchanges between equals. However, within the larger context of system reproduction, these transactions disclose themselves as aspects of a self-reproducing, compulsory, unilateral transfer from from one economic class to another. The conceptions of freedom and equality that figure in the individual transactions can both sustain and mask a process of estrangement and exploitation.

If the connection between estrangement and ideology is this tight, an account of estrangement that could be brought into smooth engagement with Rawls's ideas might yield significant insights into the problem of ideology that concerns him. While Rawls's work holds the strong admiration of many individuals (I count myself among them), not so many are prepared to say that he has succeeded in extending the limits of practical political possibility. On the contrary, I suspect that even among sympathetic and knowledgeable readers, the judgment is widespread that his proposals are unrealistically utopian, in spite of their apparent reasonableness and in spite of his efforts to stay close to what is commonly accepted in the political culture. A better understanding of estrangement and ideology might indicate that sometimes a larger rupture in the fabric of what is commonly accepted is needed to open up genuine possibilities for social progress.

## 7.3 Moral estrangement

I want to begin this section by showing how the idea of moral estrangement can figure importantly in a rebuttal of G. A. Cohen's well-known critique of Rawls's envisaged implementation of his difference principle. Then I will discuss how an alternative critique of Rawls's treatment can be grounded in the same idea of estrangement.

### 7.3.1 G. A. Cohen's critique of the difference principle

Consider the difference principle in what Rawls calls its simplest form, in which it constrains only the distribution of income.[5] It says that distributive inequalities are just only if they provide higher income prospects to everyone and moreover are necessary to make the prospects at the lower end of the distribution as high as it is possible to make them.

---

[5] Rawls says 'income and wealth', instead of just 'income', but I will suppose that income and wealth are interconvertible by means of a discount rate.

Rawls's idea is that relatively higher salaries can entice people to make more productive contributions. The productivity gain can often make it possible to benefit everyone (for example, through 'redistributive' taxation), though doing so will introduce inequalities, with some being more advantaged by the change than others. Such inequalities are just only if they are necessary to maximize the income prospects of those in the positions least advantaged by the change.

Cohen focuses on the role of incentives in Rawls's interpretation of the difference principle. He asks how we are to understand the 'necessity' that the principle says licenses inequalities. On a lax reading, this necessity can be intention relative in the sense that it exists in virtue of voluntary choices that people make (for example, they choose to make their productive contribution an increasing function of their incentives). On a strict reading, the necessity must be intention independent and the principle licenses inequalities only if they are necessary to *enable* people to make the relevant contribution, rather than merely to make them *willing* to do so. Cohen objects to the lax reading on the grounds that it is incompatible with the difference principle's intended function as a principle of justice. In a Rawlsian well-ordered society, citizens affirm the principles of justice. Hence they are not in a position to justify making their contributions conditional on the relevant incentives. If they are capable of making those contributions without getting superior advantages in return, then they cannot reasonably expect others to accept their demand for those advantages on the grounds that they are necessary to maximize the prospects of the least advantaged. For it is only in virtue of that demand that the advantages are necessary. It is hypocritical of the more advantaged intentionally to make their contribution conditional on the incentives. Since they affirm the difference principle, they ought to aim more directly in their economic choices at improving the prospects of the least advantaged. That moral incentive should suffice to motivate them, without the added material inducement. It is not sufficient to have moral requirements work only through political power or political structure; they need to have influence, through an 'ethos of justice', on which of the several structurally permissible actions individuals select.

In one of the places where Cohen advances this criticism [24, p. 134], he supplies an epigraph drawn from Marx's 'On the Jewish Question':

> Only when the actual, individual man has taken back into himself the abstract citizen and in his everyday life, his individual work, and his individual relationships has become a *species-being*, only when he

has recognized and organized his own powers as *social* powers so that social power is no longer separated from him in the form of *political* power, only then is human emancipation complete.

Cohen seems to take the rational import of this passage to be that for human emancipation to take place, moral motivation must largely supplant self-interested motivation in everyday economic decision making. However, this interpretation is strongly at odds with our earlier reading of the essay, particularly with regard to its position on morality (Section 3.6). Moreover, the following passage from *The German Ideology*, directed against Max Stirner and Arnold Ruge, comes close to an explicit rejection of Cohen's reading:

[T]he communists do not oppose egoism to selflessness or selflessness to egoism, nor do they express this contradiction theoretically either in its sentimental or in its highflown ideological form; they rather demonstrate its material source, with which it disappears of itself. The communists do not preach *morality* at all.... They do not put to people the moral demand: love one another, do not be egoists, etc.; on the contrary, they are very aware that egoism, just as much as selflessness, *is* in definite circumstances a necessary form of the self-assertion [*Durchsetzung*] of individuals. Hence, the communists by no means want... to do away with the 'private individual' for the sake of the 'general', selfless man. That is a figment of the imagination concerning which [Stirner and Ruge] could already have found the necessary explanation in the *Deutsche-Französische Jahrbücher* [93, 5:247; 94, 3:229].

Marx is referring to the short-lived journal containing 'On the Jewish Question', the very essay whose interpretation is at issue. He not only rejects a Cohen-like reading; in speaking of the general selfless man as a figment of the imagination he lends support to our 'society of these illusions' interpretation (Section 3.6). According to that interpretation, when Marx speaks of the separation between social power and political power (and the need to reintegrate them), he is referring to the abstraction of the universal (political) from the particular (social) that characterizes a political form of moral estrangement that he is in the process of criticizing. Cohen's advocacy of the replacement of self-interested by moral motivation leaves that estrangement in place and fails to give it the criticism it warrants.

Cohen's focus on the individual moral obligations of the more advantaged exposes his position to objections that could have been anticipated on the basis of Hegel's and Marx's ideas concerning the limitations of individual moral subjectivity. In an early stage of the debate he concedes to Scheffler that morality affords to each individual an agent-centered prerogative to pursue his own interests to a reasonable extent, 'even when that makes things worse than they need be for badly off people' [23, p. 302]. Later he concedes to Estlund[6] that given that agent-centered prerogative, others would be hard to deny: namely, prerogatives (a) to promote the interests of loved ones and friends, even when these interests are of little or no moral significance, (b) to meet one's special moral obligations to others that outweigh one's obligation to the disadvantaged, and (c) to pursue other morally significant purposes, within limits, whether or not they outweigh the importance of economic equality. And when Pogge [109] considers variants of a model of the disputed incentive scheme, variants that incorporate various interpretations of Cohen's special moral obligation of the more advantaged, the results seem decidedly counterintuitive. Hegel's ideas on moral estrangement—especially content estrangement and moral individualism—suggest that there are pitfalls like these that threaten efforts to criticize a form of society simply on the basis of rather intuitive and abstract reflection on the moral duties of individuals, without considering the institutional context in which they would be expected to function. Hegel and Marx would not be at all surprised by these vulnerabilities in Cohen's position, which cohere with their view of the ideological character of much moral criticism, in virtue of its tacit presupposition of social conditions that would have to be established as reasonable for it to be cogent.[7]

Moreover, if the task is to find individual moral culprits in the envisaged incentive scheme, why focus on what Kant would call the self-conceit of the more advantaged and not also on the servility of the less advantaged? Why not 'If you're an egalitarian, how come you're so poor?' as well as 'If you're an egalitarian, how come you're so rich?' To be sure, less advantaged individuals are not usually in a position to have a

---

[6]  See Cohen [24, p. 213n36] and Estlund [31].

[7]  Compare Marx's remark that the 'avaricious bourgeois have no need to deny the "promptings of conscience", "the sense of honor", etc., or to restrict themselves to the one passion of avarice alone. On the contrary, their avarice engenders a series of other passions—political, etc.—the satisfaction of which the bourgeois on no account sacrifice' (*The German Ideology* [93, 5:248; 94, 3:230]).

significant effect acting on their own, but neither are more advantaged individuals holding egalitarian views. A better question than either of these is 'If you're a free and equal citizen, a fully equal partner in a scheme of voluntary and fair social cooperation, how come you're so poor?' It is better not because it identifies the real moral culprits, but rather because it invites people to compare their actual social status— the status implicitly accorded them by actual social practice—with their 'official', formal status in the public political culture, namely their status as free and equal citizens.

### 7.3.2  An alternative critique

Rawls explains his understanding of the difference principle in terms of schemes of cooperation and corresponding 'OP curves'. A scheme of cooperation includes public rules that function to organize productive activity, specify the division of labor, and assign roles to persons engaged in production. By varying wages and salaries in a given scheme of cooperation, more may be produced, because 'the greater returns to the more advantaged serve, among other things, to cover the costs of training and education, to mark positions of responsibility and encourage persons to fill them, and to act as incentives.' If we break down society into two groups, the more advantaged and the less advantaged, then corresponding to each scheme of cooperation is an OP curve, which begins at a point of equal division and extends to plot income to the less advantaged as a function of income to the more advantaged (see Figure 7.1). If income to the more advantaged is represented on the horizontal axis and that to the less advantaged on the vertical axis, then the points on an OP curve will fall either on or below the 45 degree line extending up from the origin, since this line represents equal division. Scheme A is *more effective than* scheme B if either (i) A's OP curve reaches a higher maximum than B's or (ii) they have the same maximum, but A's maximum is to the left of B's. The difference principle directs society to aim at the maximum point on the OP curve of the most effective scheme of cooperation (point D in figure 7.1, on the assumption that the curve there represents the most effective scheme) [117, §§18.1–18.2].

What is the domain of schemes from which the most effective is to be selected? I will provisionally assume that it contains all technically and motivationally feasible schemes. That is, all schemes should be included that are compatible with available or potentially available resources,

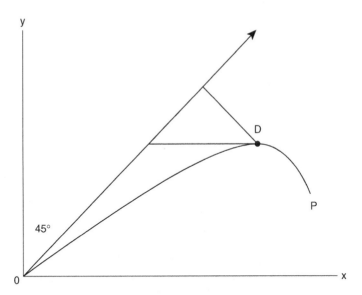

*Figure 7.1*  An envisaged operative point D and its associated triangle

abilities, knowledge, and forms of motivation.[8] On this assumption, we have reason to question Rawls's envisaged implementation of the difference principle only if we can make a reasonable case either that the sort of scheme he has in mind would not in fact fall in this domain or that the domain would contain a more effective scheme than his envisaged one.

The first possibility should not be dismissed, since the feasibility and stability of the motivational psychology required for the envisaged response to the scheme's structure of incentives are certainly open to challenge.[9] Moreover, such a challenge could reflect a concern about

---

[8] I mean this assumption to reflect the requirements of the difference principle itself, as opposed to other requirements that will eventually have to be brought into play, such as the priority of liberty or of fair equality of opportunity.

[9] Nagel [101, p. 116] claims that the required profile of attitudes is not psychologically viable. 'An economically competitive egalitarian with the appropriate partition of motives is supposed to reflect, as he signs the astronomical check for his three-star meal, that although it's a shame that business talent such as his should command such rewards while others are scraping by, there is no help for it, since he and his peers have to be allowed to earn this kind of money if the economy is to function properly. A most unfortunate situation, really, but how lucky for him!'

motivational estrangement. Because Rawls envisages a highly egalitarian scheme, the relatively abstract notion of fairness embraced in his conception might be insufficient to sustain the allegiance of citizens who stand to gain by system alterations in a less egalitarian direction, the material incentives provided by the Rawlsian scheme notwithstanding, if the potential gain would substantially support their pursuit of their deeply held though not universally shared conceptions of the good.[10]

The second possibility, too, is worth considering. Suppose for the sake of argument that the kind of scheme Rawls has in mind is in the domain. Might the domain nonetheless contain a more effective and more egalitarian scheme?

We can bring the motivational question into relief in the following way: Call the maximal point on the OP curve for society's operative scheme the *operative point*. As Rawls envisages it, this point will be a certain distance from the equality line, as a result of the aggregate influence of individuals' self-interested responses to material incentives. Consider the triangle enclosed by the line segment running due west from the operative point to the equality line, the line segment running due northwest from the operative point to the equality line, and the segment of the equality line between its two points of intersection with these line segments (see Figure 7.1). Every point in this triangle other than the operative point is preferable to the latter according to the standard given in the difference principle. That is, any scheme whose maximum is some point in the triangle other than the operative point counts as more effective than the operative scheme. It is also more egalitarian, since its maximum is closer to the equality line. Call this set of points the operative point's *associated triangle*. At every point in this triangle, distributable social product is the same or less in quantity than it is at the operative point. So it is clearly technically feasible to produce the quantities these points represent. It is hard to see what the technical barrier would be to effecting the distributions they represent. The triangle thus provides a context in which we can focus on motivational feasibility.

Like that of Hegel and Marx, Rawls's thought stands out in its recognition of the relevance of social structure to agents' self-conceptions and thus to the actualization of various forms of motivational potential. His conception of a well-ordered society is in large part an attempt to work out the social circumstances in which a political version of

---

[10] In this judgment I am in agreement with Williams [151, p. 32 and passim].

Kant's fact of reason would obtain [111, pp. 553–554]. He understands such circumstances to supply the conditions for a moral psychology of the reasonable, with its characteristic forms of motivation, to come into play. Moreover, he acknowledges not only the social dependence of motivation but its social specificity as well. For example, it is part of his case against utilitarianism as a conception of justice that it would work through a different moral psychology from justice as fairness, and moreover one that would be less effective.

In these efforts, Rawls is implicitly acknowledging the importance of Hegel's effort to identify socially determined motivational conditions for the actualization of freedom. Yet in some respects, he does not fully consider the possibilities opened up by Hegel's idea. He countenances two distinct elementary forms of concern that must be appropriately integrated in a well-ordered society: citizens' rational interests associated with their respective conceptions of the good,[11] on the one hand, and the moral concerns comprised in their sense of justice as fairness, on the other. Social variability derives from the possibility of socially integrating these two kinds of concern in different ways while maintaining the necessary priority of the sense of justice. The fact that Rawls limits himself to these two elements requires him to attempt a delicate balance. He must resist both critics on one side, like Cohen (see Section 7.3.1), who in his view want to expand the scope of egalitarian concern too far into the personal domain, and those on the other side, like Nagel, who think that even he envisages too much egalitarian concern for his conception of justice to achieve motivational feasibility and stability [101, pp. 114–118].

As we have seen, Hegel envisages a richer space of possibilities, one that includes the possibility of an organic relationship between personal concerns and the realization of a reasonable social world. He tries to realize such a relationship by incorporating into his system of ethical life concerns stemming from the individual's position in the social division of labor. If these are genuine, they cannot be analyzed as combinations of purely individual concerns and abstractly moral ones of political fairness. An egalitarian Hegel would view Rawls's system as afflicted by a form of motivational estrangement similar to what he sees in Kantian

---

[11] These concerns are not necessarily selfish in any ordinary sense [110, §43; 115, §43]. But that fact may actually increase the tension between them and the concern for fairness that is supposed to provide an effective and stable sense of justice. As we'll see, they cause difficulties not so much in virtue of their selfish character but in virtue of their independence across individuals.

morality (see Section 2.3.1), and he would appeal to his desired organic relationship as providing a fuller realization of freedom. Marx, too, envisages a richer space of motivational possibilities. His view of this space is in large part determined by his view of economic estrangement and the conditions required to overcome it. According to the analysis of Chapter 6, the susceptibility to estrangement of this kind comes from elements of independent agency operative in the social world. It is in virtue of such elements that individuals' own agency can acquire a dynamic that works against the full realization of their freedom and equality. If it were feasible, the conversion of these elements into a system of collective agency would dissolve that alien dynamic. It would do so by drawing on the distinctive motives characteristic of collective agency, which are neither independent, purely personal motives nor the abstract moral ones characteristic of Rawls's conception of justice as fairness.

We can connect Marx's idea with Hegel's as well as with the analysis of Chapter 6 by thinking of Marx's reference to a society of 'freely associated producers' as a gesture toward an idea of an economic democracy, one that comprises consumers as well as producers, and moreover one that embraces a 'deliberative' ideal.[12] According to this idea, the system of collective agency that overcomes economic estrangement is an association committed to the ideal of a 'co-deliberative' resolution of economic issues—issues of production, distribution, consumption, investment, and so forth. Here 'co-deliberative' connotes a free exchange and consideration of reasons among equal persons, undertaken in an effort to come up with a mutually justifiable joint practical orientation. Though persons may enter this process with preferences informed by their respective conceptions of their good, they modify these preferences in response to reasons so as to make their satisfaction compatible with a justifiable conception of the common good, as determined by the agreed-upon orientation. In this way, the process brings each person's individual interests into an organic relation with the general interest—in Hegel's terms, the particular into an organic relation with the universal.

Rawls does not consider the motivational potential of this form of deliberation, the extent to which it could drive a more effective scheme of cooperation. His guiding idea seems to be that persons comply with the rules of a scheme of cooperation out of moral motivation—a sense

---

[12] See Joshua Cohen [25, esp. chap. 1].

of justice; within those rules, they respond to incentives of rationality in the pursuit of their respective independently formed conceptions of the good. In occluding co-deliberative motivation, this motivational dualism is a form of moral/political estrangement. Moreover, it treats schemes of cooperation as systems of independent agency, thereby making them vulnerable to strategic estrangement (Chapter 6). As we'll see below, this feature of Rawls's conception is deeply rooted in his assumption that the fundamental interests of citizenship lie in the development and exercise of the capacity for a rational conception of the good on the one hand and the development and exercise of a sense of justice on the other. He does not consider whether there is a fundamental interest that lies in the development and exercise of a capacity for the kind of co-deliberation described above.

Rawls's insufficient sensitivity to this idea comes out in his repeated assertion that either property-owning democracy[13] or liberal-democratic socialism can satisfy the requirements of justice. For him the choice between the two systems is not a matter of their intrinsic suitability to justice, democratic social unity, or politically liberal practical reason; rather, it depends on contingent circumstances of history, tradition and culture [110, §42; 115, §42; 117, §42.2]. However, even liberal democratic socialism as Rawls himself envisages it would incorporate more collective decision making in the economy than would property-owning democracy. Yet he does not explore the potential significance of this fact.

There is a remaining issue concerning the technical feasibility requirement. Suppose that technical conditions are contributing to constraints that make a certain amount of inequality necessary. Note that this inequality need not be inequality of income, because the difference principle in its general form is intended to govern the distribution not only of wealth and income but also of what Rawls calls powers and prerogatives of offices and positions of responsibility, and what these are depends importantly on the development of technical knowledge and how it is applied in production. If such inequalities are technically conditioned, the best scheme in the domain as we have characterized it so far could well be a system of estrangement, because such systems can shape the feasibility environment in ways that contribute to their reproduction, along the lines indicated in Section 4.4. This possibility,

---

[13] Rawls takes the idea of property-owning democracy from Meade [96]. For recent discussions of the idea, see the collection edited by O'Neill and Williamson [104].

that estrangement can anchor itself in abilities and other technical conditions, means that it can be subject to a necessity that looks innocent but really isn't. A society that embraced a genuine aspiration to form a well-ordered society would have to begin with a feasibility environment determined at least in part by past systems of estrangement. It therefore could not legitimately take the inherited constraints of that environment as limiting the amount of equality it is possible to achieve. There would have to be a commitment to developing the environment in a direction more supportive of democratic equality. We should not accept without qualification technical feasibility as a constraint on the domain of potentially just schemes.

## 7.4 Economic estrangement

### 7.4.1 Economic instrumentalism

Since in the capitalist production of commodities, what counts for participation in the economy is abstract commodity value and surplus value, regardless of the specific material nature of the commodity and the specific material features of its production, economic estrangement of the sort Marx was concerned with induces an instrumental conception of production, with respect to both the product and the process, and indeed even with respect to individuals' own labor power and their relation to other individuals.[14] Though Rawls does not embrace all forms of capitalism and even explicitly rejects some forms of it ('welfare state capitalism'), his conception of justice mirrors this conception of production, through its specification of the economy's role in the provision of justice. In this respect Rawls's conception has an ideological cast. To see this, we must first consider his account of primary social goods, the goods whose distribution is to be regulated by the principles of justice.

The different primary goods are:

1. Basic rights and liberties
2. Freedom of movement and free choice of occupation against a diverse background of opportunities
3. Powers and prerogatives of offices and positions of responsibility

---

[14] Our analysis thus supports some of the claims Marx makes about the nature and the effects of estrangement in the section in his 1844 manuscripts on 'Estranged Labor' [89, pp. 322–334] without resorting to the essentialism we find there.

4. Income and wealth
5. The social bases of self-respect.

The first principle distributes rights and liberties. The first part of the second principle distributes opportunities. Both are mandated to be equal distributions. Rawls says in 'Social Unity and Primary Goods' [112] that the only permissible inequalities are in the last three categories.

However, there is a problem with the last category, the social bases of self-respect. The status of these goods is somewhat peculiar, in two respects.[15] First, they are not necessarily different goods from those in the other four categories. For example, freedom of movement, one of the primary goods distributed by the first principle of justice, is itself, on its own, a social basis of self-respect. Second, the principles of justice, as embodied in the basic structure, are themselves important social bases of self-respect. As a result of these peculiarities, how the principles of justice distribute the social bases of self-respect is a function of how they distribute the other primary goods (those in categories 1–4 above). Since the difference principle allows for unequal distributions of powers, prerogatives, income, and wealth, it opens up the abstract possibility of unequal distributions of the social bases of self-respect—a possibility Rawls wants to avoid.

Now when Rawls speaks of the social bases of self-respect as primary goods, he has in mind self-respect based on society-wide, public, political mutual recognition ('political' in the broad sense of 'having to do with citizenship'). He acknowledges that there are conditions in the internal life of various associations that have as an effect a kind of localized self-respect [115, pp. 386–388], but the principles of justice do not distribute those conditions (beyond insuring the existence of a sufficient number and variety of such associations to provide each citizen with access to a suitable one[16]). The function of the social bases of self-respect is to constitute the status of equal citizenship; the principles of justice are to insure that everyone has that status, through the way

---

[15] See Doppelt [28] for an argument similar to the one I present in the next few paragraphs.

[16] '[W]hat is necessary is that there should be for each person at least one community of shared interests to which he belongs and where he finds his endeavors confirmed by his associates' [115, p. 388]. Rawls probably thinks that such communities would arise on their own in a well-ordered society, given constitutionally guaranteed basic liberties.

they distribute the social bases of self-respect.[17] Therefore, these bases must be distributed equally; otherwise there would be a hierarchy of citizenship statuses rather than a single status of equal citizenship. Such a result would be unacceptable, since social realization of free and equal citizenship is a central aim of the conception of justice.

So if we conceive of the difference principle as actually generating inequalities in the distribution of powers, prerogatives, income, and wealth, then we cannot regard these primary goods as entering the constitution of the status of equal citizenship. Accordingly, Rawls's conception treats them instead as mere means for the exercise of the rights constitutive of that status—the rights secured by the first principle and its priority over the second principle. In this way, it accords economic life a purely instrumental role: it treats the powers, prerogatives, income, and wealth that are implicated in economic life as means for the enjoyment of democratic citizenship but not as constitutive of it. Consequently, provided the inequalities licensed by the second principle respect the priority of the first principle, they are compatible with the equality of persons as citizens. Political equality is compatible with economic inequality.

However, is the matter to be settled so easily? After all, by contraposition of the above reasoning, if the primary goods at issue in fact provide society-wide bases of self-respect, then they must be distributed equally, because otherwise, there would not be a unitary status of citizenship. By analogy with the rights of political participation, distributed equally by the first principle of justice, consider the powers and prerogatives that define rights of economic participation—rights to participation in the making of economic decisions. It seems that such rights would surely command society-wide recognition. Why then should they not count as social bases of self-respect and thus as partly constitutive of democratic citizenship? If it is correct to characterize them as such, then they should be distributed equally, if there is to be a unitary status of equal citizenship.

We can frame the issue in terms of the choices facing the parties in the original position. What reason would the parties have for not counting rights of economic participation as social bases of self-respect? Their clients might not be interested in their working lives except instrumentally, but then again they might be; the veil of ignorance precludes a definite answer. It would seem to be irrational to

---

[17] 'In a well-ordered society... self-respect is secured by the public affirmation of the status of equal citizenship for all...' [115, p. 478].

ignore the latter possibility. Consequently, wouldn't the parties then want to ensure society-wide recognition of rights of economic participation? And wouldn't then such rights count as social bases of self-respect, thereby contributing to the status of democratic citizenship, and therefore in need of equal distribution?

But Rawls does not have the parties in the original position compare his two principles to alternatives that reflect the distinctive concerns of the socialist tradition with respect to the importance of democratic control over economic life as a condition for the realization of freedom. He does not have them consider principles that would accord the highest priority to extensions of the rights of democratic political participation to encompass economic participation—for example, in collective determination of the most important sectors of the economy, including determination of what is produced and how it is produced, and in collective determination of patterns of distribution. Because of this exclusion, the agreement of the parties on merely the constitutionally guaranteed rights typical of liberal capitalist political democracies lacks the force he claims for it.[18] The exclusion makes Rawls's account open to a charge similar to Hegel's claim that Kant's categorical imperative procedure yields determinate content only in virtue of implicit presuppositions about the reasonableness of background conditions in the social environment. As a result, Rawls's conception becomes potentially vulnerable to the kind of content estrangement discussed in Section 2.3.2. That is, the charge of formalism and abstraction has some force, if not against Rawls's procedure itself, then against Rawls's own use of it. To be sure, he is explicit in asserting that his audience should be able to run an original position exercise with respect to any pairs of alternatives they wish to consider as candidate conceptions of justice, but his own lack of consideration of the alternative sketched here, an alternative, it should be noted, that stems directly from a critical concern with preventing economic estrangement, prevents his results from having the normative significance he would like to claim for them.

### 7.4.2   The index of primary goods

The difference principle in its full generality is potentially concerned with the distribution of three classes of goods: powers and prerogatives, income and wealth, and the social bases of self-respect. It is conceivable then that proper implementation of the principle will have to make use of an index that will enable comparisons of different bundles of goods

---

[18] For related discussion, see Doppelt [28].

from these heterogeneous classes. On Rawls's understanding of the simplest form of the difference principle, the one that governs distribution of income,[19] there is no need for an index.

[The] simplest form [of the difference principle] serves as an example of the use of primary goods to make interpersonal comparisons; it ignores, however, the primary goods under (c) [powers and prerogatives] and (e) [the social bases of self-respect] and hence avoids the problem of defining an index [112, pp. 162–163].

It is not clear why Rawls says this. To be sure, we don't need an index to compare one quantity of money with another. However, surely the parties in the original position would not be satisfied with measuring income in monetary terms alone. They would want to consider an income as an opportunity to choose from a set of possible combinations of goods. The combinations available to an individual depend not just on that individual's monetary income but also on the prices of the different goods. So an income is really a definite sum of monetary value along with a set of prices of the available products. An indexing problem arises because different economic schemes or policies could lead to different relative prices. It might happen that under one scheme of cooperation the worst off face one combination of monetary income and prices, while under a second scheme, those who are worst off face a different combination. Without an index, we cannot compare the relative positions of the worst off in these two schemes.[20]

The problem is still more troubling. Different schemes could lead not only to different prices for the same goods, but to different goods as well. To aim at the maximization of the monetary income prospects of the least advantaged without regard for the qualitative content of the product combinations that income can secure is in effect to conceive

---

[19] Rawls says 'income and wealth', but I am supposing that these are interconvertible by means of a discount rate.

[20] In a footnote, Rawls [112, p. 163n] cites Gibbard [39] and remarks: 'By avoiding the problem of constructing an index and considering the one primary good of income, Gibbard examines what in the text I call the difference principle in its "simplest form".' However, Gibbard avoids the index problem by using a partial ordering (thereby leaving undefined relative positions that present the sort of indexing problems we've been discussing). This construction suffices for Gibbard's purposes (among which are to show that the difference principle is incompatible with the Pareto principle), but it does not show that an index is not required for the difference principle in its simplest form to be sufficiently well defined to serve as a plausible principle of justice.

of income in the abstract way characteristic of commodity production with its category of commodity value, and thus to ignore the problem of estrangement. Surely the parties in the original position would want to take a position on whether this understanding of income as a flow of social wealth in the abstract best captures the need of democratic citizens for income. In addition, such an orientation toward social wealth in the abstract is precisely the factor appealed to by Hegel and Marx in explaining the development of a debilitating division of labor in the workshop and the factory. On the assumption that evidence supports their explanation, income prospects understood in this way would not provide a good indicator of powers and prerogatives, contrary to what Rawls typically assumes [110, p. 97; 115, p. 83].

### 7.4.3   Commodity production again

We considered an argument in Section 4.6.1 that commodity production is incompatible with Hegel's rights of moral subjectivity, which are essential to his conception of 'the free will that wills the free will', i.e., a society well-ordered by the concept of freedom. Can a similar argument be made that commodity production is incompatible with a society well-ordered by Rawls's conception of justice?

The argument in Hegel's case turned on the idea that on his view citizens must be able to understand correctly their economic activities as reason-governed participation in the social division of labor, and they must be able to understand them as such at the time of action, as part of their conscious intention. But commodity production precludes such understanding. Offhand, this argument would seem to apply to Rawls's proposals. A society well-ordered by his conception of justice, and, let us say, with the necessary stability, must be one in which citizens can act with the understanding that they are acting as free and equal participants in its realization and reproduction. But since commodity producers cannot understand their activities in this way except retrospectively (if then), commodity production is incompatible with Rawls's ideal.

This argument may seem too quick, and I want to consider an objection to it. It is true, the objection runs, that producers of commodities cannot act, at the stage of production, with an understanding of their actions as contributions to social reproduction under the description 'participating in the social division of labor', but under certain circumstances they can act with that understanding of their actions under a different description, namely as actions that serve to steer labor allocation toward the production of socially desirable products. Through the

market signals that they generate, producing activities serve this function even when they do not meet with market success, and this function
is an important element in the realization of the difference principle. So
even at the stage of production, producing activities—even those that
are market 'mistakes'—can count as co-implementations of the difference principle and thus as equal participation in the realization and
reproduction of just social arrangements.

What are we to make of this objection? Suppose for the sake of argument that commodity-market dynamics determine labor allocation in a
collectively desirable way. Initially, it may seem coherent to assume that
such a system, which runs on the self-interested, independently made
decisions of private individuals, could be so regarded at a meta-level that
all these individuals, even those that meet with failure on the market,
would count as equal partners in a collective project of labor allocation.
But for them to have this status, their market mistakes and successes
would have to count as outcomes for which they all share responsibility.
It would therefore have to be regarded as appropriate that their costs and
benefits be borne equally by all members of the group and not just by
the individuals directly involved. However, commodity production as
such precludes such equal sharing guaranteed independently of success
or failure on the market. At least it would do so in large markets, where
free-rider problems would lead self-interested individuals to depart from
what market discipline would require. For reasons of self-interest, why
should one bother to respond 'correctly' to market signals when it will
make no noticeable difference to one's distributive share?

One might object that equal sharing would not be required in the
contemplated scheme, but only the sharing required by the difference
principle. Individuals who fail on the market might thereby fall into the
least advantaged group, but that is consistent with collective responsibility for the mistakes, since the difference principle makes prospects in
the least advantaged group as high as it is possible to make them. And,
one might argue, observance of the difference principle is compatible
with commodity production.

There is a subtle confusion involved in this objection. One cannot
simply assume that the difference principle does not itself require equal
sharing in this case. To make this assumption would be to take the
necessity that licenses inequalities to be set by the dynamics of commodity production. And to do this would be to beg the question at issue,
which is whether commodity production can form part of a Rawls's
well-ordered society. If we regard collective motivation as available for
treating market mistakes as collective mistakes, then we must regard

it as available for equal sharing, in which case the difference principle requires equal sharing, contrary to what is compatible with commodity production.

If the above reasoning is correct, the consequences are far-reaching for Rawls's project. If commodity production is incompatible with Rawls's well-ordered society, then it goes without saying that so is any economic regime that joins commodity production with elements of capital, such as property-owning democracy.

Does the argument prove too much? Does it rule out liberal-democratic socialism, for example, and show, say, that only a 'command economy' can overcome estrangement as it is characterized here? Depending on the meaning of 'command economy', such a result might indeed be troubling, perhaps even a *reductio ad absurdum* of this idea of estrangement, or at least of its critical significance. I wish to offer two replies to this objection. First, the argument aims at showing that commodity production is incompatible with Rawlsian justice. If it succeeds, then, independently of whether it casts doubt on the value of the concept of estrangement as characterized here, it raises problems for Rawls's theory, since it shows that one or both of the forms of society that Rawls says can realize his conception of justice cannot in fact do so. For then, since property-owning democracy incorporates commodity production, it cannot do so, and if Rawls's conception of liberal-democratic socialism incorporates commodity production, it cannot do so either. If it is correct, the argument puts pressure on advocates of Rawls's theory to show that there is a possible non-commodity-producing socio-economic system that can satisfy his conception of justice.

Second, however, contrary to the objection, the argument does not undermine the critical significance of the idea of commodity production as a form of estrangement. Participation in the social division of labor at the stage of production requires social planning, but there is no reason to think that it must be exclusively top-down (and hence undemocratic) planning. Nor is the question to ask whether commodity production can be eliminated in one fell swoop. In commodity production producing units act independently of one another for their own separate interests. Both the independence and the separateness come in degrees. The more the independence can be constrained by democratic planning and the self-interested motivation transformed into collective motivation (which is not the same as moral motivation), the less will be the dominance of the value form and the estrangement due to commodity production.

Moreover, the planning involved need not avoid all use of prices and markets (or at least market-like machanisms). Rawls himself calls attention to the distinction between the allocative and the distributive functions of prices [110, §42]. Their allocative function is their role in the allocation of resources; their distributive function is their role in determining the income to be received by economic agents. In commodity production both of these functions hold sway. But their distinction allows for the possibility of their separation, and thus of economic practice that makes use of the allocative but not the distributive function. This possibility makes some room for the certification of producers' labor as part of the labor of society at the stage of production, by making individual income less dependent on individual success on the market. Moreover, such an arrangement is consistent with horizontal as well as vertical coordination, and it need not be part of an exclusively top-down command structure. To be sure, such practices would have to bring into play different forms of motivation from those operative in commodity production. But our analysis has already suggested that Rawls is working with too narrow a range of motivational possibilities (7.3.2).

This last observation suggests a possible interconnection between the moral/political estrangement we examined earlier and economic estrangement, a connection that, as we've seen, Marx asserted to exist (Section 3.6). Such a connection itself would indicate that the mitigation of these two forms of estrangement is not a matter of two separate acts, and that a sequential reduction of one form might need to be intertwined with a sequential reduction in the other. The implication would be that the formation of the necessary political will and the development of economic democracy need to go hand in hand. I am not claiming that the complete elimination of these forms of estrangement is an immediate prospect, or even one for the foreseeable future. But when addressing the question of utopianism it is reasonable to focus on possible progress through changes in the right direction and not just on the abstract possibility and stability of the end state to be achieved or approximated by these changes. And there have been such analyses.[21] Investigations such as these allow the idea that commodity production

---

[21] For presentation of a proposal for an evolving realization of 'multilevel democratic iterative coordination' and a comparison to several other models of socialism, see Laibman [75–77; 79]. See also Laibman [78, chaps. 9–10]. For a very different proposal from Laibman's, see Cockshott and Cottrell [20–22]. They focus on the technical feasibility of comprehensive planning in the absence of commodity production. For further discussion of the importance of horizontal as well as vertical communication and deliberation, see

is a form of economic estrangement to retain its critical significance. It points to reduction of the sway of commodity production in the context of a developing economic democracy.

At any rate, this idea is arguably no more utopian than that of property-owning democracy, one of the two forms of economy Rawls considers to be potentially just, and one that conjoins a strongly egalitarian scheme of distribution with income derived from private property. Here commodity production, with its potential to develop into a system that increasingly subjects the population to the requirements of capital accumulation, casts the egalitarianism in a utopian light. This potential is in fact another reason to doubt the compatibility of Rawlsian justice and commodity production.

## 7.5  Individualism again

There are features of Rawls's conception of justice that partially insulate it from the moral estrangement that Hegel finds in Kantian morality. Rawls's fundamental deliberative exercise is not individual reasoning about personal maxims but rather reasoning aimed at reaching agreement on principles of social justice. This approach provides some protection against the danger of illicitly presupposing the reasonableness of features of the existing social world and thereby falling into estrangement. Yet Rawls's conception remains vulnerable to problems of estrangement and individualism that have a quasi-Kantian cast.

Rawls's conception of the moral powers of democratic citizenship—the capacities for a rational conception of the good and for a reasonable sense of justice—has its origin in the Kantian conception of moral personality, with its heterogeneity between empirical and pure practical reason and its assignment of strict priority to the latter over the former. It is true that in his later work Rawls does not rely on this provenance of the ideas. Rather, he considers their extant role in the public political culture to be what makes them available for the pro tanto justification of his conception of justice. But while this move forsakes the Kantian idea of making them part of the metaphysics of practical reason, their part in the justification of the conception of justice nonetheless accords them a foundational role in generating the problems of motivational estrangement discussed in Section 7.3.2 in connection with implementation of

Cohen [25, chap. 6]. See also Lawler [80], who finds in Marx's writings a specification of stages of what I would characterize as the stepwise interdependent elimination of economic and political estrangement.

the difference principle. Their part in justification also opens the door to the estrangement that can develop out of independent agency (Chapter 6), whether it be economic estrangement narrowly construed or some other form of strategic estrangement.

As with Kant,[22] these problems of estrangement stem from a certain individualism. With Rawls it is rooted in the original position exercise, through which individual citizens subject themselves to constraints of fairness on the rational development and pursuit of their individual conceptions of the good. They do this by agreeing on principles of justice for the design of society's basic structure. These principles, and the corresponding institutional structure, are what are to enable the rational albeit fair pursuit of these individual conceptions. Beyond considerations of fairness, justice is not concerned with the contents of these conceptions, nor with the interrelations among these contents. There are no constraints on individuals to subject their interests to co-deliberative examination and possible modification in response to collectively acceptable reasons.[23] So far as justice is concerned, the pursuits of these conceptions are simply so many exercises in independent agency. This is the individualism. To be sure, the pursuits are constrained by fairness. But fairness is not enough to prevent estrangement.

One result here is similar to a condition that afflicts Kantian morality: heterogeneity and opposition between self-interested motives and those of justice that preclude an organic relationship between them.[24] Without this organic relationship, freedom is lacking, because then, in Hegel's terms, the free will does not will itself as the free will. Individuals, in pursuing their own independent interests, are not at the same time self-conscious participants in the will's self-determination.

One might question this conclusion on the grounds that in pursuing their own interests within the constraints imposed by the rules of the basic structure, individuals are 'giving each other justice'. After all, Rawls goes to great lengths to argue for the stability of his conception of justice. In the early work, he argues that in the normal course of events, individuals will acquire the appropriate sense of justice, and in addition, through congruence, they will find justice to be part of their good. In

---

[22] See Section 2.3.3.
[23] For further discussion of such deliberation, see Cohen [25].
[24] Notwithstanding the fact that this self-interest may contain moral elements. What is key is the independence of the interests rather than any narrowly selfish character.

the later work he drops the original argument for congruence, but he nonetheless argues for the possibility of an overlapping consensus on the conception of justice, a consensus among 'reasonable comprehensive doctrines' in favor of that conception.[25] Thus, one might claim, citizens can view themselves, even in the pursuit of their own individual conceptions of the good, as self-conscious participants in the reproduction of a just society, the same society that sustains them in their independent pursuits.

However, would such a social world realize the freedom appropriate for the citizens of a democratic society? Since the various independent pursuits take place within a setting of interdependence, they could, in a manner consistent with each agent's complying with the rules of a Rawlsian basic structure, form a system of independent agency vulnerable to an inversion of the kind illustrated in Chapter 6, in which individuals unwittingly turn their own agency into a system with an alien dynamic. Such an inversion might take society out of its Rawlsian condition, say by leading to violations of the equal-opportunity principle, the difference principle, the requirement that political liberties have a fair value, or the just savings principle. Some of these violations might not even be recognized, were the inversion to cloak itself in an appearance of necessity—a phenomenon also illustrated in Chapter 6. This possibility raises serious questions about the stability of Rawlsian justice. On the other hand, if the inversion did not take society out of its Rawlsian condition, then there would be estrangement within the context of Rawlsian justice.[26] Either way, there would not be a full social realization of freedom. For agents would be treating potentially important, in principle addressable circumstances and features of action as given factors lying outside the scope of decision, thereby giving them a dynamic

---

[25] Here I set aside Rawls's assertion that a 'more realistic' possibility is a consensus that focuses not on a single conception of justice but rather on a 'class of liberal conceptions that vary within a more or less narrow range' [118, p. 164]. Working with the wider focus would complicate the analysis but would not lead to different results.

[26] For example, something like the system of strategic estrangement described in Section 6.5.2 could lead to what seem to be unfair inequalities of opportunity between men and women. We can imagine that the actions taken in this system are entirely innocent in themselves, and that a coercive remedy would violate the first principle of justice, the principle requiring an adequate set of equal basic liberties. Since the first principle has priority, the behavior of the system would technically speaking not count as a breach of Rawlsian justice.

that lies beyond their control. Their reason would be in an unreasonable social form.

The problem here too lies in an individualism, understood as the pursuit of independent interests in a setting of interdependence. The solution, easy to state but hard to realize, is to make the free realization of each individual's interests a self-consciously necessary part of the free realization of the interests of each other individual.[27] Such a condition requires free, self-conscious participation in the social division of labor. There is no other solution if genuine freedom for all is to be achieved. As we've seen (Section 7.4.3), this solution requires a rejection of commodity production and of capital. In their place there must be a shared authority over economic affairs exercised through genuinely co-deliberative institutions.

Rawls argues that a conception of justice ought to have an individualistic basis:

> The essential idea is that we want to account for the social values, for the intrinsic good of institutional, community, and associative activities, by a conception of justice that in its theoretical basis is individualistic. For reasons of clarity among others, we do not want to rely on an undefined concept of community, or to suppose that society is an organic whole with a life of its own distinct from and superior to that of all its members in their relations with one another. Thus the contractual conception of the original position is worked out first [110, p. 264].

However, the organic relationship between the particular and the universal that we have referred to several times neither rests on an undefined concept of community nor implies the organicist doctrine that Rawls sketches here. It can be spelled out in terms of individuals and relations in which they stand. Yet it is an alternative to the kind of individualism specified above, which generates estrangement.

## 7.6 Conclusion

As we've seen in Section 7.2, there are several ways in which Rawls's work makes available—though he is not explicit about it—ideas of

---

[27] Compare the anticipation by Marx and Engels of 'an association in which the free development of each is the condition for the free development of all' [147, p. 491; 94, 4:482].

estrangement and related phenomena for use in contemporary political philosophy. It is instructive to read these ideas as going back through Marx and German idealism to Kant's notion of a self-critique of reason. Viewing them in this context can bring out the significance of the work of these earlier thinkers for the interpretation and assessment of Rawls's contributions. It can also enable a more direct engagement of those contributions with work that is more explicitly in the critical theory tradition.

Once we read Rawls as stepping into these waters, however, we can discern certain pressures on his ideas to develop in a certain direction. In particular, it becomes clear that his work is not sensitive enough as it stands to pitfalls connected with moral and economic estrangement, and more generally with strategic estrangement (Chapter 6).

Rawls's conceptions of justification seek to accommodate what he calls the fact of reasonable pluralism, that the conscientious exercise of reason under democratic institutions inevitably produces a pluralism of competing, fundamentally incompatible comprehensive doctrines of morality and the human good. The ideas he takes to be available for fashioning a justifiable conception of justice are in his view the products of a historical process whereby persons holding such conflicting doctrines have learned what it takes to cooperate with each other on the basis of mutual respect. I do not wish to deny this. On the contrary, my view is that Rawls's attempt to integrate political reason with reasons deriving from comprehensive views is an important contribution to the critique of estrangement and to the task of political philosophy as reconciliation. But the possibility of various forms of estrangement complicates the picture considerably. Let us acknowledge that a pluralism can distill from itself a supply of common normative ideas, such as Rawls's idea of society as a fair system of cooperation, that provide potential candidates for grounding social unity. There is no reason to think that this supply will be the same in the case of every possible pluralism. Drawing on some ideas from Hegel and Marx, I have tried to argue both that the ideas Rawls is working with may provide too thin and abstract a basis for democratic social unity and that they may have in part an ideological character, as expressions of and accommodations to various forms of estrangement in the social world as a whole. While these claims might seem to warrant a pessimism about the possibilities of democratic social unity, I don't think they do. A pluralism existing under conditions of estrangement need not be the same pluralism as would exist in a democratic social world that is relatively free of estrangement and includes a larger commitment to economic democracy. We do not yet know whether the latter form of pluralism would allow a more substantial, less ideological and hence more effective supply of ideas to serve as a basis for democratic social cooperation.

# Appendix A: Supplement to Chapter 5

## A.1 Construction of system E*

The purposes of this section are:

1. To provide details of the transformation discussed in Section 5.3 of system E into system E*
2. To use system E* to illustrate the claim argued for in Section 5.3 that Marx's Equation 5.14, which equates the rate of profit with the aggregate amount of surplus value produced in the economy divided by the value of the aggregate amount of capital advanced in the economy, holds in economies in a configuration of maximal balanced growth.

For the reader's convenience I repeat in Table A.1 the input-output relations for system E, earlier provided in Table 5.1.

Consider a hypothetical transformation of system E into a new system E* effected by eliminating the luxury sector (whiskey) and allocating its labor to the other sectors so as to allow the system to sustain a maximal rate of balanced growth. Call this rate of growth $R$. We can effect the transformation by changing the scale of the iron industry by a factor of $x$ and the corn industry by a factor of $y$, where $x$ and $y$ are such that in the resulting economy, (1) iron output equals $(1+R)$ times total iron input to the economy, (2) corn output equals $(1+R)$ times total corn input (whether as means of production or wage good), and (3) the total labor input is all the labor expended in system E, namely 24,000 units. Table A.2 thus gives us an initial description of the input-output relations of E*. The requirements that the adjustments yield balanced growth and that all 24,000 units of labor are used are captured by the following equations:

$$42,000x = (1+R)(36,000x + 3,000y),$$

$$15,000y = (1+R)(6,000y + 6,000),$$

$$6,000x + 15,000y = 24,000.$$

Table A.1  System E

| | Iron | Corn | Labor | → | Iron | Corn | Whiskey | Labor power |
|---|---|---|---|---|---|---|---|---|
| Iron industry | 36,000 | | 6,000 | | 42,000 | | | |
| Corn industry | 3,000 | 6,000 | 15,000 | | | 15,000 | | |
| Whiskey industry | 3,000 | 3,000 | 3,000 | | | | 3,000 | |
| Labor power | | 6,000 | | | | | | 3,000 |
| Totals | 42,000 | 15,000 | 24,000 | | 42,000 | 15,000 | 3,000 | 3,000 |

Table A.2  System E* (1)

| | Iron | Corn | Labor | → | Iron | Corn | Labor power |
|---|---|---|---|---|---|---|---|
| Iron industry | 36,000x | | 6,000x | | 42,000x | | |
| Corn industry | 3,000y | 6,000y | 15,000y | | | 15,000y | |
| Labor power | | 6,000 | | | | | 3,000 |
| Totals | 36,000x+ 3,000y | 6,000y+ 6,000 | 6,000x+ 15,000y | | 42,000x | 15,000y | 3,000 |

The solution is: $\{y = .82093, R = .12708, x = 1.9477\}$.[1] Using these values, we can calculate the quantities in Table A.2 to get the figures in Table A.3.

Value accounting for E* yields the same solutions for $\lambda_1$, $\lambda_{1p}$, and $\lambda_2$ as those in E, since the coefficients in their equations are proportional to those in Equations 5.15, 5.16, and 5.18, respectively. Similarly, the price accounting yields the same values for $p_1$, $p_2$, $w$, and $\pi$. However, in this case, unlike the case of system E, $S/(C + V) = \pi$, in accordance

[1] Note that the value for $R$ is the same as the value we obtained for $\pi$ in system E, thereby confirming our thought that the rate of profit reflects the growth potential of the economy.

*Table A.3* System E* (2)

| | Iron | Corn | Labor | → | Iron | Corn | Labor power |
|---|---|---|---|---|---|---|---|
| Iron industry | 70,117 | | 11,686 | | 81,803 | | |
| Corn industry | 2,463 | 4,926 | 12,314 | | | 12,314 | |
| Labor power | | 6,000 | | | | | 3,000 |
| Totals | 72,580 | 10,926 | 24,000 | | 81,803 | 12,314 | 3,000 |

with Marx's theory:[2]

$$\frac{S}{C+V} = \frac{(81,803 - 72,580)\lambda_1 + (12,314 - 10,926)\lambda_2}{72,580\lambda_1 + 10,926\lambda_2} \tag{A.1}$$

$$= \frac{11,999}{94,438} \tag{A.2}$$

$$= .12706 \tag{A.3}$$

$$= \pi \text{ (within the limits of rounding error).} \tag{A.4}$$

This result is not a coincidence. As shown in Section 5.3, Marx's theory is true of any economy in maximal balanced growth.

## A.2   A Perron-Frobenius theorem

Perron [108] and Frobenius [36–38] develop several results concerning the eignenvalues and eigenvectors of non-negative matrices. The ones appealed to in Section A.3 are stated here without proof.[3]

*Definition.*   An $m \times n$ matrix $A$ is *non-negative* (written $A \geq 0$) if each of its elements $a_{ij} \geq 0$. In general, $A \geq B$ (or $B \leq A$) if $a_{ij} \geq b_{ij}$ for all $i$ and $j$. $A$ is *positive* (written $A > 0$) if each $a_{ij} > 0$. In general, $A > B$ (or $B < A$) if $a_{ij} > b_{ij}$ for all $i$ and $j$.

---

[2] Both the numerator and the denominator of the fraction to the right of the equals sign in Equation A.1 are obtained from the last line of Table A.3. The numerator is the value of the surplus iron (output minus input) plus the value of the surplus corn produced in the economy; this value sum is the total amount of surplus value produced in the economy. The denominator is the value of the capital invested in the form of iron plus the value of the capital invested in the form of corn (whether as constant or variable capital); the result is the value of the total amount of capital advanced.

[3] See also Debreu and Herstein [27].

*Definition.* Let $A$ be an $n \times n$ matrix whose entries $a_{ij}$ are all real numbers. If there exist a real number $\alpha$ and a non-zero row vector $p = (p_1, \ldots, p_n)$ such that $pA = \alpha A$, then $\alpha$ is an *eigenvalue* of $A$ and $p$ a *left eigenvector* of $A$ corresponding to $\alpha$. Similarly, a non-zero column vector $x = (x_1, \ldots, x_n)'$ such that $Ax = \alpha x$ is a *right eigenvector* of $A$ corresponding to $\alpha$.

*Definition.* An $n \times n$ matrix $A$ is *indecomposable* (or *irreducible*) if no simultaneous permutation of its rows and corresponding columns can put it into the form:

$$\begin{bmatrix} A_{11} & A_{12} \\ 0 & A_{22} \end{bmatrix}$$

where $A_{11}$ and $A_{22}$ are square and 0 is the null matrix.

*Theorem.* Let $A \geq 0$ be indecomposable, and let $\alpha = \sup\{|\beta| : \beta$ is an eigenvalue of $A\}$. Then

1. $\alpha$ is a positive eigenvalue of $A$.
2. $\alpha$ is associated with a left eigenvector $p > 0$ (with suitable scaling)
3. $|\beta| \leq \alpha$ for all eigenvalues $\beta$ of $A$ (and thus we may call $\alpha$ the maximal (or dominant) eigenvalue of A).
4. There is no non-negative eigenvector of $A$ other than multiples of $p$.
5. $\alpha$ is an increasing function of each element of $A$; that is, $\alpha$ increases when any element of $A$ increases.
6. $\alpha$ is a simple root of the characteristic equation of $A$.

*Remark.* The theorem has been stated as applying to the left eigenvector of $A$ corresponding to $\alpha$. It also holds for a corresponding right eigenvector.

## A.3   The 'Fundamental Marxian Theorem'

This theorem states that the rate of profit is positive if and only if the rate of exploitation is positive. To see how it can be established, consider the augmented input coefficient matrix $A^+$, defined as follows:

$$A^+ = A + \frac{1}{d}BL. \tag{A.5}$$

Here $A$ is the matrix $[a_{ij}]$ of unit input coefficients of means of production. It specifies for each commodity the amounts of the various means of production needed to produce a unit of it. $B$ is the column vector

$(b_1, \ldots, b_n)'$ of commodities entering into a worker's daily subsistence needs, $L$ is the row vector of unit direct labor input coefficients, and $d$ is the length of the working day in hours. $\frac{1}{d}B$ is the real per-hour wage rate, and the matrix $\frac{1}{d}BL$ is a matrix specifying for each commodity the various amounts of worker-subsistence goods necessary to produce a unit of it. And so $A^+$ is the matrix $\lfloor a_{ij}^+ \rfloor_{n \times n}$, which specifies for each commodity its *total* input requirements, whether as means of production or wage goods. That is, $a_{ij}^+$ is the amount of commodity $i$ needed, whether as means of production or wage good, to produce a unit of commodity $j$:

$$a_{ij}^+ = a_{ij} + \frac{1}{d}b_i l_j.$$

We may now specify a complete set of price equations:

$$p = (1 + \pi)(pA + wL), \tag{A.6}$$

$$w = \frac{pB}{d}, \tag{A.7}$$

$$p_1 = 1. \tag{A.8}$$

Equations A.6 express the requirement that at equilibrium there is a uniform rate of profit $\pi$ throughout the economy and in each industry the monetary value of the gross output is equal to $(1 + \pi)$ times the monetary cost of the inputs, including the cost of the labor inputs, $wL$. Equation A.7 states that hourly wages just enable each worker to purchase the hourly real wage basket. Equation A.8 reflects an arbitrary assumption that commodity 1 is the money commodity. Combining A.6 and A.7 and using the definition of $A^+$ (A.5), we may write

$$p = (1 + \pi)pA^+ \tag{A.9}$$

$$pA^+ = \frac{1}{1 + \pi}p. \tag{A.10}$$

If we assume that there is no luxury production, then $A^+$ is non-negative and indecomposable.[4] Then by the Perron-Frobenius theorem stated in Section A.2, there is a unique pair $(\pi, p)$ satisfying Equation A.10 in which $p > 0$ is the left eigenvector of $A^+$ associated with its maximal

---

[4] For definitions of the notions of indecomposability, eigenvalue, and eigenvector used in this paragraph, see Section A.2. If there is no luxury production, then every commodity enters either directly or indirectly into the production of every commodity, and consequently there is no way to put the matrix $A^+$ into the form required for decomposability.

eigenvalue $1/(1+\pi)$. Hence $\pi$ is the equilibrium rate of profit and $p$ the equilibrium relative price vector.

By the same theorem, there is also a strictly positive right eigenvector $x$:

$$\frac{1}{1+\pi}x = A^+x \tag{A.11}$$

and so

$$x = (1+\pi)(A + \frac{1}{d}BL)x. \tag{A.12}$$

To prove the theorem,[5] pre-multiply A.12 by $\Lambda$ to get

$$\Lambda x = (1+\pi)(\Lambda A + \frac{1}{d}\Lambda BL)x. \tag{A.13}$$

We know that the rate of exploitation $e$ is defined by

$$e = \frac{d-\Lambda B}{\Lambda B} = \frac{d}{\Lambda B} - 1 \tag{A.14}$$

and hence

$$\Lambda B = \frac{d}{1+e}. \tag{A.15}$$

Substituting for $\Lambda B$ in A.13, we get:

$$\Lambda x = (1+\pi)(\Lambda A + \frac{1}{1+e}L)x. \tag{A.16}$$

Since $\Lambda > 0$, $A \geq 0$, and $x > 0$, and since we may assume that $e \geq 0$[6] and $L > 0$, we may write

$$1 + \pi = \frac{\Lambda x}{(\Lambda A + \frac{1}{1+e}L)x} \tag{A.17}$$

$$= \frac{(\Lambda A + L)x}{(\Lambda A + \frac{1}{1+e}L)x}. \tag{A.18}$$

From A.18 it is clear that

$$\pi > 0 \leftrightarrow e > 0. \tag{A.19}$$

[5] The proof given here of the fundamental Marxian Theorem essentially follows that of Roemer [125, pp. 16–17].
[6] That $e < 0$ would imply that the economy was not reproducing itself, since workers would be working for fewer hours than required to reproduce their daily subsistence.

This completes the proof of the theorem.

We can say more about the relation between the rate of profit and the rate of exploitation. The Perron-Frobenius theorem stated in Section A.2 tells us that $1/(1+\pi)$, the maximal eigenvalue of $A^+$, is a continuous, strictly increasing function of each element of $A^+$. Therefore, $\pi$ is a continuous, strictly decreasing function of each element of $A^+$. Thus, for example, if an element $a_{ij}^+$ decreases, then, other things equal,[7] $\pi$ increases. But since

$$a_{ij}^+ = a_{ij} + \frac{1}{d}b_i l_j,$$

$\pi$ is also a strictly decreasing function of $a_{ij}$, $b_i$, and $l_j$, for all $i$ and $j$, and a strictly increasing function of $d$. Now consider the rate of exploitation $e$. Using 5.11 and A.14 we may write:

$$e = \frac{d - \Lambda B}{\Lambda B} = \frac{d}{L(I-A)^{-1}B} - 1 = \frac{d}{\sum_{i=0}^{\infty} LA^i B} - 1. \tag{A.20}$$

It is clear from A.20 that $e$ is *also* a strictly decreasing function of $a_{ij}$, $b_i$, and $l_j$, for all $i$ and $j$, and a strictly increasing function of $d$.

It follows that changes in the rate of profit and the rate of exploitation are inversely related in the following sense: An increase in $e$, which must occur either through a decrease in some $a_{ij}$, $b_i$, or $l_j$ or through an increase in $d$, will increase $\pi$, other things equal.[8] Conversely, an increase in $\pi$, which must occur either through a decrease in some $a_{ij}$, $b_i$, or $l_j$ or through an increase in $d$, will increase $e$, other things equal. Similarly, a decrease in $e$ will decrease $\pi$, other things equal, and conversely. These elementary dynamic[9] relationships among price-level variables, value-level variables, and material variables, relationships that figure importantly in the volume 1 accounts of struggles over the length of the working day, of the real subjection of labor to capital, and of the reproduction of the capital-labor relationship, retain their relevance in the more generalized setting that is the focus of Volume 3. Combined with the fundamental Marxian theorem, these relationships make it possible to extend Marx's account of profits as an expression of surplus labor and of capital as estranged labor to the case of unequal organic compositions of capital.

---

[7] That is, the other elements of $A^+$ remain constant.
[8] By 'other things equal' I mean that the changes referred to in $a_{ij}$, $b_i$, $l_j$ and $d$ are not accompanied by other changes in the opposite direction.
[9] Strictly speaking, comparative-static.

# Bibliography

[1] Gilbert Abraham-Frois and Edmond Berrebi. *Theory of Value, Prices and Accumulation*. Cambridge University Press, Cambridge, 1979.

[2] Robert J. Aumann. Subjectivity and correlation in randomized strategies. *Journal of Mathematical Economics*, 1:67–96, 1974.

[3] Robert J. Aumann. Survey of repeated games. In *Essays in Game Theory and Mathematical Economics in Honor of Oskar Morgenstern*, pages 11–42. Wissenschaftsverlag, Bibliographisches Institut, Mannheim, Wien and Zurich, 1981.

[4] Robert J. Aumann. Correlated equilibrium as an expression of Bayesian rationality. *Econometrica*, 55:1–18, 1987.

[5] Shlomo Avineri. Labor and social classes in Hegel's *Realphilosophie*. *Philosophy and Public Affairs*, 1 (1):96–119, Autumn 1971.

[6] Costas Azariadis. Self-fulfilling prophecies. *Journal of Economic Theory*, 25:380–396, 1981.

[7] Nicholas Bardsley. On collective intentions: Collective action in economics and philosophy. *Synthese*, 157:141–159, 2007.

[8] William J. Baumol and Thijs ten Raa. Wassily Leontief: In appreciation. *European Journal of the History of Economic Thought*, 16 (3):511–522, September 2009.

[9] Jeffrey Bercuson. *John Rawls and the History of Political Thought: The Rousseauvian and Hegelian Heritage of Justice as Fairness*. Routledge, New York, 2014.

[10] Ladislaus von Bortkiewicz. Wertrechnung und Preisrechnung im Marxschen System, I. *Archiv für Sozialwissenschaft und Sozialpolitik*, 23 (1):1–50, 1906.

[11] Ladislaus von Bortkiewicz. Zur Berichtigung der grundlegenden theoretischen Konstruktion von Marx im 3. Band des "*Kapital*". *Jahrbücher für Nationalökonomie und Statistik*, 34:319–335, 1907.

[12] Ladislaus von Bortkiewicz. Wertrechnung und Preisrechnung im Marxschen System, II. *Archiv für Sozialwissenschaft und Sozialpolitik*, 25 (1):10–51, 1907.

[13] Ladislaus von Bortkiewicz. Wertrechnung und Preisrechnung im Marxschen System, III. *Archiv für Sozialwissenschaft und Sozialpolitik*, 25 (2):445–488, 1907.

[14] Ladislaus von Bortkiewicz. On the correction of Marx's fundamental theoretical construction in the third volume of *Capital*. In Paul M. Sweezy, editor, *Karl Marx and the Close of His System & Böhm Bawerk's Criticism of Marx*, pages 199–221. Augustus M. Kelley, New York, 1949.

[15] Ladislaus von Bortkiewicz. Value and price in the Marxian system. *International Economic Papers*, 2:5–60, 1952.

[16] Adam Brandenburger and Eddie Dekel. Rationalizability and correlated equilibria. *Econometrica*, 55:1391–1402, 1987.

[17]  Adam Brandenburger and Edie Dekel. The role of common knowledge assumptions in game theory. In Frank Hahn, editor, *The Economics of Missing Markets, Information and Games*, pages 46–61. Clarendon Press, Oxford, 1989.

[18]  Stephen Burnell. Sunspots. In Frank Hahn, editor, *The Economics of Missing Markets, Information and Games*, pages 394–409. Clarendon Press, Oxford, 1989.

[19]  David Cass and Karl Shell. Do sunspots matter? *Journal of Political Economy*, 91:193–227, 1983.

[20]  W. P. Cockshott and Allin F. Cottrell. *Towards a New Socialism*. Bertrand Russell Press, Nottingham, 1993.

[21]  W. P. Cockshott and Allin F. Cottrell. Value, markets and socialism. *Science and Society*, 61 (3):330–357, Fall 1997.

[22]  W. P. Cockshott and Allin F. Cottrell. Contribution to 'Designing socialism: Visions, projections, models'. *Science and Society*, 76 (2):151–154, 195–198, 213–215, 230–234, 251–253, April 2012.

[23]  G. A. Cohen. Incentives, inequality, and community. In Grethe B. Peterson, editor, *The Tanner Lectures on Human Values*, volume 13, pages 263–329. University of Utah Press, Salt Lake City, 1992.

[24]  G. A. Cohen. *If You're an Egalitarian, How Come You're So Rich?* Harvard University Press, Cambridge, Mass. and London, 2000.

[25]  Joshua Cohen. *Philosophy, Politics, Democracy: Selected Essays*. Harvard University Press, Cambridge, Mass. and London, 2009.

[26]  Lucio Colletti. A political and philosophical interview. *New Left Review*, (86):3–28, July–August 1974.

[27]  Gerard Debreu and I. N. Herstein. Nonnegative square matrices. *Econometrica*, 21 (4):597–607, October 1953.

[28]  Gerald Doppelt. Rawls' system of justice: A critique from the left. *Nous*, 15 (3):259–307, September 1981.

[29]  Will Dudley. *Hegel, Nietzsche, and Philosophy*. Cambridge University Press, Cambridge and New York, 2002.

[30]  Jon Elster. *Making Sense of Marx*. Cambridge University Press, Cambridge, 1985.

[31]  David Estlund. Liberalism, equality, and fraternity in Cohen's critique of Rawls. *Journal of Political Philosophy*, 6:99–112, 1998.

[32]  Ludwig Feuerbach. *Principles of the Philosophy of the Future*. Bobbs-Merrill, Indianapolis, 1966.

[33]  Ludwig Feuerbach. Preliminary theses on the reform of philosophy. *The Fiery Brook: Selected Writings of Ludwig Feuerbach*. Doubleday, Garden City, NY, 1972. Trans. Zawar Hanfi.

[34]  Ludwig Feuerbach. *The Essence of Christianity*. Prometheus Books, Amherst, NY, 1989.

[35]  Paul W. Franks. *All or Nothing: Systematicity, Transcendental Arguments, and Skepticism in German Idealism*. Harvard University Press, Cambridge, Mass. and London, 2005.

[36]  Georg Frobenius. Über Matrizen aus positiven Elementen. *Sitzungsberichte der Königlich Preussischen Akademie der Wissenschaften*, pages 471–476, 1908.

[37]  Georg Frobenius. Über Matrizen aus positiven Elementen II. *Sitzungsberichte der Königlich Preussischen Akademie der Wissenschaften*, pages 514–518, 1909.

[38]  Georg Frobenius. Über Matrizen aus nicht negativen Elementen. *Sitzungs-berichte der Königlich Preussischen Akademie der Wissenschaften*, pages 456–477, 1912.

[39]  Allan Gibbard. Disparate goods and Rawls' difference principle: A social choice theoretic treatment. *Theory and Decision*, 11:267–288, 1979.

[40]  Margaret Gilbert. *On Social Facts*. Routledge, London and New York, 1989.

[41]  Margaret Gilbert. Walking together: A paradigmatic social phenomenon. *Midwest Studies in Philosophy*, 15:1–14, 1990.

[42]  Jürgen Habermas. *Knowledge and Human Interests*. Beacon Press, Boston, 1971.

[43]  Jürgen Habermas. *Theory and Practice*. Beacon Press, Boston, 1975.

[44]  Jürgen Habermas. *The Theory of Communicative Action*, volume 1. Beacon Press, Boston, 1984.

[45]  Jürgen Habermas. *The Theory of Communicative Action*, volume 2. Beacon Press, Boston, 1989.

[46]  John C. Harsanyi and Reinhard Selten. *A General Theory of Equilibrium Selection in Games*. The MIT Press, Cambridge, Mass. and London, 1988.

[47]  G. W. F. Hegel. *Natural Law*. University of Pennsylvania Press, 1975. Trans. T. M. Knox.

[48]  G. W. F. Hegel. *Phenomenology of Spirit*. Oxford University Press, Oxford and New York, 1977. Trans. A. V. Miller.

[49]  G. W. F. Hegel. *System of Ethical Life and First Philosophy of Spirit*. State University of New York Press, Albany, 1979.

[50]  G. W. F. Hegel. *Hegel and the Human Spirit: A Translation of the Jena Lectures on the Philosophy of Spirit (1805–6)*. Wayne State University Press, 1983.

[51]  G. W. F. Hegel. *The Encyclopedia Logic*. Hackett Publishing Company, Inc., Indianapolis and Cambridge, 1991.

[52]  G. W. F. Hegel. *Elements of the Philosophy of Right*. Cambridge University Press, Cambridge, 1991. Trans. H. B. Nisbet.

[53]  G. W. F. Hegel. *Lectures on Natural Right and Political Science: The First Philosophy of Right*. University of California Press, Berkeley, Los Angeles and London, 1995. Trans. J. Michael Stewart and Peter C. Hodgson.

[54]  G. W. F. Hegel. *The Philosophy of History*. Dover Publications, Inc., New York, 1956.

[55]  G. W. F. Hegel. *On Christianity*. Harper Torchbooks, 1961.

[56]  G. W. F. Hegel. *Gesammelte Werke*. Felix Meiner Verlag, Hamburg, 1968.

[57]  G. W. F. Hegel. *Werke in zwanzig Bänden*. Suhrkamp Verlag, Frankfurt am Main, 1969.

[58]  G. W. F. Hegel. *Philosophy of Mind*. Clarendon Press, Oxford, 1971.

[59]  G. W. F. Hegel. *Philosophie des Rechts: Die Vorlesungen von 1819/1820*. Suhrkamp Verlag, Frankfurt, 1983.

[60]  Axel Honneth. *Pathologies of Reason: On the Legacy of Critical Theory*. Columbia University Press, New York, 2009.

[61]  Axel Honneth. *The Pathologies of Individual Freedom*. Princeton University Press, Princeton and Oxford, 2010.

[62]  Axel Honneth. *The I in We*. Polity Press, Cambridge, 2012.

[63]  Max Horkheimer. *Traditional and Critical Theory*. Herder and Herder, New York, 1972.

[64]  Max Horkheimer and Theodor W. Adorno. *Dialectic of Enlightenment.* Stanford University Press, Stanford, 2007.

[65]  Rahel Jaeggi. *Alienation.* Columbia University Press, New York, 2014.

[66]  Immanuel Kant. *Immanuel Kants Schriften.* W. de Gruyter, Berlin, 1902. Ausgabe der königlich preussischen Akademie der Wissenschaften.

[67]  Immanuel Kant. *Practical Philosophy.* Cambridge University Press, Cambridge, 1996.

[68]  Immanuel Kant. *Critique of Practical Reason.* Cambridge University Press, Cambridge, 1997.

[69]  Immanuel Kant. *Groundwork of the Metaphysics of Morals.* Cambridge University Press, Cambridge, 1997.

[70]  Immanuel Kant. *Religion Within the Boundaries of Mere Reason.* Cambridge Texts in the History of Philosophy. Cambridge University Press, Cambridge, 1998. Trans. Allen Wood.

[71]  Immanuel Kant. *Critique of Pure Reason.* Cambridge University Press, Cambridge, 1998.

[72]  Immanuel Kant. *Critique of Practical Reason.* Hackett Publishing Company, Inc., Indianapolis and Cambridge, 2002. Trans. Werner S. Pluhar.

[73]  Christine M. Korsgaard. Motivation, metaphysics, and the value of the self: A reply to Ginsborg, Guyer, and Schneewind. *Ethics,* 109 (1):49–66, October 1998.

[74]  Heinz D. Kurz; Erik Dietzenbacher; Christian Lager. Foundations of input-output analysis. In Heinz D. Kurz, Erik Dietzenbacher, and Christian Lager, editors, *Input-Output Analysis,* volume 1, pages xix-xxxviii. Edward Elgar Publishing, Cheltenham, UK and Northampton, Mass., 1998.

[75]  David Laibman. Market and plan: The evolution of socialist social structures in history and theory. *Science and Society,* 56 (1):60–91, 1992.

[76]  David Laibman. Contours of the maturing socialist economy. *Historical Materialism,* 9:85–110, 2001.

[77]  David Laibman. Contribution to 'Designing socialism: Visions, projections, models'. *Science and Society,* 76 (2):167–171, 191–195, 210–213, 226–230, 247–251, April 2012.

[78]  David Laibman. *Political Economy After Economics: Scientific Method and Radical Imagination.* Routledge, London and New York, 2012.

[79]  David Laibman. Multilevel, democratic, iterative coordination. *Marxism 21,* 12 (1):307–344, 2015.

[80]  James Lawler. Marx as market socialist. In Bertell Ollman, editor, *Market Socialism: The Debate among Socialists,* pages 23–52. Routledge, New York, 1998.

[81]  Georg Lukács. *History and Class Consciousness.* The MIT Press, Cambridge, Mass., 1971.

[82]  Herbert Marcuse. *Reason and Revolution: Hegel and the Rise of Social Theory.* Beacon Press, Boston, 1960.

[83]  Karl Marx. *Theories of Surplus Value, Part I.* Progress Publishers, Moscow, 1963.

[84]  Karl Marx. *Capital,* volumes 1-3. International Publishers, New York, 1967.

[85]  Karl Marx. *Theories of Surplus Value, Part II.* Progress Publishers, Moscow, 1968.

[86]  Karl Marx. *A Contribution to the Critique of Political Economy.* Progress Publishers, Moscow, 1970. Trans. S. W. Ryazanskaya.

[87]  Karl Marx. *Grundrisse: Foundations of the Critique of Political Economy (Rough Draft)*. Penguin Books, Harmondsworth, Middlesex, England, 1973. Trans. Martin Nicolaus.

[88]  Karl Marx. *Grundrisse der Kritik der politischen Ökonomie*. Dietz Verlag, Berlin, 1974.

[89]  Karl Marx. *Early Writings*. Vintage Books, New York, 1975.

[90]  Karl Marx. *Capital*, volume 1. Penguin Books, London, 1990.

[91]  Karl Marx. *Capital*, volume 2. Penguin Books, London, 1993.

[92]  Karl Marx. *Capital*, volume 3. Penguin Books, London, 1993.

[93]  Karl Marx and Frederick Engels. *Collected Works*. International Publishers, New York, 1975.

[94]  Karl Marx and Friedrich Engels. *Werke*. Dietz-Verlag, Berlin, 1972.

[95]  Karl Marx and Friedrich Engels. *Gesamtausgabe*. Dietz Verlag, Berlin, 1975.

[96]  James Edward Meade. *Efficiency, Equality and the Ownership of Property*. Harvard University Press, Cambridge, Mass., 1965.

[97]  Alfredio Medio. Profits and surplus value: Appearance and reality in capitalist production. In E. K. Hunt and Jesse G. Schwartz, editors, *A Critique of Economic Theory*. Penguin Books, Harmondsworth, 1972, pages 312–346.

[98]  Michio Morishima. *Marx's Economics*. Cambridge University Press, Cambridge, 1973.

[99]  Michio Morishima and G. Catephores. Is there an "historical transformation problem"? *The Economic Journal*, 85 (338):309–328, June 1975.

[100]  Liam Murphy and Thomas Nagel. *The Myth of Ownership*. Oxford University Press, Oxford and New York, 2002.

[101]  Thomas Nagel. *Equality and Partiality*. Oxford University Press, New York, 1991.

[102]  Frederick Neuhouser. *Foundations of Hegel's Social Theory: Actualizing Freedom*. Harvard University Press, Cambridge, Mass. and London, 2000.

[103]  N. Okishio. A mathematical note on Marxian theorems. *Weltwirtschaftliches Archiv*, 91 (2):287–299, 1963.

[104]  Martin O'Neill and Thad Williamson, editors. *Property-Owning Democracy: Rawls and Beyond*. Wiley-Blackwell, Malden, Mass. and Oxford, 2012.

[105]  Derek Parfit. *On What Matters*. Oxford University Press, Oxford, 2011.

[106]  Luigi Pasinetti. *Lectures on the Theory of Production*. Columbia University Press, New York, 1977.

[107]  Alan Patten. *Hegel's Idea of Freedom*. Oxford University Press, Oxford and New York, 1999.

[108]  Oskar Perron. Zur Theorie der Matrices. *Mathematische Annalen*, 64:248–263, July 1907.

[109]  Thomas W. Pogge. On the site of distributive justice: Reflections on Cohen and Murphy. *Philosophy and Public Affairs*, 29:137–169, 2000.

[110]  John Rawls. *A Theory of Justice*. Harvard University Press, Cambridge, Mass., 1971.

[111]  John Rawls. Kantian constructivism in moral theory. *Journal of Philosophy*, 77 (2):515–572, September 9, 1980.

[112]  John Rawls. Social unity and primary goods. In Amartya Sen and Bernard Williams, editors, *Utilitarianism and Beyond*, pages 159–186. Cambridge University Press, New York, 1982.

[113]  John Rawls. *Collected Papers*. Harvard University Press, Cambridge, Mass. and London, 1999.

[114] John Rawls. *The Law of Peoples.* Harvard University Press, Cambridge, Mass., 1999.

[115] John Rawls. *A Theory of Justice.* Harvard University Press, Cambridge, Mass., revised edition, 1999.

[116] John Rawls. *Lectures on the History of Moral Philosophy.* Harvard University Press, Cambridge, Massachusetts and London, England, 2000.

[117] John Rawls. *Justice as Fairness: A Restatement.* The Belnap Press of Harvard University Press, Cambridge, Mass., 2001.

[118] John Rawls. *Political Liberalism.* Columbia University Press, New York, expanded edition, 2005.

[119] John Rawls. *Lectures on the History of Political Philosophy.* Harvard University Press, Cambridge, Mass. and London, 2007.

[120] David Ricardo. Absolute value and exchangeable value. In Piero Sraffa and Maurice Dobb, editors, *The Works and Correspondence of David Ricardo,* volume 4, pages 357–412. Cambridge University Press, Cambridge, 1951–1973.

[121] David Ricardo. Letter to Malthus of October 9, 1820. In Piero Sraffa and Maurice Dobb, editors, *The Works and Correspondence of David Ricardo,* volume 8, pages 276–280. Cambridge University Press, Cambridge, 1951–1973.

[122] David Ricardo. Letter to Trower of July 4, 1821. In Piero Sraffa and Maurice Dobb, editors, *The Works and Correspondence of David Ricardo,* volume 9, pages 1–4. Cambridge University Press, Cambridge, 1951–1973.

[123] David Ricardo. Notes on Malthus. In Piero Sraffa and Maurice Dobb, editors, *The Works and Correspondence of David Ricardo,* volume 2. Cambridge University Press, Cambridge, 1951–1973.

[124] David Ricardo. *The Principles of Political Economy and Taxation.* In Piero Sraffa and Maurice Dobb, editors, *The Works and Correspondence of David Ricardo,* volume 1. Cambridge University Press, Cambridge, 1951–1973.

[125] John Roemer. *Analytical Foundations of Marxian Economic Theory.* Cambridge University Press, New York, 1981.

[126] John Roemer. *Free to Lose.* Harvard University Press, Cambridge, Mass., 1988.

[127] Richard Rorty. The priority of democracy to philosophy. In *Objectivity, Relativism, and Truth,* volume 1, pages 175–196. Cambridge University Press, Cambridge, 1991.

[128] Sean Sayers. *Marx and Alienation: Essays on Hegelian Themes.* Palgrave Macmillan, New York, 2011.

[129] Richard Schacht. *Alienation.* Anchor Books, Garden City, New York, 1975.

[130] Richard Schacht. *The Future of Alienation.* University of Illinois Press, Urbana and Chicago, 1994.

[131] Richard Schmitt. *Alienation and Freedom.* Westview Press, Boulder, CO and Oxford, 2003.

[132] Sibyl Schwarzenbach. Züge der Hegelschen Rechtsphilosophie in der Theorie Rawls. *Hegel-Studien,* 27:77–110, 1992.

[133] Sibyl A. Schwarzenbach. Rawls, Hegel, and communitarianism. *Political Theory,* 19 (4):539–571, November 1991.

[134] John R. Searle. Collective intentions and actions. In Jerry Morgan, Philip R. Cohen, and Martha E. Pollack, editors, *Intentions in Communication,* pages 401–415. The MIT Press, Cambridge, Mass., 1990.

[135] John R. Searle. *Making the Social World: The Structure of Human Civilization*. Oxford University Press, Oxford and New York, 2010.

[136] Sally Sedgwick. *Hegel's Critique of Kant: From Dichotomy to Identity*. Oxford University Press, Oxford and New York, 2012.

[137] Wilfrid Sellars. *Science and Metaphysics*. Humanities Press, New York, 1968.

[138] Julius Sensat. Sraffa and Ricardo on value and distribution. *Philosophical Forum*, 14 (33–34):334–368, 1983.

[139] Julius Sensat. Review of Robert Paul Wolff's *Understanding Marx*. *Philosophical Review*, 96:97–108, 1987.

[140] Julius Sensat. Reification as dependence on extrinsic information. *Synthese*, 109:361–399, 1996.

[141] Julius Sensat. Game theory and rational decision. *Erkenntnis*, 47 (3):379–410, 1997.

[142] Karl Shell. Sunspot equilibrium. In Murray Milgate and Peter Newman, editors, *The New Palgrave: A Dictionary of Economics*, volume 4, pages 549–551. New York: The Stockton Press, New York, 1987.

[143] Adam Smith. *An Inquiry into the Nature and Causes of the Wealth of Nations*. University of Chicago Press, Chicago, 1976.

[144] Robert Sugden. Thinking as a team. In E. F. Paul, F. D. Miller, and J. Paul, editors, *Altruism*. Cambridge University Press, Cambridge, 1993.

[145] David G. Sussman. *The Idea of Humanity: Anthropology and Anthroponomy in Kant's Ethics*. Routledge, New York, 2003.

[146] Paul M. Sweezy. *The Theory of Capitalist Development*. Monthly Review Press, New York, 1942.

[147] Robert C. Tucker, editor. *The Marx-Engels Reader*. W. W. Norton & Company, Inc., New York, second edition, 1978.

[148] Richard L. Velkley. *Freedom and the End of Reason: On the Moral Foundation of Kant's Critical Philosophy*. The University of Chicago Press, Chicago and London, 1989.

[149] Amy Wendling. *Karl Marx on Technology and Alienation*. Palgrave Macmillan, New York, 2011.

[150] Marcus Willaschek. The primacy of practical reason and the idea of a practical postulate. In Andrews Reath and Jens Timmermann, editors, *Kant's Critique of Practical Reason: A Critical Guide*, pages 168–196. Cambridge University Press, Cambridge, 2010.

[151] Bernard Williams. *In the Beginning Was the Deed*. Princeton University Press, Princeton and Oxford, 2005.

[152] Robert Paul Wolff. *Understanding Marx*. Princeton University Press, Princeton, 1984.

[153] Allen W. Wood. *Hegel's Ethical Thought*. Cambridge University Press, Cambridge, 1990.

[154] Allen W. Wood. Hegel's critique of morality. In Ludwig Siep, editor, *Grundlinien der Philosophie des Rechts*, chapter 7, pages 147–166. Akademie Verlag, Berlin, 1997.

[155] Allen W. Wood. *Kant's Ethical Thought*. Cambridge University Press, Cambridge and New York, 1999.

[156] Yirmiahu Yovel. *Kant and the Philosophy of History*. Princeton University Press, Princeton, 1980.

# Index

Abraham-Frois, Gilbert, 110n2
absolute freedom and terror, 3
abstract labor, 82–85, 92, 103–107
abstract moral reflection, 10, 72, 166, 171
abstract right, 42–43, 50–55, 57, 65, 70–71, 74, 78
abstraction
  of abstract right from morality and ethical life, 70–71
  of the concept from its embodiment (Hegel), 41
  from the content of the will (Kant), 37, 49
  as a moment of the free will (Hegel), 44
  as a moment of personality (Hegel), 50–51, 54
  of moral freedom from social freedom (Hegel), 43–44
  of morality from ethical life, 70–71
  of personal freedom from moral freedom (Hegel), 43–44, 54
  of the political state from civil society, 70, 72
  and Rawls's use of the original position device, 176
  as a real social process (Marx), 82–85, 92, 103–107
  theoretical, 78–79, 81–82, 112, 114–117
  of the universal from the particular, 34, 49, 165
accumulation of capital, see capital, accumulation of
admissible expectations, see expectations
Adorno, Theodor, 1
agency
  collective, 9, 15, 131, 134–135, 141–142, 151, 152, 156, 171

  as a force against itself, 4, 8, 12, 85, 92, 130, 143–151, 154, 155–156, 171, 184
  gender-structured, 144–147, 154
  independent, 9, 132, 134–141, 142–151, 152–155, 171–172, 182–184
agent-centered prerogatives, 166
alienation, see estrangement
alien powers, 71–72, 77, 85
allocative function of prices, 181
animal spirits, 93
antinomies, social, 160
Aristotle, 41
associated triangle, 168–169
associationist civil and political structure (Hegel), 63–70
Athenians, 56
atomism, 70
  see also individualism
Aumann, Robert J., 138n18, 139n21
autarkic production, 108
Avineri, Shlomo, 104n10, 110n11

Bailey, Samuel, 86
balanced growth, see growth , maximal balanced
Bardsley, Nicholas, 135n10
basic liberties, 157, 173–174, 174n16, 184, 184n26
Baumol, William J., 119n6
Bercuson, Jeffrey, 159n1, 161n3
Berrebi, Edmond, 113n2
*Bildung*, 3
Bortkiewicz, Ladislaus von, 124, 125n8
Brandenburger, Adam, 137n14, 139n21
bucket-brigade phenomenon, 93

CPSIA information can be obtained
at www.ICGtesting.com
Printed in the USA
LVOW04*1320111215

466292LV00007BB/242/P